MECHANICAL & SPATIAL APTITUDE

MECHANICAL & SPATIAL APTITUDE

New York

Copyright © 2001 LearningExpress, LLC.

All rights reserved under International and Pan-American Copyright Conventions.
Published in the United States by LearningExpress, LLC, New York.

Library of Congress Cataloging-in-Publication Data:

Mechanical and spatial aptitude.
    p. cm.—(Skill builders series)
ISBN 1-57685-357-8
    1. Mechanical Ability—Examinations, questions, etc. 2. Space perception—Examinations, questions, etc. 3. Reasoning (Psychology)—Examinations, questions, etc. I. LearningExpress (Organization) II. Skill builders series (New York, N.Y.)

BF433.M4 M44 2001
153.9'462—dc21

                                                                             2001016501

Printed in the United States of America
9 8 7 6 5 4 3 2 1
First Edition

ISBN 1-57685-357-8

For Further Information
For information or to place an order, contact LearningExpress at:
    900 Broadway
    Suite 604
    New York, NY 10003

Or visit our website at:
    www.learnatest.com

CONTENTS

1 • GETTING READY FOR A MECHANICAL/SPATIAL APTITUDE TEST

2 • THE LEARNINGEXPRESS TEST PREPARATION SYSTEM

3 • MECHANICAL APTITUDE
Shop Arithmetic
Tool Knowledge
Mechanical Insight
Mechanical Knowledge

4 • SPATIAL CONCEPTS
Hidden Figures
Block Counting
Rotated Blocks
Matching Pieces and Parts
Spatial Analysis
Understanding Patterns
Eye–hand Coordination
Reading Maps

5 • INTERPRETING SYMBOLS
Symbol Series
Symbol Analogies
Sorting and Classifying Figures
Series Reasoning Test

6 • DIAGNOSTIC TEST—PRACTICE WHAT YOU HAVE LEARNED
Practice Questions

MECHANICAL & SPATIAL APTITUDE

C·H·A·P·T·E·R 1
GETTING READY FOR A MECHANICAL/SPATIAL APTITUDE TEST

CHAPTER SUMMARY

If you're the kind of person who has always been fascinated with gears and pulleys, nuts and bolts, and electrical mazes, this book is for you! In fact, you are probably the same person who can think in 3D and can use your natural mechanical/spatial abilities for your career. Chances are your abilities will put you in a good position to take any kind of exam that tests mechanical/spatial aptitude. Remember though, that practice makes perfect in the long run. That's why you're reading this book.

The ability to understand and use mechanical devices is critical for a job in many fields. Whether you decide to enter the military, apply for a government job, or take a job in private industry, you'll have to take an entrance test that determines your skills and abilities. The military requires that all candidates take the ASVAB (Armed Services Vocational Aptitude Battery) test. Many government positions (local, state, and federal) require you to take an entrance level exam that measures your skills. If you want to be a police officer or firefighter, your ability to use mechanical devices and solve spatial concepts problems is very important and shows up on most every test.

People who work in the professions that require mechanical/spatial ability use many different mechanical devices every day. Simple hand tools such as axes and wrenches, as well as more complex systems such as pumps and internal combustion engines are standard tools of the trade. Spatial concepts go hand-in-hand with mechanical ability.

If the exam you have to take includes a section on mechanical aptitude, it may cover topics with which you are very familiar, as well as some that are new. If the exam covers spatial aptitude, you'll get lots of practice solving that kind of problem as well.

In this introductory chapter, you'll find a few sample questions to try. Next, you'll be given many practice questions designed to improve your mechanical, spatial, and symbol reasoning abilities. Last, you can take a diagnostic test to practice what you have learned. Regardless of your background, understanding the concepts in this book will benefit you on an exam designed to test your mechanical/spatial abilities.

WHAT IS MECHANICAL ABILITY?

Basically, mechanical ability means that you can understand mechanical principles, devices, and tools, and the everyday physics that make them work. You also have the ability to reason and understand the direction of movement of gears in a system of gears. In addition, you can see the patterns of moving parts in engines and machines.

Mechanical devices are an integral part of everyday life. When you imagine the numbers of cars on the highways, offices with machines and computers that make routine office duties easier, and the recreational vehicles used for vacations, you can quickly calculate that a person with mechanical abilities will have lots of work to do in a lifetime.

Mechanical aptitude questions tend to cover a wide range of topics. The questions will usually be multiple choice with four or five possible answers. Some questions may require previous knowledge of the topic while other questions will include all of the information you need to choose an answer.

A typical mechanical aptitude question will look something like this:

Which of the following is a common component of an internal combustion engine?
  a. a piston
  b. a compass
  c. a hammer
  d. a hydraulic jack

The answer is **a**, a piston. A compass is used to determine a direction on a map. A hammer is used to drive nails. A hydraulic jack is used to lift heavy items.

Some exams may test your knowledge of various systems or combinations of mechanical devices. A common example of a mechanical system is the internal combustion engine of an automobile. Other questions will require the identification of various mechanical tools or devices like hand tools, gears, pulleys, levers, fasteners, springs, valves, gauges, and pumps.

WHAT IS A MECHANICAL DEVICE?

A mechanical device is a tool invented to make a given task easier. For example, you could drive a nail into a piece of wood with a rock. However, a long time ago, a woodworker must have decided that there had to be a better way. A long slender handle with a hard piece of metal for striking the nail provided more accuracy and did not damage the wood as easily. Thus was born the hammer.

GETTING READY FOR A MECHANICAL/SPATIAL APTITUDE TEST

Most mechanical devices were invented in the same manner—people looking for easier ways to perform their everyday jobs. Some mechanical devices—the lever, the wheel, and many hand tools—are thousands of years old. Other more complex devices, such as pumps and valves, were invented more recently. Many times the idea of a new mechanical device exists but the technology to design it does not. For example, many years before the pump was invented, people probably discussed the need for an easier way to move water from the river to the town on the hill. However, the technologies of the electric motor and casting of metal had not yet been invented, so the modern pump could not possibly have been invented at that time.

Mechanical devices cover a wide range and variety of tools. In general, mechanical devices are tools that relate to physical work and are governed by mechanical forces and movements. You can usually see what they do and how they work—as opposed to, say, a light switch or a battery, which are electrical devices. Some tools are used to directly accomplish a specific task, such as when you use a handsaw to cut a piece of wood. Others, such as pulleys and gears may be used indirectly to accomplish certain tasks that would be possible without the device but are easier with the device. Still others, such as gauges, only provide feedback information on the operation of other mechanical devices. In your daily life, you see and use mechanical devices many times each day, so there's no reason to be intimidated by a mechanical aptitude section on any exam.

COMMONLY TESTED MECHANICAL DEVICES

HAND TOOLS

Hand tools are defined as tools operated not by motors but rather by human power. There are many different types of hand tools including carpentry tools and automotive hand tools as well as hand tools specific to different trades. Since it is impossible to cover every conceivable kind of hand tool, this chapter lists and defines some of the hand tools used in everyday situations—and the ones you are most likely to be tested on.

Some of the hand tools used by carpenters and other workers are listed on the table on the following page.

Some of the hand tools used in the automotive industry are listed below.

- **Wrenches** are used to tighten and loosen nuts and bolts. Examples include open end and box end wrenches, crescent, and pipe wrenches.
- **Mechanical jacks** are used to lift cars so that tires can be changed. The jack in the trunk of your car is an example.
- **Pliers** are small pincers with long jaws for holding small objects or for bending and cutting wire. Examples are cutting pliers, electrical pliers, and long-nosed pliers. In addition, vice grips are considered locking pliers.
- **Screwdrivers** are tools used for loosening, tightening, or turning screws. Examples are Phillips and straight blade screwdrivers.
- **Sockets and ratchets** are used like wrenches to loosen, remove, or tighten nuts and bolts; there are many different sizes.
- **Torque wrenches** are used to measure the tightness, i.e., the proper torque, of a nut or bolt.
- **Gear pullers** are used to remove gears and pulleys.

HAND TOOLS

Tool	Description/Function	Examples
hammer	used primarily to drive and remove nails, as well as to pound on devices such as chisels	claw hammer, rubber mallet, ball-peen hammer
saw	thin metal blade with a sharp-toothed edge used to cut wood or metal	handsaw, hacksaw, jigsaw
screwdriver	used to tighten and loosen screws and bolts	slotted (regular) head, Phillips head
level	two- to four-foot long piece of metal or plastic that contains calibrated air bubble tubes, used to ensure that things are vertically plumb or horizontally level	hand level, laser level
square	used primarily to aid in drawing a cut line on a board to insure a straight, ninety-degree cut	L-square, T-square
plane	metal tool with a handle and an adjustable blade, used to shave off thin strips of wood for the purpose of smoothing or leveling	block plane, various sizes of carpenter's planes
chisel	metal tool with a sharp, beveled edge that is struck with a hammer in order to cut and shape stone, metal, or wood	scoop chisel, beveled chisel, masonry chisel, cold chisel
protractor	half-circle with tick marks around the edge spaced at one-degree intervals, used to measure angles	only one type, made of metal or plastic
C-clamp	C-shaped metallic instrument with a threaded stop that can be adjusted to clamp together pieces of material of different thicknesses	furniture clamps, many types and sizes of metallic C-clamps
compass	V-shaped metallic instrument with a sharp point on the end of one leg and a pencil or pen on the end of the other leg, used to draw circles	only one type exists

GEARS

A gear is generally a toothed wheel or cylinder that meshes with another toothed element to transmit motion or to change speed or direction. Gears are typically attached to a rotating shaft turned by an outside energy source such as an electric motor or an internal combustion engine. Gears are used in many mechanical devices including automotive transmissions, bicycles, and carnival rides such as Ferris wheels and merry-go-rounds.

Gears can be used in several different configurations. Two gears may be connected by directly touching each other as in an automotive transmission. In this arrangement, one gear spins clockwise and the other rotates counter-clockwise. Another possible configuration is to have two gears connected by a loop of chain as on a bicycle. In this arrangement, the first gear rotates in one direction causing the chain to move. Since the chain is directly connected to the second gear, the second gear will immediately begin to rotate in the same direction as the first gear.

Many times a system will use two gears of different sizes as on a ten-speed bicycle. This will allow changes in speed of the bicycle or machine.

Problems about gears will always involve rotation or spinning. The easiest way to approach test questions that involve gears is to draw a diagram of what the question is describing. Use arrows next to each gear to indicate which direction (clockwise or counter-clockwise) it is rotating.

PULLEYS

A pulley consists of a wheel with a grooved rim in which a pulled rope or cable is run. Pulleys are commonly used with ropes or steel cables to change the direction of a pulling force.

Pulleys are often used to lift things. For instance, a pulley could be attached to the ceiling of a room. A rope could be run from the floor, up through the pulley and back down to a box sitting on the floor. The pulley would allow you to pull *down* on the rope and cause the box to go *up*. That is, the pulley caused a change in direction of the pulling force. This is the principle behind the elevator.

Another common use for a pulley is to connect an electric motor to a mechanical device such as a pump. One pulley is placed on the shaft of the motor, and a second pulley is placed on the shaft of the pump. A belt is used to connect the two pulleys. When the motor is turned on, the first pulley rotates and causes the belt to rotate. That in turn causes the second pulley to rotate and turn the pump. This arrangement is very similar to the previous example of a bicycle chain and gears.

You may have seen pulleys used in a warehouse to lift heavy loads or on construction sites on cranes. The cable on a crane extends from the object being lifted up to the top of the crane boom, across a pulley and back down to the electric winch that is used to pull on the cable. In this situation the pulley again causes a change in direction of the pulling force from the downward force of the winch that pulls the cable to the upward movement of the object being lifted.

LEVERS

A lever is a very old mechanical device. A lever typically consists of a metal or wooden bar that pivots on a fixed point. The object of using a lever is to gain a *mechanical advantage*. Mechanical advantage results when you use a mechanical device in order to make a task easier; that is, you gain an *advantage* by using a *mechanical* device. A lever allows you to complete a task, typically lifting, which would be more difficult or impossible without the lever.

The most common example of a lever is a playground seesaw. A force (a person's weight) is applied to one side of the lever, which causes the weight on the other side (the other person) to be lifted. However, since the pivot point on a seesaw is in the center, each person must weigh the same or things do not work well. You see, a seesaw is a lever with no mechanical advantage. If you push down on one side with a weight of ten pounds you can only lift a maximum of 10 pounds on the other side. This is no great advantage.

This brings us to the secret of the lever. In order to lift an object that is heavier than the force you want to apply to the other side of the lever, you must locate the pivot point closer to the object you want to lift. If two fifty-pound children sit close to the center of the seesaw, one fifty-pound child close to the end of the board on the other side will be able to lift them both.

Test questions about levers will typically require a bit of math (multiplication and division) to solve the problem. There is one simple concept which you must understand in order to solve lever problems: the product of the weight to be lifted times the distance from the weight to the pivot point must be equal to the product of the lifting force times the distance from the force to the pivot point. Stated as an equation, it would be:

$$w \times d_1 = f \times d_2.$$

For example, Bill has a 15-foot long lever and he wants to lift a 100-pound box. If he locates the pivot point 5 feet from the box, leaving 10 feet between the pivot point and the other end of the lever where he will apply the lifting force, how hard must he press on the lever to lift the box?

Use the lever formula, $w \times d_1 = f \times d_2$. The weight of 100 pounds times 5 feet must equal 10 feet times the force: $100 \times 5 = 10 \times force$. Using multiplication and division to solve for the force, you get 50 pounds of force that Bill must apply to the lever to lift the box.

FASTENERS

A mechanical fastener is similar to any mechanical device or process used to connect two or more items together. Typical examples of fastening devices are bolts, screws, nails, and rivets. *Processes* can be used to mechanically join items together including gluing and welding. There are also unique mechanical fasteners such as "hook and loop," which consist of two tapes of material with many small plastic hooks and loops that stick together. Children's sneakers often use such fastening tape instead of laces.

SPRINGS

A spring is an elastic mechanical device, normally a coil of wire, that returns to its original shape after being compressed or extended. There are many types of springs including the compression coil, spiral coil, flat spiral, extension coil, leaf spring, and torsion spring.

Springs are used for many applications such as car suspensions (compression coil and leaf springs), garage doors (extension coil and torsion springs), wind-up clocks (flat spiral and torsion springs), and some styles of ballpoint pens (compression coil).

In the kind of questions you're likely to be asked on a mechanical/spatial exam, you can assume that springs behave linearly. That is, if an extension spring stretches one inch under a pull of ten pounds, then it will stretch two inches under a pull of twenty pounds. In real life, if you pull too hard on a spring, it will not return to its original shape. This is called exceeding the spring's elastic limit. Your exam is not likely to deal with this type of spring behavior.

If several springs are used for one application, they can be arranged in one of two ways: in series or in parallel. The easiest way to remember the difference is that if the springs are all hooked together, end to end, then you have a *series* of springs. The other option is for the springs not to be hooked together but to be lined up side by side, *parallel* to each other. If two springs are arranged in *series*, they will stretch much farther than the same two springs arranged in *parallel* under the same pulling force. This is because in series, the total pulling force passes through both springs. If the same springs are arranged in parallel, the pulling force is divided equally with half going through each spring.

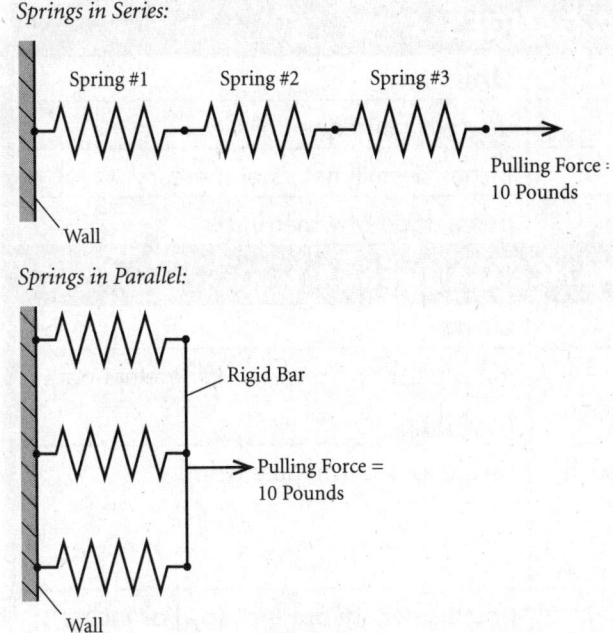

Springs in Series:

Springs in Parallel:

The key to solving spring problems is to draw a diagram of the arrangement, if one isn't already provided, and follow the pulling force through the system.

VALVES

A valve is a mechanical device that controls the flow of liquids, gases, or loose material through piping systems. There are many types of valves including butterfly valves, gate valves, plug valves, ball valves, and check valves.

A valve is basically a gate that can be closed or opened in order to permit the fluid or gas to travel in a particular direction. The type of exam question you are likely to see that involves valves will be one in which you must follow a piping flow diagram through several sets of valves. These problems are best approached by taking your time and methodically following each branch of the piping system from start to finish.

GAUGES

Gauges are used to monitor various conditions and the performance of mechanical machines such as pumps and internal combustion engines, as well as to monitor the surrounding atmospheric conditions that could indirectly affect a particular machine.

Gauges are usually marked with the *units* they are measuring. A few examples of different types of units are:

- Degrees Celsius or Fahrenheit for temperature gauges
- Pounds per square inch (psi) for pressure gauges
- Meters (or sometimes feet) for elevation gauges

You must be very careful to recognize and understand the units of a gauge that appear in a test question. For instance, a temperature gauge (commonly called a thermometer) could use either degrees Fahrenheit or degrees Celsius. Mistakes on units can cause major problems, so be careful! The table on the following page shows some common types of gauges, what they measure, and the kind of units they use.

Gauges are sometimes marked with warnings about limits of safe operation. For instance, an oil pressure gauge on an internal combustion engine may show a maximum safe working pressure of 15 psi. If you're asked about the safe operation of a device with a gauge on it, you should pay careful attention to any markings that show such a limit.

PUMPS

A pump is a device used to transfer a liquid or a gas from one location, through a piping system, to another location. There are many different types of pumps, including centrifugal pumps, positive displacement pumps,

ATMOSPHERIC GAUGES

Gauge	What It Measures	Units
Thermometer	temperature	degrees Fahrenheit or Celsius
Barometer	atmospheric pressure	inches or millimeters of mercury
Hygrometer	relative humidity	percentage of water in air

MACHINE PERFORMANCE GAUGES

Gauge	What It Measures	Units
Speedometer	velocity	miles per hour (mph) or kilometers per hour (kph)
Tachometer	speed of rotation for equipment such as pumps, internal combustion engines, or fans	revolutions per minute (rpm)
Pressure gauge	internal pressure	pounds per square inch (psi) or inches of water
Flow meter	volume of flow in a piping system	cubic feet per minute (cfm) or gallons per minute (gpm)

metering pumps, diaphragm pumps, and progressive cavity pumps.

Generally speaking, a working pump consists of the pump itself (case, bearings, impeller, seals, shaft, base, and other components) and an outside energy source. The outside energy source could be an electric motor, internal combustion engine, or battery to provide mechanical energy to the pump. This energy causes the inner workings of the pump to propel the liquid or gas through the piping system. The flow rate at which the liquid or gas is pushed through the piping system is typically measured by a flow meter in units of gallons per minute (gpm) or cubic feet per minute (cfm).

Pumps are used for many purposes. Some examples include gasoline pumps used to pump the gasoline from a holding tank in to your engine, water pumps to transfer drinking water from a reservoir to your house or business, and industrial pumps used to move industrial fluids such as chemicals or waste products from one tank to another inside a plant. A car also uses pumps to pump fuel from the gas tank to the engine and to pump coolant from the radiator to the engine block.

SYSTEMS THAT USE MECHANICAL DEVICES

Many mechanical devices are actually a combination of several simple devices that work in conjunction to form a group of interacting mechanical and electrical components called a system. Some of the systems most likely to appear on the exam are discussed below.

INTERNAL COMBUSTION ENGINES

Internal combustion engines (ICEs) are commonly used to drive many mechanical devices. However, they are very complex mechanical devices themselves. ICEs are used in cars, trucks, construction equipment, and many other devices. They can be fueled by gasoline, diesel fuel, natural gas, or other combustible fossil fuels.

An ICE is a system composed of dozens of individual mechanical (as well as electrical) systems. A few of the major systems within an ICE are discussed below.

The Cooling System

The purpose of the cooling system is to dissipate the heat generated by the engine. The system consists of a pump that moves the coolant (anti-freeze) from the radiator through piping to the engine block, where it becomes hot, and then back out to the radiator where the liquid coolant is cooled.

The Pistons, Tie Rods, and Crankshaft

The pistons, tie rods, and crankshaft are all parts of the inner workings of an ICE. When the spark plug inside the engine cylinder ignites the fuel, the piston is forced downward. The piston is mechanically fastened to the tie rod, which is therefore also driven downward. The tie rod is attached to the crankshaft and applies a rotation to the crankshaft. The crankshaft has gears attached to it that are connected to other gears on the transmission. Eventually the power is transferred to the wheels of the car, the inner workings of the pump, or whatever device the ICE is driving.

The Fuel Pump

Fuel, typically gasoline or diesel fuel, is transferred from the tank to the engine by the engine's mechanical fuel pump.

The Throttle Governor

The throttle governor is a device in an ICE that uses a spring to reduce the flow of gas back to idle level when you take your foot off of the gas pedal.

AUTOMOBILES AND OTHER VEHICLES

An automobile is one of the most complex assemblies of mechanical devices in existence. The ICE is only one of many subsystems of mechanical devices on an automobile. A few of the other devices and systems are discussed below.

The Brakes

Pressing the brake pedal compresses a piston that forces hydraulic fluid through the brake line piping, activating automobile brakes. The brake fluid presses against a set of mechanical calipers that squeeze the brake pads against the rotors. The rotation of the wheels is slowed by friction. Several springs are used to return the brake pedal and the calipers to their neutral position.

The Steering Assembly

The steering wheel is attached to a shaft with gears on it. The gears turn to rotate a series of levers that are connected by bolted connections. The levers then cause the wheels to turn.

The Exhaust System

The exhaust system includes a system of piping connected to the engine with welded joints. Several brackets are used to suspend the piping beneath the automobile. The engine's exhaust passes through the piping to the muffler, which is an acoustical chamber that reduces the engine noise.

BICYCLES

A bicycle is not nearly as complex as an automobile. However, it too uses several mechanical devices.

GETTING READY FOR A MECHANICAL/SPATIAL APTITUDE TEST

- **The chain drive.** The pedals are connected to the drive gear. A chain is used to connect the drive gear to the gears on the rear wheel.
- **The frame.** Many welded joints are used to hold the frame together.
- **The suspension system.** These days many bikes have suspension systems. The front wheel may use a hydraulic shock absorber. The rear wheel may use two springs in parallel to reduce shock to the rider.

General Mechanical Aptitude

Mechanical devices are such an integral part of everyday life that there are many real-life sources you can investigate to gain more knowledge of their design and use. A construction site is a great place to visit for a day to learn more about hand tools, cranes, pumps, and other devices. Ask the construction supervisor if you can take a tour.

Another alternative would be to hang out at an automotive repair shop. Internal combustion engines, lifts, levers, and hand tools are only a few of the types of mechanical devices you could see in use. Yet another possibility would be to visit a local manufacturer in your town. Examples include a foundry, a sheet metal fabricator, an automotive manufacturer, or a pump manufacturer. Look in the yellow pages under "manufacturing" for possibilities.

How to Answer Mechanical Aptitude Questions

- Read each problem carefully. Questions may contain words such as *not*, *all*, or *mostly*, which can be tricky unless you pay attention.
- Read the entire question once or even a few times before trying to pick an answer. Decide exactly what the question is asking. Take notes and draw pictures on scratch paper. That way you won't waste time by going in the wrong direction.
- Some questions will require the use of math (typically addition, subtraction, multiplication, and division) and science. In these situations, think about what you have learned previously in school.
- Use your common sense. Some mechanical devices can seem intimidating at first but are really a combination of a few simple items. Try to break complicated questions down into smaller, manageable pieces.
- Answer the questions that are easiest for you first. You do not have to go in order from start to finish. Read each question and, if you are not sure what to do, move on to the next question. You can go back to harder questions if you have time at the end.
- Many mechanical devices are commonly used in everyday life. You do not have to be a mechanic or an engineer to use these devices. If something seems unfamiliar, try to think of items around your house that might be similar.
- Don't be intimidated by unfamiliar terms. In most instances, there are clues in the question that will point you toward the correct answer, and some of the answers can be ruled out by common sense.

Sample Mechanical Aptitude Questions

Now use what you've learned by reading this chapter to answer the following mechanical aptitude questions. Answers are at the end of the chapter.

1. Which of the following tools is used to smooth or level a piece of wood?
   a. a wrench
   b. a screwdriver
   c. a plane
   d. a hammer

2. A compass is used for what purpose?
   a. to measure angles
   b. to tighten and loosen nuts and bolts
   c. to drive and remove nails
   d. to draw circles of various sizes

3. Which of the following is NOT a carpenter's hand tool?
   a. a winch
   b. a level
   c. a compass
   d. a chisel

4. Vice grips are a type of
   a. ax
   b. locking pliers
   c. ladder
   d. mechanical jack

5. How can gears be used to change the speed of a machine?
   a. use more gears
   b. use two gears of the same size
   c. use two gears of different sizes
   d. use two large gears

6. What is the main function of a pulley?
   a. to decrease the strength of a construction crane
   b. to override the power of an electric motor
   c. to add energy to a system
   d. to change the direction of a pulling force

7. Steve has a lever whose pivot point is 3 feet from the 50-pound box he wants to lift. Steve is standing at the other end of the lever, 6 feet from the pivot point. How much force must he apply to lift the box?

   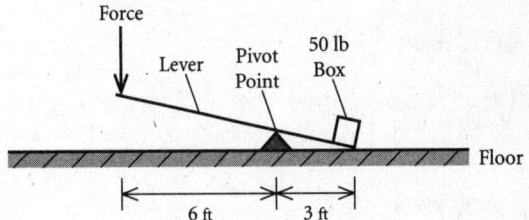

   a. 50 pounds
   b. 25 pounds
   c. 100 pounds
   d. 6 pounds

8. Which of the following is NOT a mechanical process for fastening?
   a. welding
   b. buttoning
   c. bolting
   d. covalent bonding

9. When three identical springs are arranged in a series and a pulling force of 10 pounds is applied, the total stretch is 9 inches. If these same three springs were arranged in parallel and the same 10-pound force is applied to the new arrangement, what will be the total distance of stretch?

Springs in Series:

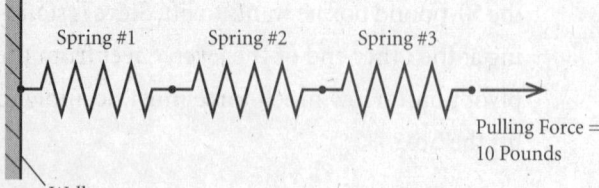

Springs in Parallel:

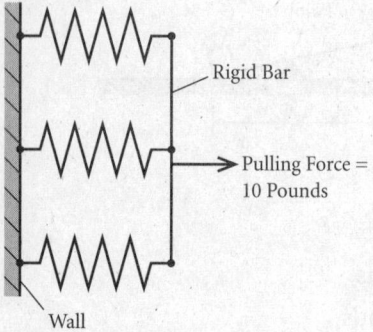

   a. 3 inches
   b. 4.5 inches
   c. 9 inches
   d. 18 inches

10. What type of gauge uses units of rpm?
    a. a pressure gauge
    b. a tachometer
    c. a speedometer
    d. a thermometer

11. What type of outside energy source could be used to operate a pump?
    a. a battery
    b. an internal combustion engine
    c. an electric motor
    d. all of the above

12. What type of mechanical device is used to aid in the cooling of an internal combustion engine?
    a. a pump
    b. a lever
    c. a gauge
    d. a hammer

13. Of the following mechanical devices on an automobile, which one uses friction to accomplish its purpose?
    a. the steering system
    b. the exhaust system
    c. the braking system
    d. the internal combustion engine

14. The suspension system on a bicycle is likely to use which of the following mechanical devices?
    a. a chain
    b. a pulley
    c. a gear
    d. a spring

Answers to Sample Questions

1. **c.** See the table under "Hand Tools" earlier in this chapter for the functions of the items listed.
2. **d.** As defined under "Hand Tools," a compass is used to draw circles.
3. **a.** A level, a compass, and a chisel are all carpenter's hand tools.
4. **b.** Vice grips are a type of locking pliers.
5. **c.** Changing gears on a ten-speed bicycle is a good example of using different size gears to change speed.
6. **d.** Pulleys are used to change not the strength of a force but its direction.
7. **b.** Apply the distance formula, $w \times d_1 = f \times d_2$, to come up with the equation $50 \times 3 = f \times 6$. Solve for the unknown f by multiplying 3 times 50 to get 50 and then dividing by 6 to get 25 pounds.
8. **d.** A covalent bond is a chemical bond. Welding, buttoning, and bolting are all mechanical fastening processes.
9. **a.** The total pulling force will be divided equally, with each spring experiencing one-third of the total force. Since the force is divided by 3, the amount of movement will be divided by 3 also. The original configuration stretched 9 inches, so the new arrangement will stretch only 3 inches.
10. **b.** A tachometer measures rotation in units of revolutions per minute or rpm.
11. **d.** Any of the energy sources listed could be used to operate a pump.
12. **a.** As discussed in the section "Internal Combustion Engines" earlier in this chapter, a pump is used to help cool an ICE.
13. **c.** The braking system uses friction to slow or stop the rotation of the wheels.
14. **d.** Springs are commonly used in suspension systems.

What is Spatial Aptitude?

If you can imagine a box unfolded, see two-dimensional objects in three dimensions, read maps, or see hidden figures in geometric shapes, you have spatial aptitude.

Imagine you are shopping in a local mall. You look at the store directory to find the closest restaurant. You locate the arrow that says, "You Are Here." Do you know where you are? Do you know which way to go to find the restaurant?

The store directory has just asked a typical spatial relations question. Spatial relations can be defined as the ability to visualize in three dimensions. As the store directory example suggests, everyone needs to be able to translate a two-dimensional representation into a three-dimensional sense in order to know location and direction. But this ability is particularly important for people who want to enter fields that rely on these skills. For instance, if you want to be a firefighter, a police officer, electrician, carpenter, plumber, or an emergency medical technician, these skills are essential. Similar skills are needed to read electric mazes and schematics.

Spatial relations questions, especially in the map-reading skills section, are based on floor plans, pictures, or maps. Test questions will often ask you to locate certain points or routes on the diagram. While the answer is there in the diagram, you must know how to read it correctly and how to pay attention to details.

In addition to the map-reading exercises, sections of this book are devoted to other spatial ability aptitudes such as hidden figures, block counting, rotated blocks, matching parts, spatial analysis, understanding patterns, and eye-hand coordination.

READING A MAP

Many spatial relations questions are based on maps because map-reading skills are essential in many professions. Firefighters and police officers are expected to be able to figure out the quickest route to the scene of an emergency without hesitation; ambulance drivers would be required to do the same. Truck drivers, electricians, plumbers, and repairmen have to know the shortest routes to make their jobs easier and faster. Carpenters have to be able to read floor plans. And, in many of those professions, you may find that you need to give directions to motorists or pedestrians.

Questions On The Most Direct Route

Map-based questions typically ask for the most direct route between two points. As you answer such questions, keep in mind that you must choose the best legal route, observing one-way streets and traffic rules. When giving directions to pedestrians, you would not have to consider the flow of traffic, so providing them with the shortest route may be easier to do. Take a systematic approach to answering a map question by using the following procedure:

1. **Look at the map.** Take a moment to scan the buildings and streets. Locate the legend, if any; it tells you which way is north and explains any special symbols, such as those indicating one-way streets.
2. **Read the question.** Read carefully and be sure you understand what is being asked. Do not read the answer choices at this time. Read only the question so that you can plot the route yourself. That way, you're less likely to be confused by incorrect choices purposely included to distract you.
3. **Return to the map.** Locate the information asked for in the question. Look at the street names and traffic patterns.
4. **Prepare your answer by tracing your route.** Remember to observe any traffic rules that are necessary. Write down the route you have selected. Read the question again. Have you understood what was asked, and have you answered correctly?
5. **Read the answer choices.** Be very observant, as the choices may be very similar to each other. Does one of the choices match your route exactly? Some answers may almost match your route but contain one wrong direction. For example, the answer may use north when you are supposed to go south. If you do not find an answer choice that matches yours exactly, reread the question and try again. Carefully review the question to see what is being asked. Do you understand the question? Have you mapped out the correct directions in selecting this route?

A street map is on the next page. Following the map are questions that ask you to find the best route, based on the map. After each question is a detailed explanation of how to use the procedure outlined above to find the correct answer.

The map below shows a section of the city where some public buildings are located. Each of the squares represents one city block. Street names are as shown. If there is an arrow next to the street name, it means the street traffic is one way in the direction of the arrow. If there is no arrow next to the street name, two-way traffic is allowed. Answer questions 1–4 on the basis of this map.

GETTING READY FOR A MECHANICAL/SPATIAL APTITUDE TEST

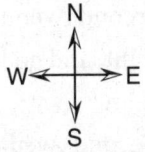

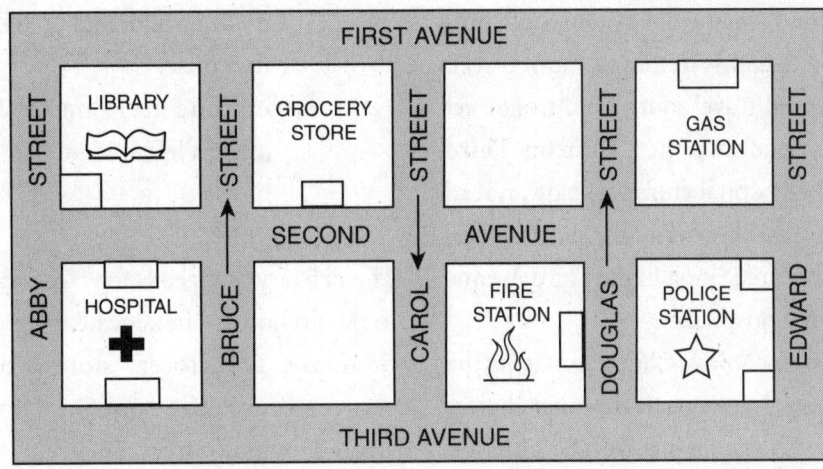

1. What is the shortest legal route from the Fire Station to the Third Avenue entrance of the hospital?
   a. south on Douglas Street, west on Second Avenue, north on Carol Street, and west on Third Avenue to the hospital entrance
   b. north on Douglas Street, west on Second Avenue, south on Bruce Street, and west on Third Avenue to the hospital entrance
   c. north on Douglas Street, west on Second Avenue, south on Carol Street, and west on Third Avenue to the hospital entrance
   d. north on Douglas Street, west on First Avenue, south on Abby Street, and east on Second Avenue to the hospital entrance

Here's how you would use the map-reading procedure to answer question #1.

1. **Look at the map.** Notice that some streets are one way and that avenues permit two-way traffic. Locate north, south, east, and west. What are the names of the buildings shown?

2. **Read the question.** Take note of key words and directions, in this case, shortest legal route. Remember that the starting point must be the Fire Station. The hospital has two entrances, one on Second Avenue and another on Third Avenue. You are being asked to go from the entrance of the Fire Station to the Third Avenue entrance of the hospital using the shortest legal route.

3. **Return to the map.** Locate the Fire Station entrance. It is on Douglas Street between Second Avenue and Third Avenue. Douglas Street is one way going north. The hospital entrance you are asked to report to is on Third Avenue between Abby Street and Bruce Street. Avenues allow two-way traffic, but Bruce Street is one way going north. You need to go south in order to get to Third Avenue. Abby Street is a two-way street but you would have to go past the hospital to use it. Carol Street, which is one-way going south, is the better option.

LearningExpress Mechanical & Spatial Aptitude • CHAPTER 1   15

4. **Prepare your answer by tracing your route.** After careful consideration, you find that the shortest legal route would be to start on Douglas Street at the Fire Station entrance and go north to Second Avenue. Then you would proceed west on Second Avenue to Carol Street. Then you would travel south on Carol Street to Third Avenue and then west on Third Avenue to the hospital entrance. Now, reread the question. You have found the shortest legal route from the Fire Station to the Third Avenue entrance of the hospital.

5. **Read the answer choices.** Choice c matches the route you chose, but examine the other choices to make sure. Choice a is incorrect because you can't legally travel south on Douglas Street, and, if you could, it wouldn't lead you to Second Avenue. Choice b is close to your chosen route, but it becomes incorrect when it sends you south on Bruce Street, which allows northbound traffic only. Choice d will get you to the hospital legally but takes you to the Second Avenue entrance of the hospital instead of the Third Avenue entrance. It also takes you out of the way by traveling on First Avenue to Abby Street.

Use the same procedure to answer the next question.

2. The delivery boy from the grocery store calls to ask directions to the firehouse so that he can deliver the order. You should direct him to walk
   a. west on Second Avenue to Douglas Street, make a left, and go half a block to the firehouse.
   b. east on Second Avenue to Douglas Street, make a right, and go half a block to the firehouse.
   c. west on Second Avenue to Douglas Street, make a right, and go half a block to the firehouse.
   d. east on First Avenue to Douglas Street, make a left, and go half a block to the firehouse.

The delivery boy needs to walk from the grocery store to the firehouse. First, locate the grocery store and the firehouse. The grocery store is on Second Avenue between Bruce Street and Carol Street. The firehouse is on Douglas Street between Second and Third Avenues. Since the delivery boy is walking, you can ignore the one-way streets. Trace a route. Beginning at the grocery store, the delivery boy should walk east on Second Avenue to Douglas Street, turn right, and go half a block to the firehouse.

Now read the answer choices. Choice b is the route you would have directed the delivery boy to use to get from the grocery store to the firehouse. Choices a and c have him walking west on Second Avenue, which is not the correct direction from the grocery store to the firehouse. Choice d has the delivery boy walking on First Avenue, which is not where the entrance to the grocery store is located, and left on Douglas Street, which will not take him to the firehouse.

Questions on Finding Your Location or Direction

Map questions may also ask you for your location after following a series of directions. These questions, while worded differently, should be answered using the same procedure:

1. Look at the map.
2. Read the question.

3. Return to the map and follow the directions given.
4. Go back to the question and examine the answer choices to see which one matches the direction or location you found in step 3.

Try this procedure on the questions that follow, using the same map given previously.

3. You are on the corner of First Avenue and Abby Street. Drive east two blocks, south one block, and west half a block. You are in front of the
   a. hospital.
   b. library.
   c. fire station.
   d. grocery store.

Trace the steps given in the question on the map, paying careful attention to the specific directions, north, south, east, and west. Turn the map as you go to help you keep track of where you are. You have arrived in front of the grocery store, choice **d**.

4. You are walking north on Bruce Street. You turn right on Second Avenue, walk two blocks to Douglas Street, and turn right. What direction are you now facing?
   a. north
   b. south
   c. east
   d. west

The answer to this question is also found by tracing the steps given in the question. Again, turn the map as you are reading the directions indicated. If you are facing north on Bruce Street, a right turn will leave you walking east. Turning right onto Douglas Street, leaves you facing south, choice **b**.

READING A FLOOR PLAN

A floor plan is a map of the interior of a building, apartment, or house. The ability to read floor plans and visualize your position is critical for many professions. In questions based on floor plans, your ability to observe, plan, judge location, and anticipate potential hazards is being tested. The floor plan may be accompanied by a brief explanation of what the picture shows. The questions may ask the number of exits, windows, bedrooms, etc. You may be asked where you would position a ladder to attempt a rescue or which room you are in based on a set of directions.

Handle floor-plan questions in the same manner as those on maps. Before attempting to answer any questions, look at the diagram. Familiarize yourself with such features as doors, windows, doorways, patio doors, fire extinguishers, and smoke detectors. Read each question carefully. Then return to the diagram to find the answer. After you've determined your answer, try to match it to the choices. The correct answer should be apparent, but read each choice carefully to avoid making unnecessary errors. Never jump at one option without carefully reading all the others.

A floor plan is on the next page. Apply the procedure outlined above to answer the questions that come after it.

Office buildings and apartment buildings may post floor plans at the front entrance or by the elevators to assist visitors. Firefighters arriving at the scene of a fire must be able to read a floor plan quickly and develop a mental picture of the interior. When there is a fire, the smoke can be very thick, so firefighters need to know their way in and out without seeing where they are. The diagram on the next page shows two apartments on the first floor of a building. Answer questions 5–8 based on this diagram.

GETTING READY FOR A MECHANICAL/SPATIAL APTITUDE TEST

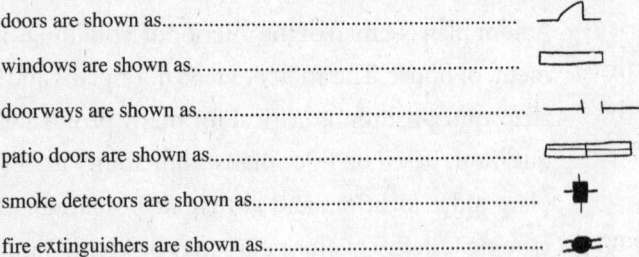

doors are shown as..
windows are shown as..
doorways are shown as..
patio doors are shown as..
smoke detectors are shown as..................................
fire extinguishers are shown as................................

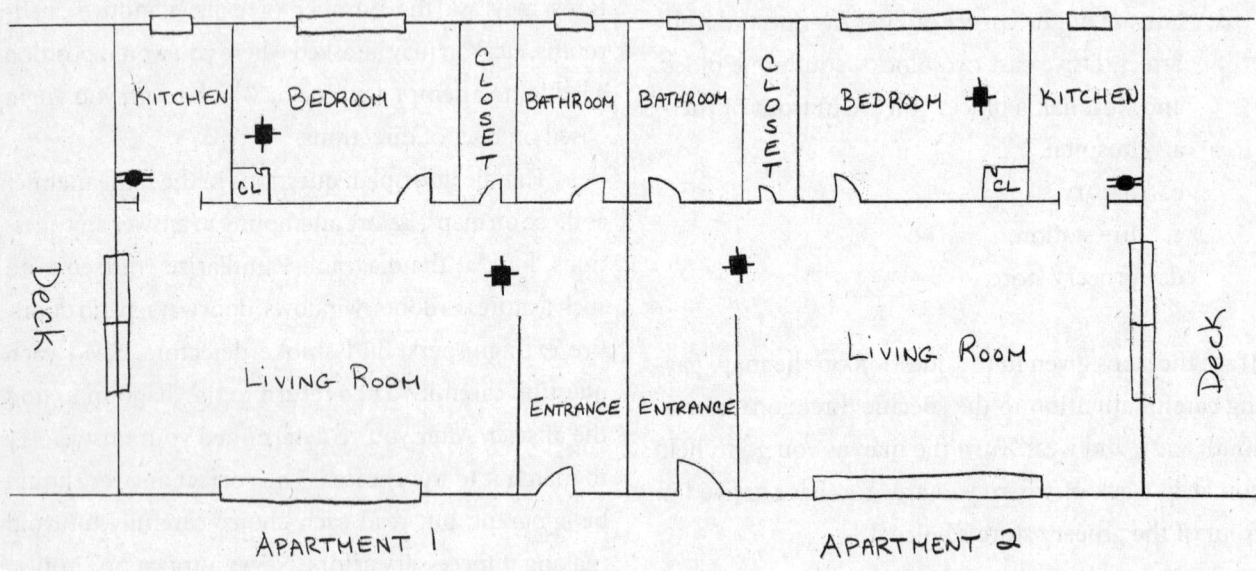

5. Firefighters arrive at the scene to find that there is a woman trapped in the bedroom of apartment 2. There is a fire in the living room, and the entrance to the apartment is blocked by fire. What would be the most direct way to rescue the trapped woman?
   a. Go into the apartment through the patio doors.
   b. Climb through the kitchen window.
   c. Climb through the bedroom window.
   d. Climb through the bathroom window.

The question asks for an alternate way to reach the bedroom of apartment 2, since the entrance is blocked. A look at the floor plan shows that choices **a**, **b**, and **d** would bring the firefighters through the living room, where the fire is located. Choice **c**, which brings you directly into the bedroom, is the fastest and safest means of entering the apartment and rescuing the woman with the least risk of injuring either her or the rescuers.

GETTING READY FOR A MECHANICAL/SPATIAL APTITUDE TEST

6. A fire in the kitchen has filled apartment 1 with smoke. You must reach the bedroom to search for sleeping occupants. Visibility is near zero as you are crawling down the entry hall. How many doors will you encounter before you reach the bedroom?
   a. none
   b. six
   c. four
   d. two

To answer this question, locate the entrance to apartment 1 and trace a route down the hall and to the bedroom. You would pass the bathroom door and a closet door before the bedroom: two doors, choice **d**.

7. How many bathrooms are there in apartment 1?
   a. one
   b. two
   c. three
   d. four

Review the diagram. Two apartments are shown, labeled 1 and 2. The question asks for the number of bathrooms in apartment 1. Apartment 1 contains one bathroom, choice **a**. If you counted all the bathrooms shown on the diagram, you would incorrectly choose **b**.

8. How many smoke detectors and fire extinguishers are there in apartments 1 and 2?
   a. six
   b. ten
   c. four
   d. three

The answer is **a**. You must read the question carefully to see that it asks you to look at both apartments and to find two items, the smoke detectors and the fire extinguishers. There are two smoke detectors and one fire extinguisher in each apartment. If you counted the smoke detectors (but not the fire extinguishers) in both apartments, you would have chosen **c**. On the other hand, if you counted both smoke detectors and fire extinguishers, but only in one apartment, you would have thought choice **d** was correct.

The ability to understand spatial relations is an important tool. Can you apply what you see and mentally navigate yourself through the city or a building, while paying close attention to detail? That's what these questions try to assess.

How to Answer Spatial Relations Questions

- First, familiarize yourself with the map or diagram.
- Next, read the question carefully to determine what you are being asked to do.
- Return to the diagram and find your own answer before reading the choices given.
- Reread the question and the answer choices. Don't rush; read all the possible choices. Misleading answers are placed on the test to see if you can be caught *not* paying attention.
- If the answer you found does not match the choices, look at the question thoroughly, return to the diagram, and go over your options to see what you missed.
- Remember, the answers to the questions are right there in the map or diagram. Take your time, read to understand, and think through your answers.

GETTING READY FOR A MECHANICAL/SPATIAL APTITUDE TEST

SYMBOLS

Last, but not least, employers will want to know whether you have the ability to reason using symbols. Chapter 5 of this book gives you the practice you'll need to pass this section of a mechanical/spatial exam. Here you will find exercises entitled Symbol Series, Symbol Analogies, Sorting and Classifying Figures, and Series Reasoning Tests.

WHAT KINDS OF JOBS REQUIRE MECHANICAL/SPATIAL APTITUDE?

There are many kinds of jobs that require mechanical/spatial abilities. These are only a few.

Aircraft Mechanic	Furniture Manufacturer
Automobile Technician/ Mechanic	Hardware Store Manager
	Painter
Bicycle Repairman	Pipefitter
Camera Repairman	Plumber
Carpenter	Police Officer
Computer Programmer	Printer
Dental Lab Technician	Radio/TV Repairman
Drafter	Roofer
Electrician	Sheet-Metal Worker
Emergency Medical Technician	Telephone Repairman
	Tool/Die Maker
Firefighter	Truck Driver
Framer	

C·H·A·P·T·E·R 2
THE LEARNINGEXPRESS TEST PREPARATION SYSTEM

CHAPTER SUMMARY

Taking any test can be tough. But, don't let the written test scare you! If you prepare ahead of time, you can achieve a top score. The LearningExpress Test Preparation System, developed exclusively for LearningExpress by leading test experts, gives you the discipline and attitude you need to be a winner.

First, the bad news: Getting ready for any test takes work! If you plan to enter a field that requires mechanical/spatial abilities, you'll need to know how to answer questions in Shop Arithmetic, Tool Knowledge, Mechanical Insight, Rotated Blocks, Symbol Series, and Map Reading, to name a few. By honing in on these skills, you will take your first step toward achieving the career of your dreams. However, there are all sorts of pitfalls that can prevent you from doing your best on exams. Here are some obstacles that can stand in the way of your success.

- Being unfamiliar with the format of the exam
- Being paralyzed by test anxiety
- Leaving your preparation to the last minute
- Not preparing at all

THE LEARNINGEXPRESS TEST PREPARATION SYSTEM

- Not knowing vital test-taking skills like:
  - how to pace yourself through the exam
  - how to use the process of elimination
  - when to guess
- Not being in tip-top mental and physical shape
- Forgetting to eat breakfast and having to take the test on an empty stomach
- Forgetting a sweater or jacket and shivering through the exam

What's the common denominator in all these test-taking pitfalls? One word: *control*. Who's in control, you or the exam?

Now the good news: The LearningExpress Test Preparation System puts *you* in control. In just nine easy-to-follow steps, you will learn everything you need to know to make sure that *you* are in charge of your preparation and your performance on the exam. *Other* test-takers may let the test get the better of them; *other* test-takers may be unprepared or out of shape, but not *you*. *You* will have taken all the steps you need to take for a passing score.

Here's how the LearningExpress Test Preparation System works: Nine easy steps lead you through everything you need to know and do to get ready to master your exam. Each of the steps listed below gives you tips and activities to help you prepare for any exam. It's important that you follow the advice and do the activities, or you won't be getting the full benefit of the system. Each step gives you an approximate time estimate.

Step 1. Get Information	30 minutes
Step 2. Conquer Test Anxiety	20 minutes
Step 3. Make a Plan	50 minutes
Step 4. Learn to Manage Your Time	10 minutes
Step 5. Learn to Use the Process of Elimination	20 minutes
Step 6. Know When to Guess	20 minutes
Step 7. Reach Your Peak Performance Zone	10 minutes
Step 8. Get Your Act Together	10 minutes
Step 9. Do it!	10 minutes
Total	**3 hours**

We estimate that working through the entire system will take you approximately three hours, though it's perfectly okay if you work faster or slower than the time estimates say. If you can take a whole afternoon or evening, you can work through the entire LearningExpress Test Preparation System in one sitting. Otherwise, you can break it up, and do just one or two steps a day for the next several days. It's up to you—remember, *you're* in control.

THE LEARNINGEXPRESS TEST PREPARATION SYSTEM

STEP 1: GET INFORMATION

Time to complete: 30 minutes
Activities: Read Chapter 1. "Getting Ready for a Mechanical/Spatial Test."
Knowledge is power. The first step in the LearningExpress Test Preparation System is finding out everything you can about the types of questions that will be asked on any mechanical/spatial test. Practicing and studying the exercises in this book will help prepare you for those tests.

PART A: JOBS THAT TEST MECHANICAL/SPATIAL ABILITY

If you already know that you have mechanical/spatial abilities, that's great! But, employers need to know what your abilities are and if you can learn new ones. While some of the aptitudes and problem-solving skills tested in this book are important in almost any job, others, such as mechanical insight or eye-hand coordination, are quite specialized. It is vital to give your attention to these kinds of questions to get the kind of job you want.

PART B: THE KINDS OF SKILLS TESTED

This book has seventeen subtests that help employers determine your mechanical/spatial abilities.

- Shop Arithmetic
- Tool Knowledge
- Mechanical Insight
- Mechanical Knowledge
- Hidden Figures
- Block Counting
- Rotated Blocks
- Matching Pieces and Parts
- Spatial Analysis
- Understanding Patterns
- Eye-Hand Coordination
- Reading Maps
- Symbol Series
- Symbol Analogies
- Sorting and Classifying Figures
- Series Reasoning Tests

If you haven't already done so, stop here and read Chapter 1 of this book. Here, you'll read an overview of the definitions of mechanical and spatial aptitudes and the kinds of jobs that use these skills.

Step 2: Conquer Test Anxiety

Time to complete: 20 minutes
Activity: Take the Test Stress Test

Having complete information about the exam is the first step in getting control of the exam. Next, you have to overcome one of the biggest obstacles to test success: test anxiety. Test anxiety not only impairs your performance on the exam itself, but it can even keep you from preparing! In Step 2, you'll learn stress management techniques that will help you succeed on your exam. Learn these strategies now, and practice them as you work through the exams in this book, so they'll be second nature to you by exam day.

COMBATING TEST ANXIETY

The first thing you need to know is that a little test anxiety is a good thing. Everyone gets nervous before a big exam—and if that nervousness motivates you to prepare thoroughly, so much the better. It's said that Sir Laurence Olivier, one of the foremost British actors of this century, threw up before every performance. His stage fright didn't impair his performance; in fact, it probably gave him a little extra edge—just the kind of edge you need to do well, whether on a stage or in an exam room.

On page 5 is the Test Stress Test. Stop here and answer the questions on that page, to find out whether your level of test anxiety is something you should worry about.

Stress Management Before the Test

If you feel your level of anxiety getting the best of you in the weeks before the test, here is what you need to do to bring the level down again:

- **Get prepared.** There's nothing like knowing what to expect. Being prepared will put you in control of test anxiety. That's why you're reading this book. Use it faithfully, and remind yourself that you're better prepared than most of the people taking the test.
- **Practice self-confidence.** A positive attitude is a great way to combat test anxiety. This is no time to be humble or shy. Stand in front of the mirror and say to your reflection, "I'm prepared. I'm full of self-confidence. I'm going to ace this test. I know I can do it." Say it into a tape recorder and play it back once a day. If you hear it often enough, you'll believe it.
- **Fight negative messages.** Every time someone starts telling you how hard the exam is or how it's almost impossible to get a high score, start telling them your self-confidence messages above. If the someone with the negative messages is you—telling yourself you don't do well on exams, you just can't do this—don't listen. Turn on your tape recorder and listen to your self-confidence messages.
- **Visualize.** Imagine yourself reporting for your first day on the job. Visualizing success can help make it happen—and it reminds you why you're preparing for the exam so diligently.
- **Exercise.** Physical activity helps calm your body down and focus your mind. Besides, being in good

Test Stress Test

You only need to worry about test anxiety if it is extreme enough to impair your performance. The following questionnaire will provide a diagnosis of your level of test anxiety. In the blank before each statement, write the number that most accurately describes your experience.

0 = Never   1 = Once or twice   2 = Sometimes   3 = Often

_____ I have gotten so nervous before an exam that I simply put down the books and didn't study for it.

_____ I have experienced disabling physical symptoms such as vomiting and severe headaches because I was nervous about an exam.

_____ I have simply not showed up for an exam because I was scared to take it.

_____ I have experienced dizziness and disorientation while taking an exam.

_____ I have had trouble filling in the little circles because my hands were shaking too hard.

_____ I have failed an exam because I was too nervous to complete it.

_____ **Total: Add up the numbers in the blanks above.**

Your Test Stress Score

Here are the steps you should take, depending on your score. If you scored:

- **Below 3,** your level of test anxiety is nothing to worry about; it's probably just enough to give you that little extra edge.
- **Between 3 and 6,** your test anxiety may be enough to impair your performance, and you should practice the stress management techniques listed in this section to try to bring your test anxiety down to manageable levels.
- **Above 6,** your level of test anxiety is a serious concern. In addition to practicing the stress management techniques listed in this section, you may want to seek additional, personal help. Call your local high school or community college and ask for the academic counselor. Alternatively, contact a counselor affiliated with your department. Tell the counselor that you have a level of test anxiety that sometimes keeps you from being able to take exams. The counselor may be willing to help you or may suggest someone else you should talk to.

THE LEARNINGEXPRESS TEST PREPARATION SYSTEM

physical shape can actually help you do well on the exam. Go for a run, lift weights, go swimming—and do it regularly.

Stress Management on Test Day

There are several ways you can bring down your level of test anxiety on test day. To find a comfort level, practice these in the weeks before the test, and use the ones that work best for you.

- **Deep breathing.** Take a deep breath while you count to five. Hold it for a count of one, then let it out on a count of five. Repeat several times.
- **Move your body.** Try rolling your head in a circle. Rotate your shoulders. Shake your hands from the wrist. Many people find these movements very relaxing.
- **Visualize again.** Think of the place where you are most relaxed: lying on the beach in the sun, walking through the park, or whatever. Now close your eyes and imagine you're actually there. If you practice in advance, you'll find that you only need a few seconds of this exercise to experience a significant increase in your sense of well-being.

When anxiety threatens to overwhelm you right there during the exam, there are still things you can do to manage the stress level:

- **Repeat your self-confidence messages.** You should have them memorized by now. Say them quietly to yourself, and believe them!
- **Visualize one more time.** This time, visualize yourself moving smoothly and quickly through the test answering every question right and finishing just before time is up. Like most visualization techniques, this one works best if you've practiced it ahead of time.
- **Find an easy question.** Skim over the test until you find an easy question, and answer it. Getting even one circle filled in gets you into the test-taking groove.
- **Take a mental break.** Everyone loses concentration once in a while during a long test. It's normal, so you shouldn't worry about it. Instead, accept what has happened. Say to yourself, "Hey, I lost it there for a minute. My brain is taking a break." Put down your pencil, close your eyes, and do some deep breathing for a few seconds. Then you're ready to go back to work.

Try these techniques ahead of time, and see if they work for you!

Step 3: Make a Plan

Time to complete: 50 minutes
Activity: Construct a study plan

Maybe the most important thing you can do to get control of yourself and your exam is to make a study plan. Too many people fail to prepare simply because they fail to plan. Spending hours on the day before the exam poring over sample test questions not only raises your level of test anxiety, it also is simply no substitute for careful preparation and practice.

Don't fall into the cram trap. Take control of your preparation time by mapping out a study schedule. If you're the kind of person who needs deadlines and assignments to motivate you for a project, here they are. If you're the kind of person who doesn't like to follow other people's plans, you can use the suggested schedules here to construct your own.

Even more important than making a plan is making a commitment. You can't review everything you need to know for a mechanical/spatial test in one night. You have to set aside some time every day for study and practice. Try for at least 20 minutes a day. Twenty minutes daily will do you much more good than two hours on Saturday.

Don't put off your study until the day before the exam. Start now. A few minutes a day, with half an hour or more on weekends can make a big difference in your score.

If you have months before the exam, you're lucky. Don't put off your study until the week before the exam! Start now. Even ten minutes a day, with half an hour or more on weekends, can make a big difference in your score—and in your chances of making the grade you want!

THE LEARNINGEXPRESS TEST PREPARATION SYSTEM

SCHEDULE A: THE 30-DAY PLAN

If you have at least a month before you take your test, you have plenty of time to prepare—as long as you don't waste it! If you have less than a month, turn to Schedule B.

Time	Preparation
Days 1–4	Skim over the written materials from any courses or training programs you may have taken, particularly noting 1) areas you expect to be emphasized on the exam and 2) areas you don't remember well. On Day 4, concentrate on those areas.
Day 5	Take the diagnostic test at the end of the book.
Day 6	Score the exam. Make a note of your strongest and weakest areas. Identify two areas that you will concentrate on before you practice the exam a second time.
Days 7–10	Study the two areas you identified as your weak points. Don't worry about the other areas. Go back to the sections in the book and review these skills again.
Day 11	Take the diagnostic test once again.
Day 12	Score your second diagnostic test. Identify one area, turn back to the chapter in the book for more review.
Days 13–18	Study the one area you identified for review. In addition, review both diagnostic tests, and give special attention to the answer explanations and the length of time it takes you to complete the exam.
Day 19	Take the diagnostic test for a third time.
Day 20	Once again, identify one area to review, based on your score on the third practice exam.
Days 20–21	Study the one area you identified for review.
Days 22–25	Take an overview of any training material you may have.
Days 26–27	Review all the areas that have given you the most trouble in the three diagnostic tests you've taken so far.
Day 28	Take the diagnostic one final time. Note how much you've improved!
Day 29	Review one or two weak areas.
Day before the exam	Relax. Do something unrelated to the exam and go to bed at a reasonable hour.

CHAPTER 2 • *LearningExpress Mechanical & Spatial Aptitude*

SCHEDULE B: THE 10-DAY PLAN

If you have two weeks or less before you take your exam, you may have your work cut out for you. Use this 10-day schedule to help you make the most of your time.

Time	Preparation
Day 1	Take the practice exam and score it using the answer key at the end. Turn to the list of subject areas on the exam in the Table of Contents to find out which areas need the most work—based on your exam score.
Day 2	Review one area that gave you trouble on the diagnostic test.
Day 3	Review another area that gave you trouble on the diagnostic test.
Day 4	Take the diagnostic test again and score it.
Day 5	If your score on the second diagnostic test doesn't show improvement on the two areas you studied, review them. If you did improve in those areas, choose a different trouble spot to study today.
Day 6	Take the diagnostic test a third time and score it.
Day 7	Choose your weakest area from the third diagnostic test to review.
Day 8	Review any areas that you have neglected in this schedule.
Day 9	Take the diagnostic test a final time and score it.
Day 10	Use your last study day to brush up on any areas that are still giving you trouble.
Day before the exam	Relax. Do something unrelated to the exam and go to bed at a reasonable hour.

STEP 4: LEARN TO MANAGE YOUR TIME

Time to complete: 10 minutes to read, many hours of practice!
Activities: Practice these strategies as you take the sample tests in this book

Steps 4, 5, and 6 of the LearningExpress Test Preparation System put you in charge of your exam by showing you test-taking strategies that work. Practice these strategies as you take the sample tests in this book, and then you'll be ready to use them on test day.

First, take control of your time on the exam. Mechanical/Spatial exams have a time limit, which may give you more than enough time to complete all the questions—or may not. It's a terrible feeling to hear the examiner say, "Five minutes left," when you're only three-quarters of the way through the test. Here are some tips to keep that from happening to *you*.

- **Follow directions.** If the directions are given orally, listen closely. If they're written on the exam booklet, read them carefully. Ask questions *before* the exam begins if there is anything you don't understand. If you're allowed to write in your exam booklet, write down the beginning time and the ending time of the exam.
- **Pace yourself.** Glance at your watch every few minutes, and compare the time to how far you've gotten in the test. When one-quarter of the time has elapsed, you should be a quarter of the way through the section, and so on. If you're falling behind, pick up the pace a bit.
- **Keep moving.** Don't waste time on one question. If you don't know the answer, skip the question and move on. Circle the number of the question in your test booklet in case you have time to come back to it later.
- **Keep track of your place on the answer sheet.** If you skip a question, make sure you skip it on the answer sheet, too. Check yourself every 5–10 questions to make sure the question number and the answer sheet number are still the same.
- **Don't rush.** Though you should keep moving, rushing won't help. Try to keep calm and work methodically and quickly.

STEP 5: LEARN TO USE THE PROCESS OF ELIMINATION

Time to complete: 20 minutes
Activity: Complete worksheet on Using the Process of Elimination

After time management, your next most important tool for taking control of your exam is using the process of elimination wisely. It's standard test-taking wisdom that you should always read all the answer choices before choosing your answer. This helps you find the right answer by eliminating wrong answer choices.

THE LEARNINGEXPRESS TEST PREPARATION SYSTEM

CHOOSING THE RIGHT ANSWER BY PROCESS OF ELIMINATION

As you read a question, you may find it helpful to underline important information or make some notes about what you're reading. When you get to the heart of the question, circle it and make sure you understand what it is asking. If you're not sure of what's being asked, you'll never know whether you've chosen the right answer. What you do next depends on the type of question you're answering.

- If it's math, take a quick look at the answer choices for some clues. Sometimes this helps to put the question in a new perspective and makes it easier to answer. Then make a plan of attack to solve the problem.
- Otherwise, follow this simple process of elimination plan to manage your testing time as efficiently as possible: Read each answer choice and make a quick decision about what to do with it, marking your test book accordingly:

    If the answer seems reasonable; keep it. Put a ✓ next to the answer.

    If the answer is awful, get rid of it. Put an X next to the answer.

    If you can't make up your mind about the answer, or you don't understand it, keep it for now. Put a ? next to it.

Whatever you do, don't waste time with any one answer choice. If you can't figure out what an answer choice means, don't worry about it. If it's the right answer, you'll probably be able to eliminate all the others, and, if it's the wrong answer, another answer will probably strike you more obviously as the right answer.

If you haven't eliminated any answers at all, skip the question temporarily, but don't forget to mark the question so you can come back to it later if you have time. If the test has no penalty for wrong answers, and you're certain that you could never answer this question in a million years, pick an answer and move on!

If you've eliminated all but one answer, just reread the circled part of the question to make sure you're answering exactly what's asked. Mark your answer sheet and move on to the next question.

Here's what to do when you've eliminated some, but not all of the answer choices. Compare the remaining answers looking for similarities and differences, reasoning your way through these choices. Try to eliminate those choices that don't seem as strong to you. But *don't* eliminate an answer just because you don't understand it. You may even be able to use relevant information from other parts of the test. If you've narrowed it down to a single answer, check it against the circled question to be sure you've answered it. Then mark your answer sheet and move on. If you're down to only two or three answer choices, you've improved your odds of getting the question right. Make an educated guess and move on. However, if you think you can do better with more time, mark the question as one to return to later.

IF YOU'RE PENALIZED FOR WRONG ANSWERS

You must know whether you'll be penalized for wrong answers before you begin the test. If you don't, ask the proctor before the test begins. Whether you make a guess or not depends upon the penalty. Some standardized tests are scored in such a way that every wrong answer reduces your score by a fraction of a point, and these can

THE LEARNINGEXPRESS TEST PREPARATION SYSTEM

really add up against you! Whatever the penalty, if you can eliminate enough choices to make the odds of answering the question better than the penalty for getting it wrong, make a guess. This is called educated guessing.

Let's imagine you are taking a test in which each answer has five choices and you are penalized $\frac{1}{4}$ of a point for each wrong answer. If you cannot eliminate any of the answer choices, you're better off leaving the answer blank because the odds of guessing correctly are one in five. However, if you can eliminate two of the choices as definitely wrong, the odds are now in your favor. You have a one in three chance of answering the question correctly. Fortunately, few tests are scored using such elaborate means, but if your test is one of them, know the penalties and calculate your odds before you take a guess on a question.

IF YOU FINISH EARLY

Use any time you have left to do the following:

- Go back to any unanswered questions you marked and try them again.
- Check your work on all the other questions. If you have a good reason for thinking a response is wrong, change it.
- Review your answer sheet. Make sure that you've put the answers in the right places and that you've marked only one answer for each question. (Most tests are scored in such a way that questions with more than one answer are marked wrong.)
- If you've erased an answer, make sure you've done a good job of it.
- Check for stray marks on your answer sheet that could distort your score.

Whatever you do, don't waste time when you've finished a test section. Make every second count by checking your work over and over again until time is called.

Try using your powers of elimination on the questions in the worksheet on the next page called "Using the Process of Elimination." The answer explanations that follow show one possible way you might use the process to arrive at the right answer.

The process of elimination is your tool for the next step, which is knowing when to guess.

USING THE PROCESS OF ELIMINATION

Use the process of elimination to answer the following questions.

1. Ilsa is as old as Meghan will be in five years. The difference between Ed's age and Meghan's age is twice the difference between Ilsa's age and Meghan's age. Ed is 29. How old is Ilsa?
    a. 4
    b. 10
    c. 19
    d. 24

THE LEARNINGEXPRESS TEST PREPARATION SYSTEM

2. "All drivers of commercial vehicles must carry a valid commercial driver's license whenever operating a commercial vehicle." According to this sentence, which of the following people need NOT carry a commercial driver's license?
   a. a truck driver idling his engine while waiting to be directed to a loading dock
   b. a bus operator backing her bus out of the way of another bus in the bus lot
   c. a taxi driver driving his personal car to the grocery store
   d. a limousine driver taking the limousine to her home after dropping off her last passenger of the evening

3. Smoking tobacco has been linked to
   a. an increased risk of stroke and heart attack.
   b. all forms of respiratory disease.
   c. increasing mortality rates over the past ten years.
   d. juvenile delinquency.

4. Which of the following words is spelled correctly?
   a. incorrigible
   b. outragous
   c. domestickated
   d. understandible

ANSWERS

Here are the answers, as well as some suggestions as to how you might have used the process of elimination to find them.

1. **d.** You should have eliminated choice **a** immediately. Ilsa can't be four years old if Meghan is going to be Ilsa's age in five years. The best way to eliminate other answer choices is to try plugging them in to the information given in the problem. For instance, for choice **b**, if Ilsa is 10, then Meghan must be 5. The difference in their ages is 5. The difference between Ed's age, 29, and Meghan's age, 5, is 24. Is 24 two times 5? No. Then choice **b** is wrong. You could eliminate choice **c** in the same way and be left with choice **d**.

2. **c.** Note the word not in the question, and go through the answers one by one. Is the truck driver in choice **a** "operating a commercial vehicle"? Yes, idling counts as "operating," so he needs to have a commercial driver's license. Likewise, the bus operator in choice **b** is operating a commercial vehicle; the question doesn't say the operator has to be on the street. The limo driver in choice **d** is operating a commercial vehicle, even if it doesn't have a passenger in it. However, the cabbie in choice **c** is not operating a commercial vehicle, but his own private car.

LearningExpress Mechanical & Spatial Aptitude • CHAPTER 2

3. a. You could eliminate choice **b** simply because of the presence of the word all. Such absolutes hardly ever appear in correct answer choices. Choice **c** looks attractive until you think a little about what you know—aren't fewer people smoking these days, rather than more? So how could smoking be responsible for a higher mortality rate? (If you didn't know that mortality rate means the rate at which people die, you might keep this choice as a possibility, but you'd still be able to eliminate two answers and have only two to choose from.) Choice **d** can't be proven, so you could eliminate that one, too. Now you're left with the correct choice, **a**.

4. a. How you used the process of elimination here depends on which words you recognized as being spelled incorrectly. If you knew that the correct spellings were outrageous, domesticated, and understandable, then you were home free. Surely you knew that at least one of those words was wrong.

STEP 6: KNOW WHEN TO GUESS

Time to complete: 20 minutes
Activity: Complete worksheet on Your Guessing Ability

Armed with the process of elimination, you're ready to take control of one of the big questions in test-taking: Should I guess? The first and main answer is, Yes. Some exams have what's called a "guessing penalty," in which a fraction of your wrong answers is subtracted from your right answers. Check with the administrators of your particular exam to see if this is the case. In many instances, the number of questions you answer correctly yields your raw score. So you have nothing to lose and everything to gain by guessing.

The more complicated answer to the question, "Should I guess?" depends on you, your personality, and your "guessing intutition." There are two things you need to know about yourself before you go into the exam:

- Are you a risk-taker?
- Are you a good guesser?

You'll have to decide about your risk-taking quotient on your own. To find out if you're a good guesser, complete the worksheet called Your Guessing Ability that begins on page 15. Frankly, even if you're a play-it-safe person with terrible intuition, you're still safe in guessing every time. The best thing would be if you could overcome your anxieties and go ahead and mark an answer. But you may want to have a sense of how good your intuition is before you go into the exam.

(continued on page 18)

THE LEARNINGEXPRESS TEST PREPARATION SYSTEM

Your Guessing Ability

The following are ten really hard questions. You're not supposed to know the answers. Rather, this is an assessment of your ability to guess when you don't have a clue. Read each question carefully, just as if you did expect to answer it. If you have any knowledge at all of the subject of the question, use that knowledge to help you eliminate wrong answer choices. Fill in the correct answer.

ANSWER GRID

1. ⓐ ⓑ ⓒ ⓓ   5. ⓐ ⓑ ⓒ ⓓ   9. ⓐ ⓑ ⓒ ⓓ
2. ⓐ ⓑ ⓒ ⓓ   6. ⓐ ⓑ ⓒ ⓓ   10. ⓐ ⓑ ⓒ ⓓ
3. ⓐ ⓑ ⓒ ⓓ   7. ⓐ ⓑ ⓒ ⓓ
4. ⓐ ⓑ ⓒ ⓓ   8. ⓐ ⓑ ⓒ ⓓ

1. September 7 is Independence Day in
    a. India.
    b. Costa Rica.
    c. Brazil.
    d. Australia.

2. Which of the following is the formula for determining the momentum of an object?
    a. $p = mv$
    b. $F = ma$
    c. $P = IV$
    d. $E = mc^2$

3. Because of the expansion of the universe, the stars and other celestial bodies are all moving away from each other. This phenomenon is known as
    a. Newton's first law.
    b. the big bang.
    c. gravitational collapse.
    d. Hubble flow.

4. American author Gertrude Stein was born in
    a. 1713.
    b. 1830.
    c. 1874.
    d. 1901.

5. Which of the following is **not** one of the Five Classics attributed to Confucius?
   a. the I Ching
   b. the Book of Holiness
   c. the Spring and Autumn Annals
   d. the Book of History

6. The religious and philosophical doctrine that holds that the universe is constantly in a struggle between good and evil is known as
   a. Pelagianism.
   b. Manichaeanism.
   c. neo-Hegelianism.
   d. Epicureanism.

7. The third Chief Justice of the Supreme Court was
   a. John Blair.
   b. William Cushing.
   c. James Wilson.
   d. John Jay.

8. Which of the following is the poisonous portion of a daffodil?
   a. the bulb
   b. the leaves
   c. the stem
   d. the flowers

9. The winner of the Masters golf tournament in 1953 was
   a. Sam Snead.
   b. Cary Middlecoff.
   c. Arnold Palmer.
   d. Ben Hogan.

10. The state with the highest per capita personal income in 1980 was
    a. Alaska.
    b. Connecticut.
    c. New York.
    d. Texas.

THE LEARNINGEXPRESS TEST PREPARATION SYSTEM

Answers

Check your answers against the correct answers below.

1. c.	**5.** b.	**9.** d.
2. a.	**6.** b.	**10.** a.
3. d.	**7.** b.	
4. c.	**8.** a.	

HOW DID YOU DO?

You may have simply gotten lucky and actually known the answer to one or two questions. In addition, your guessing was more successful if you were able to use the process of elimination on any of the questions. Maybe you didn't know who the third Chief Justice was (question 7), but you knew that John Jay was the first. In that case, you would have eliminated answer **d** and therefore improved your odds of guessing correctly from one in four to one in three.

According to probability, you should get $2\frac{1}{2}$ answers correct by guessing, so getting either two or three right would be average. If you got four or more right, you may be a really terrific guesser. If you got one or none right, you may decide not to guess.

Keep in mind, though, that this is only a small sample. You should continue to keep track of your guessing ability as you work through the practice questions in this book. Circle the numbers of questions you guess; or, if you don't have time during the practice tests, go back afterward and try to remember which questions you guessed. Remember, on a test with four answer choices, your chances of getting a right answer is one in four. So keep a separate "guessing" score for each exam. How many questions did you guess? How many did you get right? If the number you got right is at least one-fourth of the number of questions you guessed, you are at least an average guesser, maybe better—and you should always go ahead and guess on the real exam. If the number you got right is significantly lower than one-fourth of the number you guessed on, you should not guess on exams where there is a guessing penalty unless you can eliminate a wrong answer. If there's no guessing penalty, you would, frankly, be safe in guessing anyway, but maybe you'd feel more comfortable if you guessed only selectively, when you can eliminate a wrong answer or at least have a good feeling about one of the answer choices.

THE LEARNINGEXPRESS TEST PREPARATION SYSTEM

STEP 7: REACH YOUR PEAK PERFORMANCE ZONE

Time to complete: 10 minutes to read; weeks to complete!
Activity: Complete the Physical Preparation Checklist

To get ready for a challenge like a big exam, you have to take control of your physical, as well as your mental state. Exercise, proper diet, and rest will ensure that your body works with, rather than against, your mind on test day, as well as during your preparation.

EXERCISE

If you don't already have a regular exercise program going, the time during which you're preparing for an exam is actually an excellent time to start one. If you're already keeping fit—or trying to get that way—don't let the pressure of preparing for an exam fool you into quitting now. Exercise helps reduce stress by pumping wonderful good-feeling hormones called endorphins into your system. It also increases the oxygen supply throughout your body and your brain, so you'll be at peak performance on test day.

A half hour of vigorous activity—enough to raise a sweat—every day should be your aim. If you're really pressed for time, every other day is ok. Choose an activity you like and get out there and do it. Jogging with a friend always makes the time go faster as does listening to music.

But don't overdo. You don't want to exhaust yourself. Moderation is the key.

DIET

First of all, cut out the junk. Go easy on caffeine and nicotine, and eliminate alcohol and any other drugs from your system at least two weeks before the exam. Promise yourself a binge the night after the exam, if need be.

What your body needs for peak performance is simply a balanced diet. Eat plenty of fruits and vegetables, along with protein and carbohydrates. Foods that are high in lecithin (an amino acid), such as fish and beans, are especially good "brain foods."

REST

You probably know how much sleep you need every night to be at your best, even if you don't always get it. Make sure you do get that much sleep though, for at least a week before the exam. Moderation is important here, too. Extra sleep will just make you groggy.

If you're not a morning person and your exam will be given in the morning, you should reset your internal clock so that your body doesn't think you're taking an exam at 3 A.M. You have to start this process well before the exam. The way it works is to get up half an hour earlier each morning, and then go to bed half an hour earlier that night. Don't try it the other way around; you'll just toss and turn if you go to bed early without getting up early. The next morning, get up another half an hour earlier, and so on. How long you will have to do this depends on how late you're used to getting up. Use the Physical Preparation Checklist on the next page to make sure you're in tip-top form.

(continued on page 20)

THE LEARNINGEXPRESS TEST PREPARATION SYSTEM

Physical Preparation Checklist

For the week before the test, write down 1) what physical exercise you engaged in and for how long and 2) what you ate for each meal. Remember, you're trying for at least half an hour of exercise every other day (preferably every day) and a balanced diet that's light on junk food.

Exam minus 7 days
Exercise: _____ for _____ minutes
Breakfast: _____
Lunch: _____
Dinner: _____
Snacks: _____

Exam minus 6 days
Exercise: _____ for _____ minutes
Breakfast: _____
Lunch: _____
Dinner: _____
Snacks: _____

Exam minus 5 days
Exercise: _____ for _____ minutes
Breakfast: _____
Lunch: _____
Dinner: _____
Snacks: _____

Exam minus 4 days
Exercise: _____ for _____ minutes
Breakfast: _____
Lunch: _____
Dinner: _____
Snacks: _____

Exam minus 3 days
Exercise: _____ for _____ minutes
Breakfast: _____
Lunch: _____
Dinner: _____
Snacks: _____

Exam minus 2 days
Exercise: _____ for _____ minutes
Breakfast: _____
Lunch: _____
Dinner: _____
Snacks: _____

Exam minus 1 day
Exercise: _____ for _____ minutes
Breakfast: _____
Lunch: _____
Dinner: _____
Snacks: _____

STEP 8: GET YOUR ACT TOGETHER

Time to complete: 10 minutes to read; time to complete will vary
Activity: Complete Final Preparations worksheet

Once you feel in control of your mind and body, you're in charge of test anxiety, test preparation, and test-taking strategies. Now it's time to make charts and gather the materials you need to take to the exam.

GATHER YOUR MATERIALS

The night before the exam, lay out the clothes you will wear and the materials you have to bring with you to the exam. Plan on dressing in layers because you won't have any control over the temperature of the exam room. Have a sweater or jacket you can take off if it's warm. Use the checklist on the worksheet entitled Final Preparations on page 21 to help you pull together what you'll need.

DON'T SKIP BREAKFAST

Even if you don't usually eat breakfast, do so on exam morning. A cup of coffee doesn't count. Don't eat doughnuts or other sweet foods, either. A sugar high will leave you with a sugar low in the middle of the exam. A mix of protein and carbohydrates is best: cereal with milk and just a little sugar or eggs with toast will do your body a world of good.

Step 9: Do It!

Time to complete: 10 minutes, plus test-taking time
Activity: Ace Your Test!

Fast forward to exam day. You're ready. You made a study plan and followed through. You practiced your test-taking strategies while working through this book. You're in control of your physical, mental, and emotional state. You know when and where to show up and what to bring with you. In other words, you're better prepared than most of the other people taking the test with you. You're psyched!

Just one more thing. When you're done with the exam, you will have earned a reward. Plan a celebration. Call your friends and plan a party, or have a nice dinner for two—whatever your heart desires. Give yourself something to look forward to.

And then do it. Go into the exam full of confidence, armed with test-taking strategies you've practiced until they're second nature. You're in control of yourself, your environment, and your performance on exam day. You're ready to succeed. So do it. Go in there and ace the exam! And, then, look forward to your new career.

Final Preparations

Getting to the Exam Site

Location of exam: _____

Date of exam: _____

Time of exam: _____

Do I know how to get to the exam site? Yes _____ No _____

If no, make a trial run.

Time it will take to get to the exam site: _____

Things to lay out the night before

Clothes I will wear _____

Sweater/jacket _____

Watch _____

Photo ID _____

Admission card _____

4 No. 2 pencils _____

_____ _____

_____ _____

CHAPTER 3
MECHANICAL APTITUDE

CHAPTER SUMMARY

This chapter addresses topics specific to fields involving mechanical work, electronics, and machinery. The Shop Arithmetic section deals with basic math skills needed on the job. Later sections focus on the recognition and usage of common tools (Tool Knowledge), the ability to make calculations involving tools and mechanical equipment (Mechanical Insight), and general mechanical aptitude (Mechanical Knowledge). If you will be tested for a job involving mechanical skills, this chapter is for you.

LEARNINGEXPRESS MECHANICAL/SPATIAL EXAM ANSWER SHEET

SHOP ARITHMETIC

TOOL KNOWLEDGE

MECHANICAL INSIGHT

MECHANICAL KNOWLEDGE

MECHANICAL APTITUDE

SHOP ARITHMETIC

Does the idea of adding a list of fractions make you wince? Does your heart pound when a question begins "An eastbound train leaves the station at 8 A.M."? Relax! Here's where we brush up on lots of basic math, dust off all those old area formulas, and even make sense of those wordy word problems that bring forth nightmares.

Typical Shop Arithmetic questions deal with basic mathematics: fractions, decimals, proportions, percentages, mean (average), unit conversion, and geometry. These arithmetic skills are important in mechanical work because of the extensive measuring and calculations associated with this field. In addition to hands-on calculations, it is also necessary to be able to determine a time frame for a given task, approximate expenses, and generate price estimates.

Although you don't see many trains driving through the shop, these—albeit annoying—questions represent an additional category of questions: those of a more formula based nature. How long will it take to deliver a product by truck? How much weight is necessary to balance a lever? How many watts are used during a given period of time?

$$\text{Average (mean)} = \frac{\text{sum of all values}}{\text{\# of values}}$$

Conversions to Know:
12″ = 1′ (12 inches equal 1 foot)
3′ = 1 yard (3 feet equal one yard)
60 minutes = 1 hour
60 seconds = 1 minute
1 gross = 12 dozen (or 144)
1 ton = 2000 lbs

Formulas to Know:
$$\text{distance} = \text{constant rate} \times \text{time}$$
$$\text{torque} = \text{force} \times \text{lever arm}$$
$$\text{power in watts} = \frac{\text{energy in joules}}{\text{time in seconds}}$$

GEOMETRY FORMULAS

Triangle: Area = $\frac{1}{2} bh$

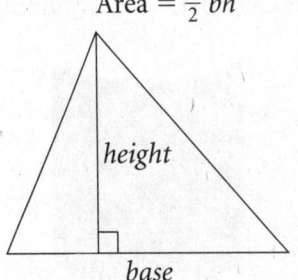

There are 180° in a triangle.

Rectangle: Area = lw

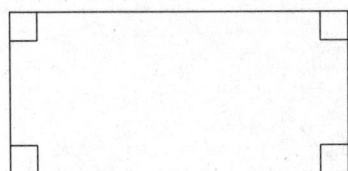

Circle: Area = πr^2

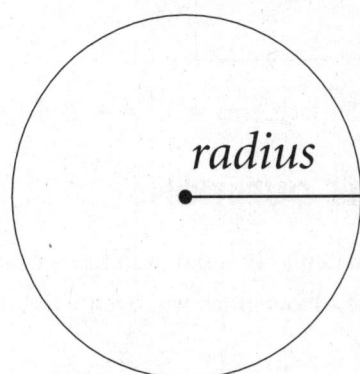

Circumference = $\pi d = 2\pi r$
(Use 3.14 or $\frac{22}{7}$ for π.)

LearningExpress Mechanical & Spatial Aptitude • CHAPTER 3

MECHANICAL APTITUDE

Pythagorean theorem: $a^2 + b^2 = c^2$

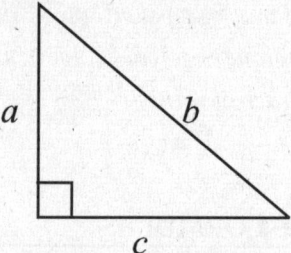

Right Circular Cylinder: Volume = $\pi r^2 h$

Total Surface Area = $2\pi RH + 2\pi r^2$

Rectangular Solid: Volume = lwh

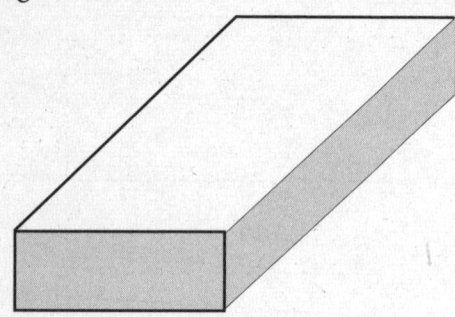

Total Surface Area = $2(lw) + 2(hw) + 2(lh)$

3 SAMPLE QUESTIONS

1. A particular brand of wall base costs $.60 per 8 inches. How much will twenty feet of wall base cost?
   a. $10.60
   b. $12.60
   c. $16
   d. $18

d. Some questions are straightforward unit conversions, but for the most part, questions (like this one) will be a combination of unit conversions *and* proportions. You should always convert your units *before* you set up a proportion. You know that 8 inches of wall base costs $.60, and you need to order 20 feet of it. First, you would convert the 20 feet into inches. You know 1 ft = 12 in, so you multiply:

$$20 \text{ ft} \times \frac{12 \text{ in}}{1 \text{ ft}} = 240 \text{ in.}$$

Notice that you crossed out the units you didn't want (feet) and ended up with the units you needed (inches). $\frac{12 \text{ in}}{1 \text{ ft}}$ is known as a *conversion factor*. Having the feet in the denominator of this conversion factor lets us cross out the "ft" unit in the original 20 ft. In other instances you may want to cross out inches and convert to feet. The conversion factor to use would be $\frac{1 \text{ ft}}{12 \text{ in}}$.

Tip: When dealing with "unwanted units," place the unit you want to cross out in the denominator (bottom part) of your conversion factor.

When dealing with "/ unwanted units," place the unit you want to cross out in the numerator (top part) of your conversion factor.

Now you know that you need a price for 240 inches. You set up a proportion:

$$\frac{8 \text{ inches}}{\$.60} = \frac{240 \text{ inches}}{\$ x}$$
$$8x = (.60)(240)$$
$$8x = 144$$
$$x = 18$$

MECHANICAL APTITUDE

2. An eastbound train destined for Station 2 leaves Station 1 at 8 A.M. traveling at a rate of 50 mph. At the same time, a westbound train leaves Station 2 for Station 1, traveling at a rate of 65 mph. If Station 1 is located 632.5 miles west of Station 2, then at what time will the two trains pass each other?
   a. 10:45 A.M.
   b. 12 noon
   c. 1:30 P.M.
   d. 2:15 P.M.

   c. This question deals with the constant rate formula: *distance = constant rate × time*, or $D = RT$. Drawing a diagram is a major asset:

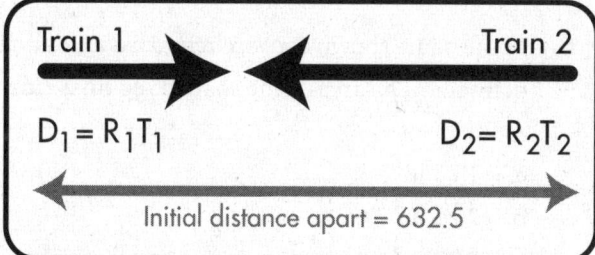

The total distance between the 2 stations will equal the sum of the distances traveled by each train for the period of time in question.

$$\text{Total Distance} = D_1 + D_2$$
$$\text{Total Distance} = R_1T + R_2T$$
$$632.5 = (50)(t) + (65)(t)$$
$$632.5 = 115\,t$$
$$5.5 = t$$

It will take 5.5 hours, or 5 and one half hours until the trains pass each other. If both trains left at 8 A.M., they would pass each other at 1:30 P.M.

Material	Pounds per cubic inch
brass	.303–.314
copper	.323
cast iron	.0254–.258
Tin	.264

3. Use the information in the table above to calculate the approximate weight of a copper cube with a side equal to $6\frac{1}{16}$ inches.
   a. 63 lbs
   b. 115 lbs
   c. 223 lbs
   d. 285 lbs

   c. Upon examining the table, you'll note that copper weighs .323 pounds per cubic inch. In order to determine the weight of the given cube, you'll need to find out how many cubic inches there are in the cube. Cubic inches, or in^3, represent the unit for *volume*. What is the volume of a cube? $V = side^3$, so $V = (6\frac{1}{16})^3 = 222.82056$ in^3, for those of you who are incredibly accurate. You then round up to 223 lbs, choice **c**. Or, for those of you who noticed that the answer choices are pretty spaced apart and contain no decimals, $V_{approx} = (6)^3 = 216$. You know you underestimated a bit, so you pick **c**. And the moral is: *Peek at the answers before you do an exceedingly tedious calculation by hand.*

LearningExpress Mechanical & Spatial Aptitude • CHAPTER 3

MECHANICAL APTITUDE

30 PRACTICE QUESTIONS

1. Of the choices listed, the greatest weight a chain hoist with $\frac{1}{4}$ ton capacity can safely lift is
   a. 294 lbs.
   b. 482 lbs.
   c. 524 lbs.
   d. 600 lbs.

2. A foreman originally scheduled a construction job for 12 workers, allowing eight days for completion. Due to an emergency at another site, he pulled four workers off the construction job. If the remaining workers work at the same rate, how many days should it take them to complete construction?
   a. 9 days
   b. 10 days
   c. 11 days
   d. 12 days

3. The area of a floor 7 yards by 16.5 feet is
   a. 18.5 yd^2
   b. 38.5 yd^2
   c. 72.5 yd^2
   d. 115.5 yd^2

4. A mechanic who earns a gross pay of $10.25 per hour notices that approximately 10% of his gross salary gets taken out for taxes. If he works 76 hours during a given pay period, his paycheck should be approximately what amount?
   a. $600
   b. $680
   c. $700
   d. $780

5. Given that cast iron weighs approximately .25 lb per cubic inch, how much would a cast iron bar 5.5' × 6" × 2" weigh?
   a. 198 lbs
   b. 214.4 lbs
   c. 265 lbs
   d. 312 lbs

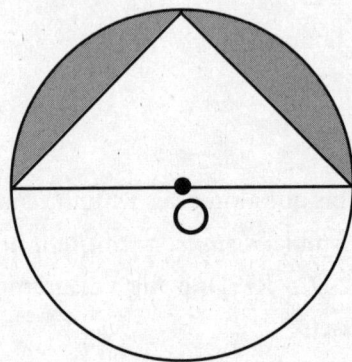

6. In the figure shown above, circle O has a 12-inch diameter. The area of the shaded region is closest to
   a. 18.3 in^2
   b. 20.5 in^2
   c. 24.2 in^2
   d. 30.0 in^2

7. Two crates that have a combined weight of 200 lbs, and two more weighing 150 lbs and 178 lbs, respectively, are all part of the same shipment. What is the average weight of the crates in this shipment?
   a. 80 lbs
   b. 90 lbs
   c. 100 lbs
   d. 132 lbs

MECHANICAL APTITUDE

8. What is the value of $\frac{5}{8}" + \frac{3}{16}" + \frac{1}{2}" + 2\frac{3}{4}"$?
   a. $3\frac{3}{16}"$
   b. $3\frac{12}{16}"$
   c. $4\frac{1}{16}"$
   d. $4\frac{11}{16}"$

9. If, in order to make 11 wooden coat racks you need 33 nails, then how many nails are needed for three coat racks?
   a. 9
   b. 8
   c. 7
   d. 6

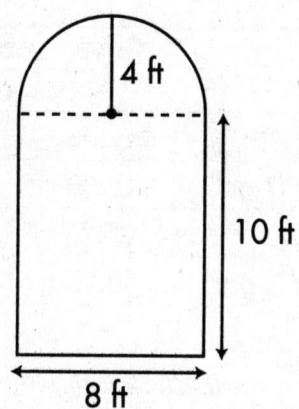

10. Athena wants to tile the floor pictured above with 12" × 12" tiles. If tiles come 20 to a box, how many boxes should she purchase?
    a. 5
    b. 6
    c. 7
    d. 8

11. Ralph is making metal boxes, each of which requires a six-inch hinge at the top. When cut, five pieces of piano hinge, each two yards long, will provide enough hinges for how many metal boxes?
    a. 100
    b. 60
    c. 30
    d. 12

12. How much more energy will be consumed by a 100-watt bulb in five minutes than a 50-watt bulb during the same period of time? (1 kJ = 1000 joules)
    a. 0 kJ
    b. 5 kJ
    c. 10 kJ
    d. 15 kJ

13. A metal spring has 1135 coils with radii equal to 5 inches. When it is unwound and measured, approximately how long will the wire be?
    a. 5,675 inches
    b. 15,135 inches
    c. 35,639 inches
    d. 39,725 inches

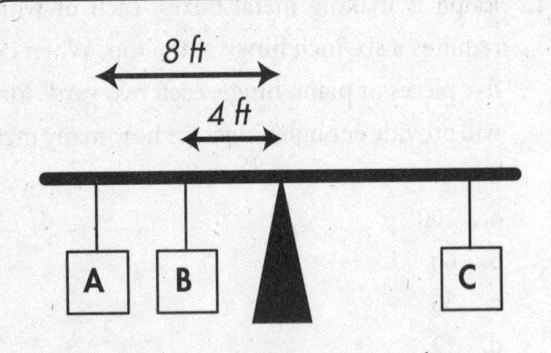

Note: Figure not drawn to scale.

14. In the figure above, block A weighs 10 pounds, block B weighs 15 pounds, and block C weighs 14 pounds. If the lever is perfectly balanced, then how far is Block C from the fulcrum?
   a. 10 ft
   b. 6 ft
   c. 12 ft
   d. 3 ft

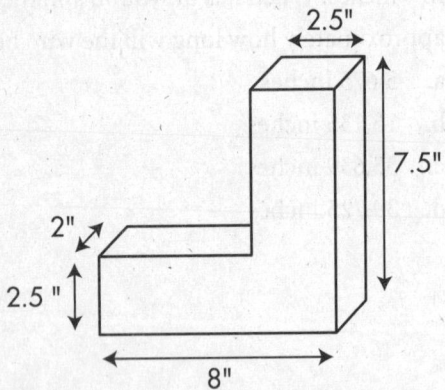

15. What is the volume of the three-dimensional solid in the figure above?
   a. 22.5 in³
   b. 40.3 in³
   c. 65.0 in³
   d. 83.5 in³

16. Train A is traveling northbound at 60 mph. On an adjacent track up north, Train B is traveling at 75 mph in a southbound direction. If the two trains departed from their respective stations at the same time, and pass each other after 120 minutes, then how far apart were they initially?
   a. 150 miles
   b. 270 miles
   c. 340 miles
   d. 420 miles

Use the table and the client information provided below to answer questions 17–18.

	Cost	Square ft. covered
primer (1 gal)	$12.00	400
latex paint (1 gal)	$15.00	400
primer ($\frac{1}{2}$ gal)	$7.25	200
latex paint ($\frac{1}{2}$ gal)	$8.75	200

Client Name: Erik L.
Information provided: Client wants bedroom painted; 2 walls with dimensions 3 yds × 8 ft, two walls with dimensions 4 yd × 8 ft, one window 3 ft × 2 ft (not to be painted), and one door (to be painted).

17. What is the total area of the room requiring paint and primer?
   a. 330 ft²
   b. 336 ft²
   c. 340 ft²
   d. 346 ft²

18. What is the least expensive combination of cans that would be ample for applying *one* coat of primer and *two* coats of paint to the client's room?
    a. one $\frac{1}{2}$ gal can of primer, one 1 gal can of latex paint
    b. one 1 gal can of primer, three $\frac{1}{2}$ gal cans of latex paint
    c. one 1 gal can of primer, one 1 gal can of latex paint, one $\frac{1}{2}$ gal can of latex paint
    d. one 1 gal can of primer, two 1 gal cans of latex paint

19. Given that dry sand weighs .059 lbs/in^3, approximately how much would a cubic foot of dry sand weigh?
    a. 70
    b. 98
    c. 100
    d. 102

20. Frank used 12 ft of wood to make a sign. After the project was finished, three ft of wood was left over. What percent of the wood did Frank use for the sign?
    a. 25%
    b. 50%
    c. 75%
    d. 85%

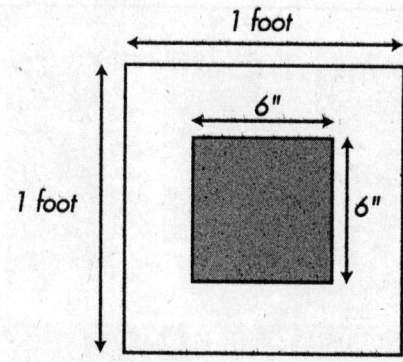

21. After the shaded region is removed from the figure above, what is the surface area of the remaining template material?
    a. 108 in^2
    b. 108 ft^2
    c. 110 in^2
    d. 110 ft^2

22. If the average speed limit along a truck's route is 50 mph, then approximately how long should it take for the driver to make a delivery 400 miles away, allowing for two 30 minute rest stops along the way?
    a. 9 hrs
    b. $8\frac{1}{2}$ hrs
    c. 8 hrs
    d. $7\frac{1}{2}$ hrs

MECHANICAL APTITUDE

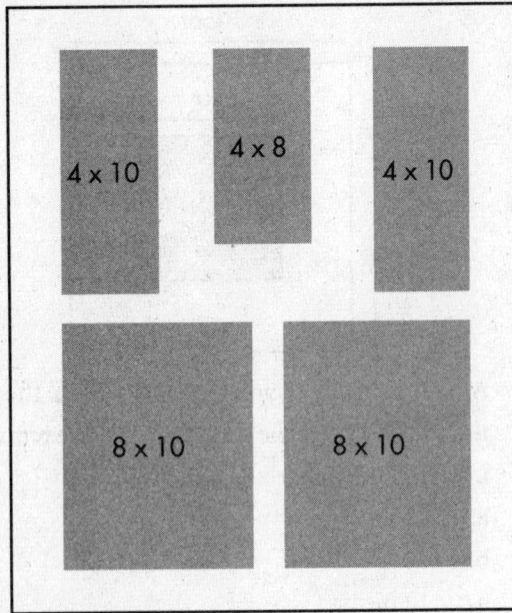

Day	Hours Worked
Monday	5.5
Tuesday	7
Wednesday	—
Thursday	—
Friday	6.5
Saturday	7
Sunday	7

23. *Refer to the figure above.* When assembled, what will the volume of the box be?
   a. 300 in³
   b. 320 in³
   c. 340 in³
   d. 360 in³

24. Jade's time sheet is pictured above. Normally, she gets $12/hr and she gets paid time and a half on Sunday. How much should her gross pay be for the week?
   a. $126
   b. $312
   c. $438
   d. $512

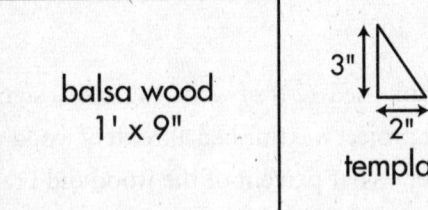

25. Referring to the above diagram, what is the maximum number of triangles that can be cut from the rectangular piece of balsa wood?
   a. 18
   b. 24
   c. 30
   d. 36

26. If a calculation is acceptable, it is figured to be ±.025 within the actual value. An acceptable calculation for an actual value equaling 57.683 would be
a. 57.433
b. 57.705
c. 57.933
d. 58.333

Type of Wood	Pounds per in³	Pounds per ft³
Red cedar	.014	24
Elm	.022	37
Maple	.027	47
Redwood	.016	28
Willow	.015	26

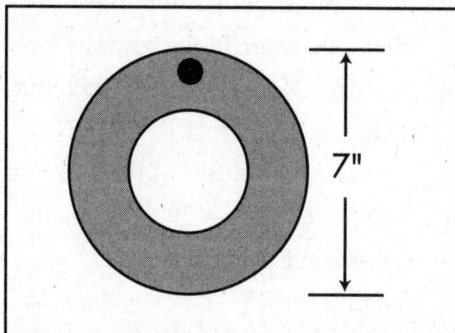

27. Of the choices below, which distance represents the number of feet traveled by the wheel pictured above as it revolves 20 times along its path?
a. $36\frac{2}{3}$
b. 40
c. $42\frac{1}{3}$
d. 45

28. What is the mean weight in pounds per cubic foot of all the wood types listed in the table above?
a. .019
b. .022
c. 30.8
d. 32.4

29. A shop brought in $6500 in April. In May, the amount made decreased by 10%. In June, the amount brought in increased 20% over May. How much money was made in June?
a. $8580
b. $7150
c. $7020
d. $6580

30. In the figure above, each spoke protrudes $\frac{1}{2}''$ into the outer rim, and $\frac{1}{2}''$ into the inner hub, leaving $4\frac{3}{4}''$ of each spoke visible in the finished wheel. The minimum dowel size necessary to cut enough spokes for two wheels would be
- a. 2′
- b. 4′
- c. 6′
- d. 8′

SHOP ARITHMETIC ANSWER EXPLANATIONS

1. **b.** One ton is equal to 2000 lbs, so a chain hoist with $\frac{1}{4}$-ton capacity can safely lift $\frac{1}{4}$ × 2000 lbs = 500 lbs. Answer **b** is the greatest value that doesn't exceed this 500 lb limit.

2. **d.** If it takes 12 workers 8 days to do a job, you can set up an equation to find out how long it will take the remaining 8 workers to do the same job.
   (12 workers)(8 days) = (8 workers)(x days)
   96 = 8x
   12 = x

3. **b.** First, you need to convert the 16.5 feet into yards. 16.5 feet × 1 yard/3 feet = 5.5 yd. Area = $l \times w$ = (7 yd)(5.5 yd) = 38.5 yd²

4. **c.** He earns $10.25 × 76 hrs or $779 as his gross pay. Since 10% of this amount will go to taxes, you multiply 10% × $779 = (.10)(779) = $77.9, to find that about 78 dollars will be subtracted from his gross pay. $779 − $78 = $701. Of the choices, c: 700 is the closest to this approximation.

5. **a.** Because you are given a weight per cubic inch, you must find out how many cubic inches there are in the bar. The length of the bar, 5.5′, must be converted into inches: 5.5′ x 12 in/1 ft = 66″. Next, you calculate the volume of the bar, V = lwh = (66″)(6″)(2″) = 792 in³. Finally, you can set up a proportion to calculate the weight:
   .25 lb/1 in³ = x lb/792 in³
   Cross multiply to get:
   (.25)(792) = (x)(1)
   198 = x

6. **b.** The shaded area is equal to the area of half the circle minus the area of the triangle:
   Shaded Area = $\frac{1}{2}$ Area of Circle − Area of Triangle
   Circle O has a diameter of 12″, so its radius is 6″. The area formula for a circle is A = πr^2, and we need $\frac{1}{2}$A = $\frac{1}{2}\pi r^2$ = $\frac{1}{2}$(3.14)(6²) = $\frac{1}{2}$(3.14)(36) = 18(3.14) = 56.52. The area formula for a triangle is A = $\frac{1}{2}bh$. Looking at the triangle in the figure, you can see the base is the diameter and the height is the radius of the circle:

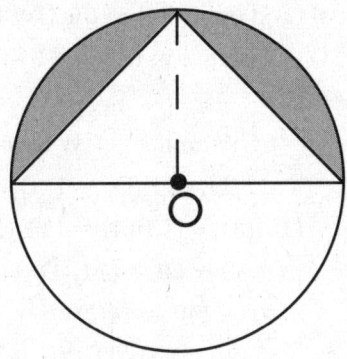

$$A = \tfrac{1}{2}bh = \tfrac{1}{2}(12)(6) = (6)(6) = 36$$

Substituting these area values into our formula:

Shaded Area = $\tfrac{1}{2}$ Area of Circle − Area of Triangle

Shaded Area = 56.52 − 36 = 20.52

Choice **b**, 20.5, represents the closest value.

7. d. Remember that there are 4 crates being averaged. You are given that the sum of the first two is 200, so you need to add in the 150 and 178 in order to find the total weight. Average = total weight/#crates = (200 + 150 + 178)/4 = 528/4 = 132 lbs.

8. c. First, you look at the denominator, or bottom part, of each of the fractions. What is the least common denominator? 16. Next, you convert all of the fractions so that they have a denominator of 16. For instance, to convert $\tfrac{5}{8}''$ you will multiply top and bottom by 2. Thus, $\tfrac{5}{8}''$ becomes $\tfrac{(5 \times 2)}{(8 \times 2)}$, which is $\tfrac{10}{16}''$. Next, you change the remaining fractions:

$$\tfrac{10}{16}'' + \tfrac{3}{16}'' + \tfrac{8}{16}'' + 2\tfrac{12}{16}''$$

Adding you get:

$$2\tfrac{33}{16}''$$

$\tfrac{33}{16}''$ is 33 divided by 16. 16 goes into 33 twice with a remainder of one. You stick the remainder over the denominator, 16. So, $\tfrac{33}{16}''$ reduces to $2\tfrac{1}{16}''$.

Now you have:

$$2'' + 2\tfrac{1}{16}''$$
$$4\tfrac{1}{16}''$$

9. a. Here you would set up a proportion:

$$\tfrac{11 \text{ racks}}{33 \text{ nails}} = \tfrac{3 \text{ racks}}{x \text{ nails}}$$

Cross-multiply to get:

$$(11)(x) = (33)(3)$$
$$(11)(x) = 99$$
$$(x) = 9$$

10. b. Since the tiles are 12″ × 12″, it is easy to see that they are 1′ × 1′, or 1 ft² each. The rectangular section of the floor is 10 ft × 8 ft = 80 ft², and thus will need 80 tiles. 80 tiles represents 4 boxes. The $\tfrac{1}{2}$ circle is a little trickier. Look at the diagram below:

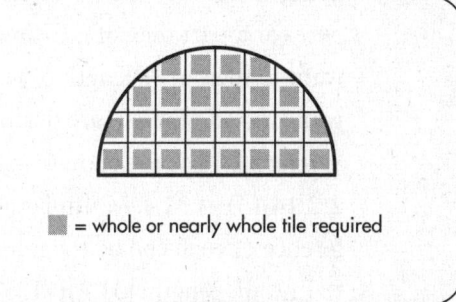

= whole or nearly whole tile required

As you can see, 1 box of 20 tiles will not be enough for this section. Therefore, she must buy 6 boxes in all.

11. b. Each piece of piano hinge is 2 yards long. First, convert this length into feet by multiplying: 2 yards × 3 feet/1 yard = 6 feet. Each piano hinge is 6 feet long, and will be cut into 6″, or $\tfrac{1}{2}$ ft, pieces. Each uncut hinge can be cut into 6 feet divided by $\tfrac{1}{2}$ ft = 6/.5 = 12 hinges of the proper length. Because you are starting with 5 long hinges you will get 5 × 12 = 60 hinges for the boxes.

12. d. Use the formula:

$$\text{power in watts} = \frac{\text{energy in joules}}{\text{time in seconds}}$$

Rearranging, you know *energy = power × time*. Converting the time into seconds, you get 5 minutes × 60 seconds/1 min = 300 seconds. Now all your units are correct, so you proceed with the calculations. For the 100-watt bulb, *energy* = (100)(300) = 30,000 joules. For the 50-watt bulb, *energy* = (50)(300) = 15,000 joules. Thus, the 100-watt bulb uses 30,000 − 15,000 = 15,000 joules more than the 50-watt bulb. Using 1 kJ = 1000 joules, 15,000 joules = 15 kJ.

13. c. No matter how menacing a question might look, if it has to do with circles, it is going to boil down to: *area* or *circumference* (or a part thereof). Ultimately, you want to measure a length of wire, so this is the tip off that you are dealing with *circumference*. For each coil $C = 2\pi r = 2(3.14)(5) = 31.4$. Multiply the circumference of each coil by the number of coils to find the length: (31.4)(1135) = 35,639.

14. a. If the lever is perfectly balanced, then all the weight on one side is counteracted by the weight on the other side. Blocks A and B would tend to pull the lever in a counterclockwise (CCW) direction, and Block C would tend to pull the lever in a clockwise (CW) direction. You will apply the torque equation: *torque = force × lever arm*. Here, each torque = *force × distance from pivot point*. Because there is no net rotation, you know the CCW torques are equal (and opposite) to the CW torque. Let D = distance in feet and F = force in pounds:

$$CCW\ torque = CW\ torque$$
$$F_A D_A + F_B D_B = F_C D_C$$
$$(10)(8) + (15)(4) = (14)(D_C)$$
$$80 + 60 = (14)(D_C)$$
$$140 = 14(D_C)$$
$$10 = D_C$$

15. c. The three-dimensional figure can be envisioned as two rectangular solids, each with Volume, $V = lwh$.

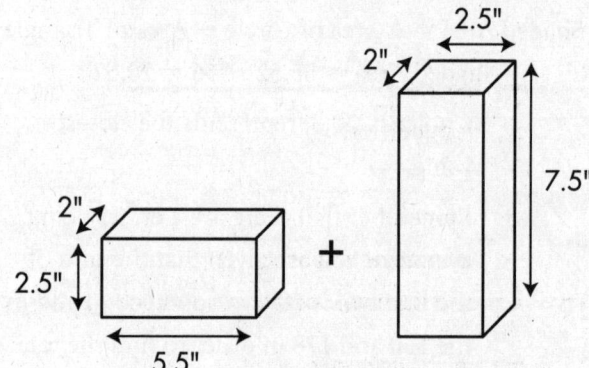

Thus, the volume of the shorter solid = lwh = (5.5)(2)(2.5), or 27.5. The volume of the taller solid = lwh = (2.5)(2)(7.5), or 37.5. Combined the volume is 27.5 + 37.5 = 65.

16. b. First, notice that the speed is in mph, and the time is given in minutes. Luckily, it is easy to convert the 120 minutes into 2 hours by inspection alone. (Mathematically: 120 min × 1 hr/60 min = 2 hr.) Next, make yourself a diagram:

MECHANICAL APTITUDE

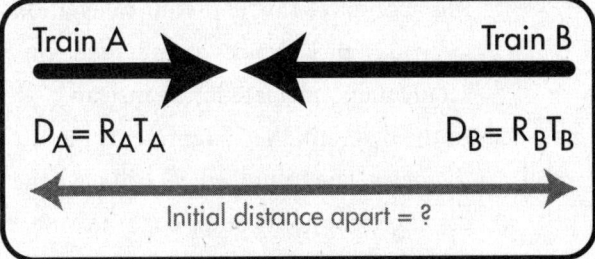

$$\text{Total Distance} = D_A + D_B$$
$$= R_A T + R_B T$$
$$= (60)(2) + (75)(2)$$
$$= 120 + 150$$
$$= 270 \text{ miles}$$

17. **a.** First, convert the dimensions of both walls into feet: 3 yd × 3 ft/yd = 9 feet. Thus, 2 walls are 9 ft × 8 ft. Also, 4 yd × 3 ft/yd = 12 feet, so there are 2 walls with dimensions 12 ft × 8 ft. Next, express the area of each wall in square feet. The first pair of walls take up 2 × (9 ft × 8 ft) = 2 × (72 ft²) = 144 ft². The second pair of walls take up 2 × (12 ft × 8 ft) = 2 × (96 ft²) = 192 ft². Together, all four walls have an area of 144 + 192 = 336 ft², but you need to subtract the area of the window. 336 ft² − (3 ft × 2 ft) = 336 ft² − 6 ft² = 330 ft².

18. **d.** 330 ft² requires primer, making the $\frac{1}{2}$ gallon can (covers only 200 ft²) insufficient. So, one 1 gallon can of primer must be purchased. Because two coats of paint will be applied, 660 ft² requires the latex paint. Purchasing one 1 gallon can of paint will cover 400 ft², leaving 660 ft² − 400 ft² = 260 ft² left to paint. Again, the $\frac{1}{2}$ gallon will not be enough. A second 1 gallon can of latex paint is required. In all, you need one 1 gallon can of primer and two 1 gallon cans of latex paint.

19. **d.** First, you must make yourself a conversion factor to convert the in³ into ft³. You know 1 ft = 12 in, so (1 ft)³ = (12 in)³. Cubing the 12, you know 1 ft³ = 1728 in³. The conversion factor to use is 1728 in³/1 ft³. Next, multiply: .059 lbs/in³ × 1728 in³/1 ft³ = 101.952 lbs/ft³. Choice **d** is the closest approximation.

20. **c.** Set up a proportion:
$$\frac{9 \text{ ft used}}{12 \text{ ft total}} = \frac{x}{100}$$
$$(100)(9) = (12)(x)$$
$$(900) = (12)(x)$$
$$75 = x$$

75% of the wood was used.

21. **a.** The surface area of the original piece of template material is 1′ × 1′ or 12″ × 12″ = 144 in². The inner square is 6″ × 6″, so its surface area is 36 in². Subtracting out the smaller piece you get: 144 in² − 36 in² = 108 in². Notice that choices **b** and **d** are way too large. Since **a** and **c** represent values in in², you know to solve this question using inches and in², and not feet.

22. **a.** You know that the driver has a total of 1 hour allotted for rest stops (30 min + 30 min). To calculate the time on the road, use the formula: *distance = constant rate × time*, or $D = RT$. This formula can be rearranged, so $T = D/R$. Substituting in the given values, you have: $T = 400/50 = 8$ hours. Add in the 1 hour for rest stops to get 9 hrs.

23. b. The two sets of matching pieces will be opposite sides in the assembled box. The lone 4 × 8 will be the bottom.

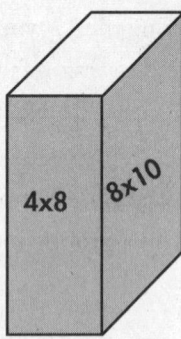

Using $V = lwh = 8 \times 4 \times 10 = 320$ in³.

24. c. Calculate the total number of hours at the normal rate: $5.5 + 7 + 6.5 + 7 = 26$. 26 hrs × $12/hr yields $312 so far. Next, figure out her wage when she works for time and a half. The "time" part is $12 and the "half" part is $\frac{1}{2} \times \$12 = \$6$. This means that on Sundays she makes $12 + 6 = \$18/hr$. From viewing the table, you know she worked 7 hours at this rate: $7 \times 18 = \$126$. Add this to the $312 to get $438.

25. d. These questions are best tackled by drawing a diagram:

As you can see, if you lay out your templates in an organized fashion, you can cut out 36 triangles.

26. b. $57.683 - .025 = 57.658$ and $57.683 + 0.25 = 57.708$. Thus, your answer must be between 57.658 and 57.708, inclusive. Choice **b**, 57.705 is the only value within this acceptable range. If your calculations led you to pick choices **a**, or **c**, then you accidentally calculated ±.25 instead.

27. a. In the diagram, the 7″ represents the *diameter*. The rolling wheel will have the distance around its outer edge in contact with the ground as it revolves. This question boils down to a *circumference* question. Using $C = \pi d$, with $\frac{22}{7}$ substituted in for π, this equation becomes: $C = \frac{22}{7}(7) = 22$ inches. If the wheel revolves 20 times we multiply 22×20 to get the number of inches traveled. This value, 440″, can be then converted into feet: $440″ \times 1\text{ ft}/12″ = 36\frac{2}{3}$ ft.

28. d. Notice that you will be using the information provided in the *last column* of the table. Mean (average) = sum of all values/# of values. The sum of the five values is: $24 + 37 + 47 + 28 + 26 = 162$. Putting this value into the equation: mean $= \frac{162}{5} = 32.4$

29. c. First, calculate the earnings for May. This amount is a 10% decrease from April's money. $6500 − 10% ($6500) = 6500 − (.10)(6500) = 6500 − 650 = $5850 for May. Next, calculate the 20% increase over this new amount for June. $5850 + 20%($5850) = 5850 + 1170 = $7020.

30. d. Each spoke is $4.75″ + .5″ + .5″ = 5.75″$ long. Each wheel needs 8 spokes, and you need enough spokes for *two* wheels, or 16 spokes. 16 × 5.75″ = 92″ required length. $92″ \times 1\text{ ft}/12″ = 7\frac{2}{3}$ ft. Of the choices listed, only an 8′ dowel would be long enough.

MECHANICAL APTITUDE

TOOL KNOWLEDGE

If you are planning to work with tools, you may find yourself sitting in front of a Tool Knowledge test. It probably comes as no surprise that this type of test is designed to test how familiar you are with specific tools. You simply match the tool to its function. In a matching question scenario, save any unfamiliar tools for last. Even though you might not know what a tool does, chances are you will be able to eliminate a couple of answers by deciding what it cannot do. For example, it would be a safe bet to assume that something with a jagged, sharp edge would not be used for measuring diameters or sanding. Just use your best judgment.

Perhaps you're a seasoned carpenter or maybe you've never touched a tool in your life. In any case, the following exercises were created with the intention of gauging and honing your tool knowledge. Although you may not be certified in a particular trade, chances are you've used or seen a conventional array of hand or power tools. This knowledge is exactly what you need to determine the correct answers in the following exercises.

TOOL MATCHING

Study the pictures of these tools and pick the answer that you think best fits the task described in the 1–5 listing.

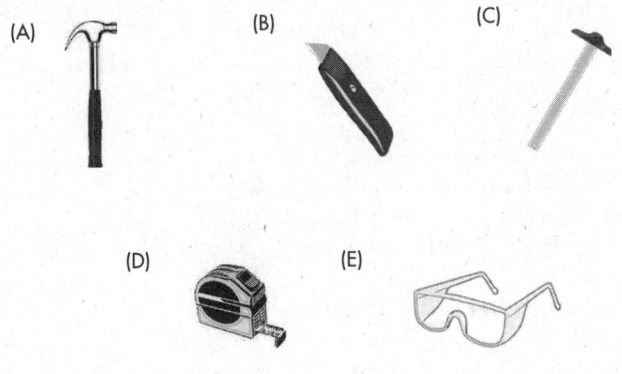

1. This is used to make straight lines for cutting on wooden boards or sheetrock.
2. This is used to measure distances and size.
3. This is used to both remove and install nails.
4. This is used to keep your eyes safe while using power tools.
5. This is used to make cuts in sheetrock and other soft building materials.

Although you may not recognize each of these tools for their specific use, a method of logical elimination can be used to answer the questions correctly. Take Question #2 for instance. Described in this task is a simple measuring tool and among the choices only one appropriate answer seems to fit. This is more obvious in Questions #4 and #5. Number 4 describes safety equipment used for the eyes and number 5 describes a cutting tool of some sort. Among the choices there is only one choice per question that would be appropriate. Check your answers against the answer explanation.

ANSWER EXPLANATIONS:

1. c.
2. d.
3. a.
4. e.
5. b.

Picture A is a basic claw hammer used for hammering and extracting nails.

Picture B is a common razor knife used for most light duty cutting purposes.

Picture C is a T-square commonly used for making straight lines.

Picture D is a tape measure commonly used for most measuring purposes.

Picture E is a pair of safety goggles used to protect your eyes while using equipment.

MECHANICAL APTITUDE

30 PRACTICE QUESTIONS
Tool Recognition

In the first part of this exercise there are three tool groups followed by five questions each. Each question will list a particular task involving a tool. Choose the tool that you think best fits the task described.

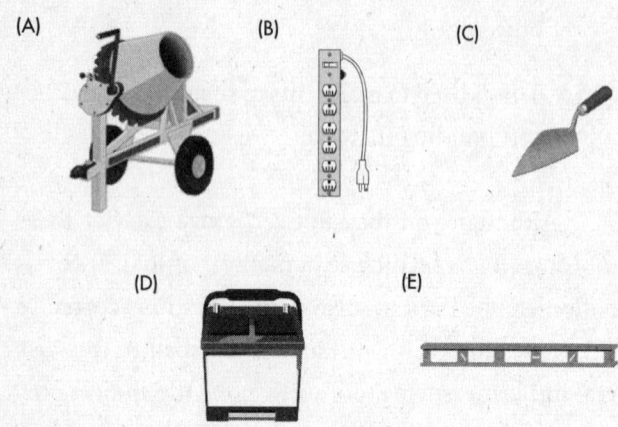

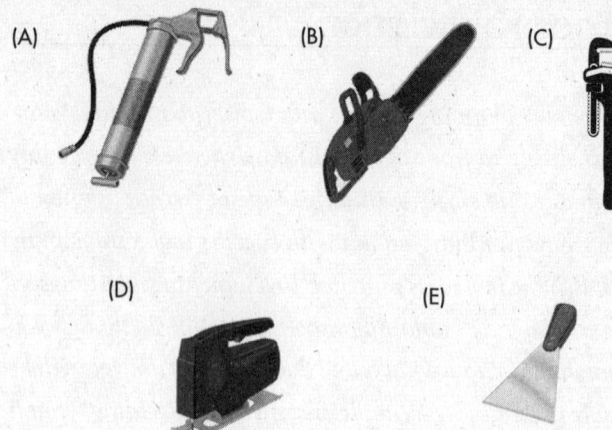

1. used as a remote power source
2. used to handle and level mortar while building a brick wall
3. used to verify if a structure is level or not
4. used to supply power to many electric tools
5. mixes water and powdered cement
6. used to loosen or tighten plumbing pipes
7. used to apply spackle or correction putty
8. used to apply lubrication to gears and machinery
9. used to cut large pieces of lumber or wood
10. used to cut round corners or designs in wooden boards

MECHANICAL APTITUDE

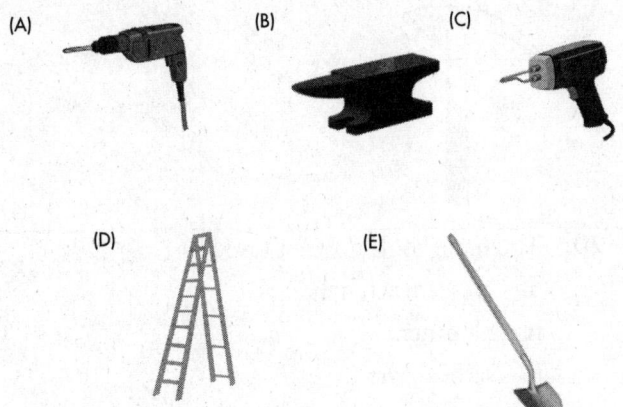

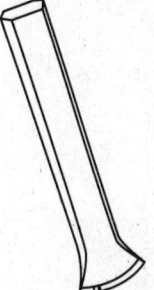

11. used with forging hammer to manipulate hot metal

12. used for dirt removal or ditch digging

13. used to help reach high places

14. used with bit to drill holes into wood

15. used with solder to fuse metal pieces together

17. The tool shown above would most likely be used to
    a. drive nails.
    b. weld metal.
    c. tighten bolts.
    d. carve wood.

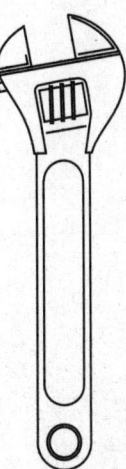

For questions 16–20, choose the best answer based on the picture shown.

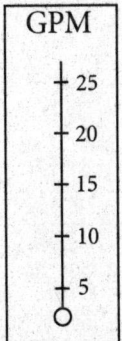

16. Which of the following is the type of gauge shown above? (Note: GPM = gallons per minute.)
    a. pressure gauge
    b. altitude gauge
    c. temperature gauge
    d. flow meter gauge

18. The hand tool shown above is a
    a. a crescent wrench.
    b. an offset wrench.
    c. a box wrench.
    d. a socket wrench.

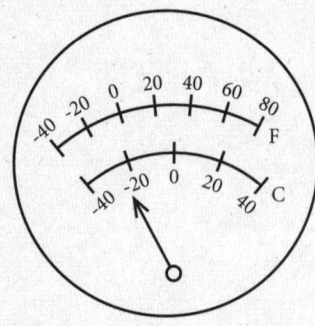

19. The gauge shown above is
   a. a pressure gauge.
   b. an altitude gauge.
   c. a temperature gauge.
   d. a flow meter gauge.

20. The hand tool shown above is a
   a. crescent wrench.
   b. hammer.
   c. screwdriver.
   d. pair of pliers.

MECHANICAL APTITUDE

TOOL ANALOGY

When you open up your toolbox, chances are you are not about to start composing essays. So why should a test on tools consist of elaborate text? It shouldn't. And luckily, these tests don't. For Tool Analogy questions, your job is to recognize the tool in the question and choose the most closely related tool or object from the given choices. If you are ever unsure of the tool in question, use your judgment and eliminate answer choices that do not look like they could have a related function.

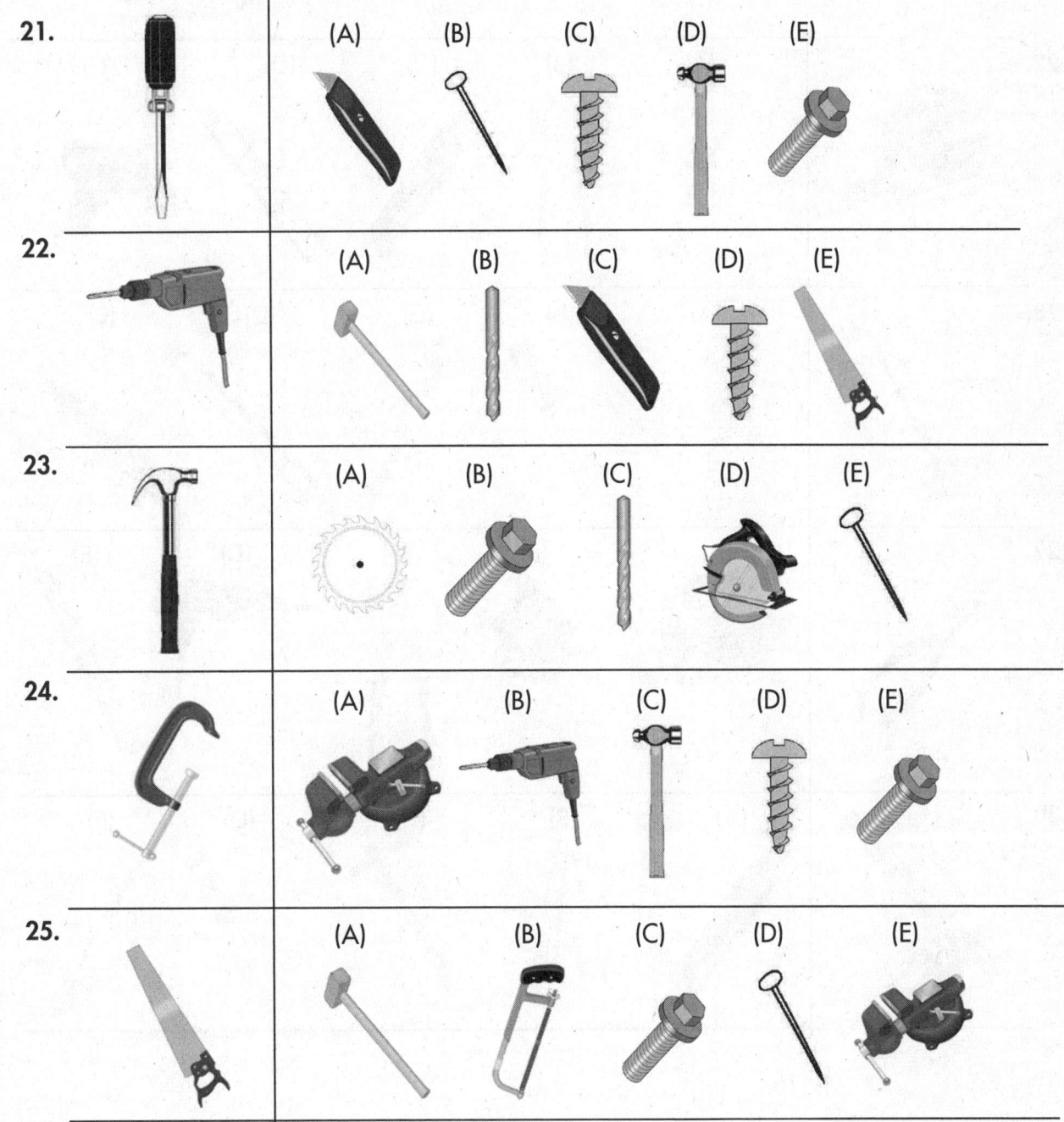

TOOL KNOWLEDGE ANSWER EXPLANATIONS

Tool Recognition

1. **d.** The picture in choice **d** is that of a conventional car battery which supplies a remote source of power for heavy equipment.
2. **c.** The picture in choice **c** is that of a trowel which is commonly used to handle and spread bricklaying mortar.
3. **e.** Choice **e** is a picture of a carpenter's level which is used to determine whether a structure is built level to the ground.
4. **b.** Choice **b** is a picture of a common electrical power strip that allows for many power tools to be used safely at once.
5. **a.** The picture shown in choice **a** is of a cement mixer that requires powdered cement and water.
6. **c.** Choice **c** is an image of a monkey wrench used to tighten and loosen pipes and large bolts.
7. **e.** The putty knife, which is represented in choice **e**, is used to apply and remove excess spackle and other substances like it.
8. **a.** The tool shown in choice **a** is a grease gun used to neatly apply grease to open gears and other pieces of machinery.
9. **b.** The chainsaw shown in choice **b** is used for chopping down trees or to make cuts into large pieces of lumber.
10. **d.** The jigsaw, choice **d**, is used to cut intricate designs and round corners into wooden planks.
11. **b.** The anvil, choice **b**, is a common tool used to fit and manipulate metal pieces usually with a hammer.
12. **e.** Choice **e** is a shovel that has virtually no other use than to displace dirt in some manner.
13. **d.** Choice **d** is a ladder that is used to work in high places not usually able to be reached without assistance.
14. **a.** Choice **a** is a power drill used with a drill bit to produce holes in metal or wood.
15. **c.** A soldering gun is shown in choice **c**. Used with an easily molten metal substance called solder, it is usually used to attach wires or to fuse metal together.
16. **d.** The flow meter gauge measures liquid flow rate, which is typically measured in units of volume per unit time, such as gallons per minute or cubic meters per second.
17. **d.** This tool carves wood. Hammers are used to drive nails; welders or torches are used to weld metal; wrenches are used to tighten bolts.
18. **a.** The correct answer is a crescent wrench.
19. **c.** The fact that this gauge measures temperature can be determined by the units of degrees Fahrenheit and degrees Celsius shown on the gauge.
20. **b.** A hammer is used for driving nails and other general carpentry functions.

Tool Analogy

21. **c.** The picture given is of a simple conventional flathead screwdriver and is most commonly associated with choice **c**, the screw.
22. **b.** The picture given is of an electric drill. Answer **b**, a drill bit, is the most relative choice.

23. **e.** The picture shown is that of a conventional claw hammer which is most commonly associated with choice **e**, the nail.
24. **a.** The picture shown is that of a common C-Clamp. From the answers given, choice **a**, the vice would be most relative.
25. **b.** The picture shown is of a common wood saw. From the answers given, choice **b**, the hack saw is the most relative.
26. **b.** The picture shown is that of a socket wrench. From the choices given, answer **b**, a hex-head bolt which is tightened and loosened by a socket wrench, is most relative.
27. **d.** The picture shown is that of a tape measure. Answer **d** is best because it shows a ruler which is a similar tool.
28. **b.** The picture shown is that of a stone chisel. The best response is answer **b**, a wood chisel, which is a similar tool.
29. **c.** The picture shown is a pair of needle-nose pliers. Among the choices given, choice **c**, an adjustable set of pliers, is the best answer.
30. **c.** The picture shown is an adjustable square. Choice **c** is a T-square. Both of these tools are used to make accurate markings for cutting.

MECHANICAL INSIGHT

Can you analyze the components of a machine and relate them to its function? Mechanical experience is helpful on these types of test questions, but notice the focus on the word insight, because it really means mechanical aptitude. If you like working with machines and need to take a Civil Service or private company's placement test, the questions in this section will help you get prepared and gauge your skill.

30 PRACTICE QUESTIONS

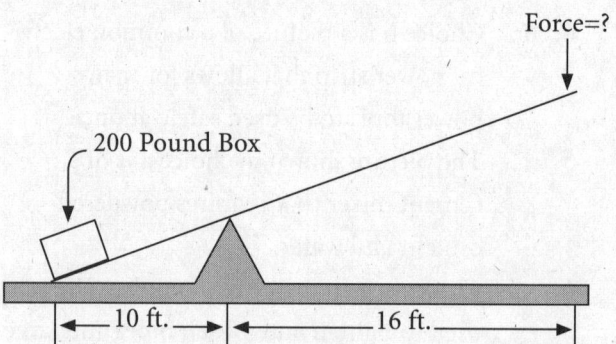

1. In the diagram shown above, Frank must lift a 200-pound box using a lever. How many pounds of force must Frank apply to the right side of the lever to lift the box? w^x
    a. 100 pounds
    b. 125 pounds
    c. 200 pounds
    d. 320 pounds

2. What units are used to measure velocity?
    a. feet per minute
    b. feet per second
    c. miles per hour
    d. all of the above

MECHANICAL APTITUDE

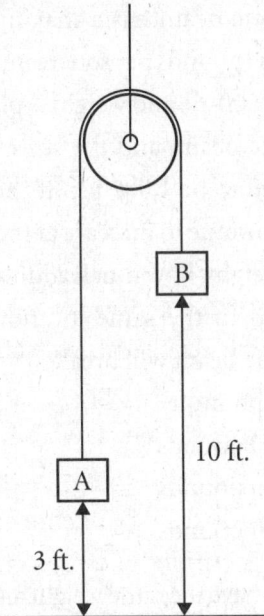

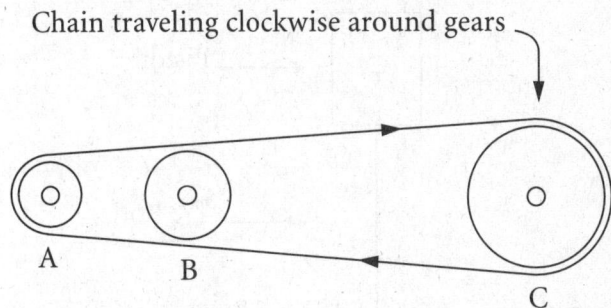

3. In the diagram shown above, how much must block A be raised to allow block B to rest on the floor beneath it?
   a. 3 feet
   b. 10 feet
   c. 13 feet
   d. 7 feet

4. Which of the following items listed below most resembles a lever?
   a. a seesaw
   b. an elevator
   c. a car
   d. a door

5. Lori and Steve are sitting in separate cars at a stop sign. Lori accelerates at twice the rate that Steve accelerates. After five minutes of constant acceleration, who has traveled a longer distance?
   a. Steve
   b. Lori
   c. they have traveled the same distance
   d. not enough information to answer the question

6. In the diagram shown above, gears A, B, and C are connected by a chain. The diameters of the gears are 1 inch, 2 inches, and 4 inches respectively. If gear A is turning at 20 revolutions per minute (RPM), what is the turning rate of gear C?
   a. 5 RPM
   b. 20 RPM
   c. 40 RPM
   d. 80 RPM

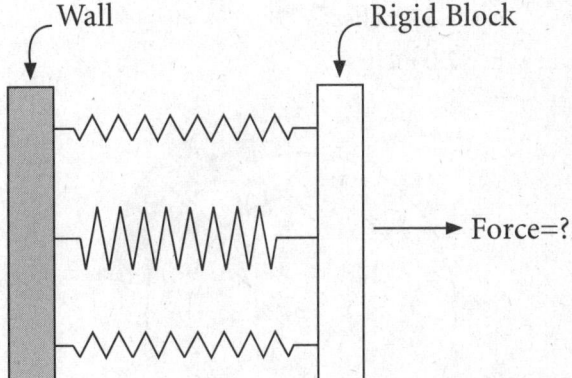

7. Three springs are arranged in parallel between a wall and a rigid block, as shown above. The spring constants are 5 pounds per inch, 12 pounds per inch, and 5 pounds per inch respectively. What force is required to move the block 2 inches to the right?
   a. 12 pounds
   b. 44 pounds
   c. 22 pounds
   d. 10 pounds

MECHANICAL APTITUDE

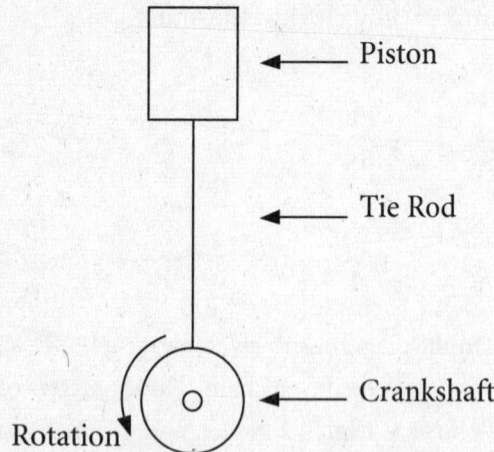

8. The figure above shows a piston that is connected to a crankshaft by a tie rod. The crankshaft has a radius of 1.0 inch. If the crankshaft rotates 180 degrees (one half of a revolution), how far downward will the piston be pulled?
   a. 0.5 inches
   b. 1.0 inch
   c. 1.33 inches
   d. 2.0 inches

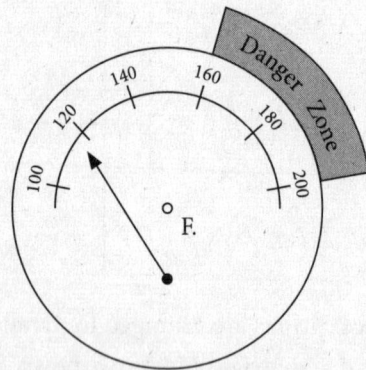

9. On the temperature gauge shown above, what is the maximum recommended operating temperature (degrees Fahrenheit) for this gauge in order to remain in a safe zone?
   a. 120
   b. 140
   c. 160
   d. 180

10. A concrete beam has a maximum strength of 3,000 psi (pounds per square inch). In an experiment, a 500-pound weight is placed in the center of the beam, and the stress in the beam is measured to be 1,000 psi. If the stresses in the beam continue to increase at the same rate with added weight, how much additional weight can be added to the same location on the beam before the beam will break?
    a. 500 pounds
    b. 1,000 pounds
    c. 1,500 pounds
    d. 3,000 pounds

11. Two cars have the same weight and the same type of engine and travel at the same speed. One is a boxy minivan and the other a low, sleek sports car. Which factor below best explains why the sports car gets better gas mileage than the minivan?
    a. friction
    b. wind resistance
    c. acceleration
    d. all of the above

12. Which principle of mechanical motion is used in the design of a roller coaster?
    a. momentum
    b. friction
    c. acceleration
    d. all of the above

13. Two balls of the same density, one large and one small, are rolled toward each other at the same speed. When they collide, what will happen to the smaller ball?
   a. It will be propelled backwards in the opposite direction.
   b. It will continue forward in the same direction.
   c. It will stop and stay at the point of impact.
   d. It will jump over the heavier ball.

14. A seesaw works best when both people weigh the same. This demonstrates which principle of mechanical motion?
   a. relative velocity
   b. centrifugal force
   c. acceleration
   d. equilibrium

15. A grandfather clock typically has a long pendulum that swings back and forth to keep time. Which description below best describes the action of this pendulum?
   a. periodic motion
   b. relative velocity
   c. free-falling body
   d. all of the above

16. Which term below best describes the OPPOSITE of "an increase in speed"?
   a. velocity
   b. friction
   c. deceleration
   d. rotation

17. When a load is applied to a structural beam, which of the following does the beam experience?
   a. deflection
   b. stress
   c. strain
   d. all of the above

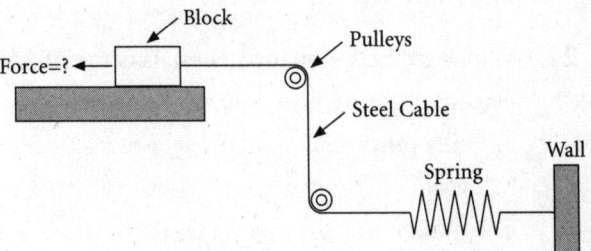

18. In the diagram shown above, the spring is very stiff and can be stretched 1 inch by a pulling force of 100 pounds. How much force must be applied to the block in order to move the wall 3.5 inches to the left?
   a. 100 pounds
   b. 300 pounds
   c. 350 pounds
   d. 3.5 pounds

19. When a cannon ball is fired at an upward angle from the surface of the earth, which of the following causes it to come back to the surface of the earth?
   a. friction
   b. centrifugal force
   c. gravity
   d. momentum

20. Which of the following best describes the location of the center of gravity of a steel bar that is four feet long and is the same diameter along its length?
    a. two feet from the left end of the bar
    b. three feet from the right end of the bar
    c. on the right end of the bar
    b. on the left end of the bar

21. Which of the following materials is the LEAST elastic?
    a. silly putty
    b. wax
    c. rubber
    d. paper

22. Block A is twice as big as Block B. Block B is made of a material that is three times as dense as the material in Block A. Which block is heavier?
    a. Block A
    b. Block B
    c. both blocks weigh the same amount
    d. not enough information

23. A block of steel has a density of 0.29 pounds per cubic inch. If the block has dimensions of 1 inch by 1 inch by 2 inches, what is its weight?
    a. 0.29 pounds
    b. 0.58 pounds
    c. 2.0 pounds
    d. 4.0 pounds

24. What is the structural principle behind the use of snowshoes?
    a. to spread the load out on the snow
    b. to increase the weight on the snow
    c. to slow down the person using them
    d. to prevent slippage in the snow

25. There are three beams that are each 10 feet long and all of the same size. One is made of wood, another of steel, and the third of concrete. If identical loads are applied to these three beams, which of the following will occur?
    a. The concrete beam will deflect more than the other two.
    b. The wood beam will deflect less than the steel beam.
    c. The steel beam will deflect less than the wood beam.
    d. The wood beam will deflect less than the concrete beam.

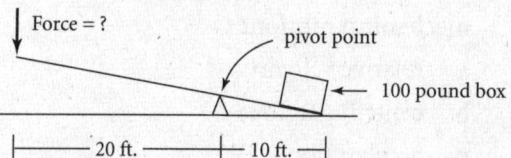

26. In the diagram shown above, Joe must lift a 100-pound box using a lever. How many pounds of force must Joe apply to the left side of the lever to lift the box? ($w \times d_1 = f \times d_2$)
    a. 100 pounds
    b. 200 pounds
    c. 50 pounds
    d. 33 pounds

MECHANICAL APTITUDE

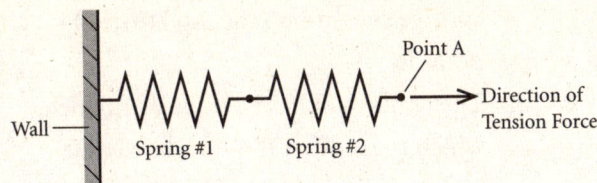

27. Two springs are arranged in series as shown above. Spring #1 is very stiff and will become 1 inch longer when a tension force of 10 pounds is applied to it. Spring #2 is very soft and will become 2 inches longer when a tension force of 5 pounds is applied to it. What will be the change in length of the two springs (that is, how far will point A move to the right) when a force of 20 pounds is applied?
    a. 10 inches
    b. 6 inches
    c. 8 inches
    d. 3 inches

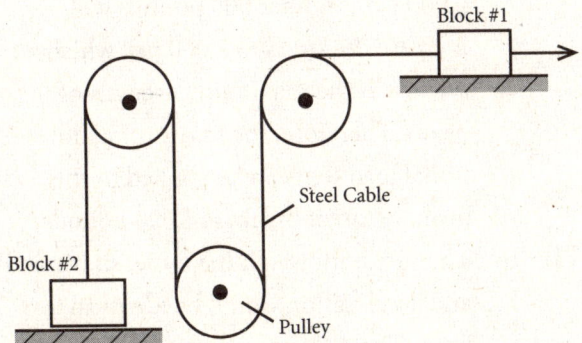

28. In the diagram shown above, if block #1 is moved 10 feet to the right, how far upward is block #2 lifted?
    a. 3 feet
    b. 5 feet
    c. 10 feet
    d. 20 feet

29. Which of the following groups of items listed below consists entirely of fasteners—that is, of devices that are used to connect two items together?
    a. chairs, tables, and windows
    b. string, scissors, and glue
    c. rivets, levers, and bolts
    d. snaps, buckles, and buttons

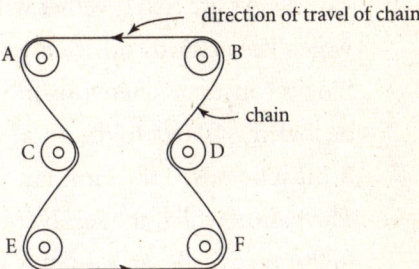

30. In the diagram shown above, which gears are turning clockwise?
    a. A, C, and E
    b. B, D, and F
    c. C and D
    d. E and F

MECHANICAL INSIGHT ANSWER EXPLANATIONS

1. **b.** (200 pounds)(10 feet) = f(16 feet). Solving for f gives 125 pounds.
2. **d.** All the choices are true. Velocity is measured in units of distance in a certain amount of time. All of the answers use these units.
3. **b.** The blocks are tied together with a cable, which keeps the distance between the blocks constant. Therefore, if block B is to be lowered 10 feet to the floor, then block A must be raised the same amount.
4. **a.** The bar on which the seesaw pivots is the fulcrum of the lever. Also, the seesaw raises and lowers a load (person) on one end when a force (pushing off the ground) is applied on the other end.
5. **b.** Lori's acceleration rate is twice Steve's rate. Since they both started at the same time and accelerated for the same amount of time, Lori will travel twice as far as Steve.
6. **a.** Gear C is 4 times the diameter of gear A. Since the gears are all connected by a chain, the tip velocity of all the gears must be the same; otherwise, the chain would come off the gears. Therefore, if the tip velocity is to be the same for all gears and gear C is 4 times larger than gear A, then gear C must be turning 4 times slower than gear A. Twenty RPM divided by 4 equals 5 RPM.
7. **b.** All three springs must be stretched 2 inches. The question tells you that it takes 5 pounds to stretch spring A one inch. Therefore, it takes 10 pounds to stretch it 2 inches. Apply this to the other two springs and add up the total to get 44 pounds.
8. **d.** The crankshaft has a radius of 1.0 inch, which means that the diameter is 2.0 inches. If the crankshaft rotates one-half revolution (180 degrees) from its starting point, the attachment of the tie rod to the crankshaft will move from the top of the crankshaft down to the bottom. This is equivalent to the diameter of the crankshaft, which is 2.0 inches.
9. **c.** The indicated danger zone on the gauge is from 160 degrees to 200 degrees Fahrenheit. Thus, it is acceptable to operate up to 160 degrees for this gauge.
10. **b.** The first 500 pounds generated 1,000 psi of stress in the beam; therefore, 500 more pounds will increase the total stress to 2,000 psi. Another 500 pounds will increase the stress to 3,000 psi, which we are told is the maximum strength of the beam. Therefore, the maximum additional load that can be applied to this beam before it breaks is 1,000 pounds.
11. **b.** The cars both weigh the same, so friction and acceleration would be identical for both. The difference is that a sports car has a low, sleek shape compared to a minivan and therefore has less drag from the wind.
12. **d.** Acceleration must be considered in designing the maximum rise of the first hill. Momentum must be considered to ensure the train gets back to the starting point, since it has no motor. Friction must be considered in the design of the braking system.

MECHANICAL APTITUDE

13. a. This is a demonstration of momentum. Momentum is defined as mass (weight) multiplied by velocity. Since both balls have the same speed (velocity), the heavier ball (the larger one in this case, since both balls have the same density) will have more momentum. Therefore, upon impact, the heavier ball will be slowed but continue in the same direction and knock the smaller, lighter ball backward.

14. d. When an object is at equilibrium, it has equal forces acting on it. When both people on a seesaw weigh the same, the seesaw is in equilibrium, and it is easier for each person to push off the ground.

15. a. In the equilibrium position, the pendulum hangs straight down. When displaced from this position, the pendulum does not simply return to the equilibrium position, but swings back and forth in a regular, repetitive manner. This is the definition of periodic motion.

16. c. By definition, deceleration means slowing down.

17. d. The beam will move, or deflect, under the load. The beam will also undergo internal stresses and strains caused by the load.

18. c. 3.5 inches multiplied by 100 pounds per inch equals 350 pounds.

19. c. On earth, the force of gravity pulls objects toward its surface. The force of a cannon is not enough to allow the cannon ball to escape this pull.

20. a. The center of gravity of an object is loosely defined as "the middle of its weight" or "the point at which you could balance it on your finger;" in this case, that would be two feet from the left end (or two feet from the right end).

21. d. Elasticity is defined as "stretchiness." It is a measure of how easy it is to deform a material. Paper is the stiffest or least elastic of the material listed.

22. b. Block B is smaller, but we are told it is made of a material that is three times more dense (density is weight per unit volume) than Block A. Therefore, since Block A is only twice as big as Block B, it is actually 50 percent lighter.

23. b. The volume of the block can be calculated by multiplying its length by its width by its height, or 1 times 1 times 2, which equals 2 cubic inches. The weight is the density multiplied by its volume, which is 2 cubic inches multiplied by 0.29 pounds per cubic inch, which equals 0.58 pounds.

24. a. Snowshoes distribute the weight of the person over a larger area than boots alone and reduce the pressure on the snow. This keeps the person from sinking so far into the snow.

25. c. The steel beam will deflect less than the wood beam. Choice **a** is not correct since the concrete beam will deflect less than the wood beam—concrete is stiffer than wood.

26. c. The distance from the pivot point to the point of application of the force (20 feet) is twice the distance from the pivot point to the box (10 feet). Therefore, in order to lift the box, the required force will be one half of the weight of the box, or 50 pounds.

27. a. Because the springs are in series, their amount of stretch is additive. Spring #1

LearningExpress Mechanical & Spatial Aptitude • CHAPTER 3

will stretch 1 inch under 10 pounds. So its total stretch under 20 pounds will be 2 inches. Spring number 2 is being subjected to a load of 20 pounds, which is four times the load that will stretch it 2 inches. Therefore, its total stretch will be 8 inches. Adding the amount of stretch for the two springs together gives you 10 inches.

28. c. The two blocks are directly connected by a fixed length of steel cable. Therefore, regardless of the number of pulleys between the two blocks, the distance moved by one block will be the same as the other block.

29. d. The items listed that are *not* fasteners are chairs, tables, windows, scissors, and levers.

30. c. The other gears are turning counter-clockwise. It helps to follow the direction of the chain, which is connected to all of the gears.

MECHANICAL KNOWLEDGE

If you work with machines or plan on testing for a job or military position that deals with mechanical equipment, you will probably be faced with a test of your mechanical know-how. Mechanical Knowledge tests represent a paper and pencil test of hands-on experience. Of course a stressful test-taking environment is nothing like actual on-the-job experience. This section will help you brush up on the knowledge you need to do well on these tests and get you used to the test format.

30 PRACTICE QUESTIONS

1. The purpose of a camshaft in an internal combustion engine is to
    a. provide ignition of the fuel.
    b. provide cooling of the engine.
    c. provide lubrication of the engine.
    d. transfer energy to the drive train.

2. Vernier calipers are used to perform which of the following functions?
    a. tightening
    b. measuring
    c. cutting
    d. drilling

3. Which of the following items is used to gain a mechanical advantage?
    a. a lever
    b. a protractor
    c. a spring
    d. a gear

4. Which of the following wrenches is adjustable?
    a. a crescent wrench
    b. a pipe wrench
    c. channel locks
    d. all of the above

MECHANICAL APTITUDE

5. What type of gauge would be read in units of mph (miles per hour)?
   a. a speed gauge
   b. a depth gauge
   c. a pressure gauge
   d. a temperature gauge

6. The main purpose of a muffler on a car is to
   a. cool the engine.
   b. conserve fuel.
   c. reduce engine noise.
   d. increase horsepower.

7. Which of the following mechanical devices is typically found on an automobile?
   a. an electric router
   b. a hinge
   c. a skimmer float
   d. a drill

8. Of the definitions shown below, which one best describes "preventive maintenance"?
   a. fixing a device after it fails for the first time
   b. periodically making small adjustments to a device to prevent failure
   c. purchasing a new device in anticipation of the old one's wearing out
   d. purchasing a new device after an old one wears out

9. Which tool listed below is the best for cutting metal?
   a. a handsaw
   b. a circular saw
   c. a hacksaw
   d. a back saw

10. Gears are used in which of the following automotive systems?
    a. the cooling system
    b. the suspension system
    c. the exhaust system
    d. the transmission system

11. In the United States, most speedometers on automobiles have two different scales: mph, which stands for miles per hour, and kph, which stands for
    a. kilometers per mile.
    b. kilometers per hour.
    c. kilograms per hour.
    d. kilobytes per hour.

12. Which of the following items is typically part of the suspension of a car?
    a. the carburetor
    b. the wheels
    c. the rods
    d. the pistons

13. "Stilson," "strap," "torque," and "spanner" all denote types of
    a. saws.
    b. hammers.
    c. pliers.
    d. wrenches.

14. Which of the following portions of a building must be constructed before all the others listed?
    a. flooring
    b. framing
    c. foundation
    d. walls

MECHANICAL APTITUDE

15. Which of the following building materials may be used for structural purposes?
    a. wood
    b. plasterboard
    c. glass
    d. fiberglass insulation

16. Which construction procedure listed below is most likely to require the use of a saw for cutting wood?
    a. building a foundation for a bridge
    b. building a wall for an apartment building
    c. building a deck for a house
    d. all of the above

17. What is the name of the building procedure that is used to pinpoint the exact location of a corner of a building or the exact elevation of a bridge deck?
    a. forming
    b. surveying
    c. masonry
    d. all of the above

18. The sub-flooring of a typical residential house in the United States is normally made of which of the following materials?
    a. plastic
    b. wood
    c. fiberglass
    d. resin

19. Which of the following are types of screwdrivers?
    a. Phillips
    b. Allen
    c. socket
    d. all of the above

20. Which automotive system uses the following components: water pump, radiator, and thermostat?
    a. the interior heating system
    b. the engine cooling system
    c. the exhaust system
    d. the braking system

21. Which of the following refers to a kind of chisel?
    a. diamond point
    b. dovetail
    c. coping
    d. duck bill

22. If your car will not start due to a dead battery, which of the following measures should be taken to get the car started?
    a. install a new starter
    b. check the fuel level
    d. use jumper cables
    d. replace all of the fuses

23. A spring is most likely to be used on which of the following?
    a. a cabinet door
    b. a table
    c. an electric cord
    d. a pogo stick

24. Which of the following items listed below most resembles a lever?
    a. a seesaw
    b. an elevator
    c. a car
    d. a door

MECHANICAL APTITUDE

25. An elevator uses which of the following mechanical devices?
    a. a cable
    b. a pulley
    c. a motor
    d. all of the above

26. Water is flowing through a piping system. Eventually, due to friction losses and a rise in elevation of the piping, the flow rate of the water becomes very slow. What mechanical device can best be used to increase the flow of the water?
    a. a gear
    b. a winch
    c. a pump
    d. a compressor

27. What common mechanical device is typically used on a push button, such as on a push-button telephone, a computer keyboard, and an electric garage door opener, in order to return the button to its original position?
    a. a wheel
    b. a pulley
    c. a spring
    d. a gear

28. Which of the following types of wire cutter would allow a worker to cut a heavy piece of wire using the least force?
    a. a wire cutter with very thick handles
    b. a wire cutter whose handles are longer than its blades
    c. a wire cutter with finger grooves on the grip
    d. a wire cutter whose blades are longer than its handles

29. What type of gauge is read in units of psi (pounds per square inch)?
    a. a pressure gauge
    b. a depth gauge
    c. a speed gauge
    d. an RPM gauge

30. Engine overheating can be caused by which of the following?
    a. a low fuel level
    b. too much motor oil
    c. a faulty transmission
    d. a faulty thermostat

MECHANICAL KNOWLEDGE ANSWER EXPLANATIONS

1. **d.** The camshaft is rotated by the up and down movement of the piston and transfers the energy from the internal combustion engine to the drive train (transmission). The spark plugs provide fuel ignition. The radiator provides engine cooling. The oil provides lubrication.
2. **b.** Vernier calipers are used to determine precise internal or external measurement.
3. **a.** A lever is the correct choice. A protractor is used to measure angles. A spring is used for many purposes but not to gain a mechanical advantage. A gear is used to change rotational speeds of shafts.
4. **d.** All of these wrenches can be used on different size objects.
5. **a.** A speed gauge is the correct answer. A depth gauge would use units of length such as feet or meters. A pressure gauge would use units of pressure such as psi (pounds per square inch) or bar (barometric atmospheric pressure) and is usually measured in inches of mercury. A temperature gauge would use units of temperature such as degrees Celsius or degrees Fahrenheit.
6. **c.** The muffler is placed at the end of the exhaust system of an automobile to reduce engine noise. It is a chamber that dampens the noise coming from the internal combustion engine.
7. **b.** Hinges are found on car doors, as well as on other parts such as the trunk lid, the hood, and the gas cap lid.
8. **b.** Preventive maintenance is periodically making small changes and adjustments on a device to prevent failure. Examples include changing the oil in a car engine, adjusting the brakes on a car, lubricating the moving parts on a pump, and changing the fan belts and hoses on a truck.
9. **c.** A hacksaw is the correct answer. This type of saw is similar to a saw for cutting wood except that the teeth are very small and close together.
10. **d.** The transmission uses different size gears in order to adjust for different speeds. With a manual transmission, the driver changes these gears with the gear shift. An automatic transmission changes the gears at preset speeds.
11. **b.** Kilometers per hour is the correct answer. A kilometer is a unit of distance in the metric system that is roughly equivalent to 0.6 miles.
12. **b.** The suspension of an automobile is typically composed of springs, shocks, wheels, and tires.
13. **d.** All of these are names applied to various kinds of wrenches.
14. **c.** The foundation is the base upon which the building is constructed. Therefore, it must be constructed before the framing, the walls, or the flooring.
15. **a.** Wood is typically used to build the walls of houses or pedestrian bridges. The other materials listed are used in buildings for purposes other than structural support.
16. **d.** The saw could be used to cut the wood used for the forms for a concrete bridge foundation. It could be used for cutting the studs for the apartment building wall.

MECHANICAL APTITUDE

It could also be used for cutting the wood for a cedar deck railing.

17. **b.** Surveying is the practice of determining locations and elevations of structures and roadways. This is accomplished through the use of many instruments and tools, including levels for measuring elevations or heights, tape measures for measuring distances, and transits for measuring angles.

18. **b.** The sub-floor of a residential house consists of joists to support the structural load and decking for the surface. The joists are usually made of 2-inch by 10-inch lumber, and the decking is usually made of $\frac{3}{4}$-inch plywood.

19. **a.** A Phillips screwdriver is a very common type and is used on screws that have an indented cross on the head. You may find this type of screw on objects such as door hinges, television sets, and bicycles.

20. **b.** The internal combustion engine in an automobile generates heat and must be cooled. The typical cooling system is based on pumping water around the hot engine block. The heated water is then pumped into the radiator, where it is cooled and then re-circulated back to the engine block. The thermostat is used to regulate the flow of water to keep the engine warm but not let it overheat.

21. **a.** *Diamond point* is a kind of chisel. *Dovetail* and *coping* describe kinds of saws. *Duck bill* describes a kind of pliers.

22. **c.** Use jumper cables to get a charge from another battery. Installing a new starter will not help; the battery will still be dead. Adding fuel and changing fuses also will not recharge the battery. Jumper cables can be used to connect your dead battery to another live car battery to start the car.

23. **d.** Of all the items, only a pogo stick uses springs.

24. **a.** The bar on which the seesaw pivots is the fulcrum of the lever. Also, the seesaw raises and lowers a load (person) on one end when a force (pushing off the ground) is applied on the other end.

25. **d.** All of the answers are correct. A motor is used to wind a cable around a pulley in order to raise and lower the car.

26. **c.** Pumps are used to move liquids through piping systems.

27. **c.** A compression coil spring is typically placed behind the button. When the button is pressed, the spring is compressed and then springs back to return the button to its original position.

28. **b.** A wire cutter whose handles are longer than its blades provides the mechanical advantage of a lever.

29. **a.** A pressure gauge is measured in psi. The other gauges are read in the following units: A depth gauge uses a unit of length such as feet or meters; a speed gauge uses a unit of velocity such as miles per hour (mph) or kilometers per hour (kph); the RPM gauge measures revolutions per minute.

30. **d.** A faulty thermostat can cause engine overheating. If the thermostat is stuck in the closed position, the coolant cannot circulate and cool the engine.

C·H·A·P·T·E·R

SPATIAL CONCEPTS

CHAPTER SUMMARY

It's a 3-D world, but when you're quizzed about it on a 2-D piece of paper, things can get nerve wracking. In this chapter we'll have you folding up boxes, counting cubes, spinning and rotating 3–D figures, and that's just the beginning. We'll also look at hidden figures, maps, and test your eye–hand coordination.

LEARNINGEXPRESS MECHANICAL/SPATIAL EXAM ANSWER SHEET

HIDDEN FIGURES

BLOCK COUNTING

ROTATED BLOCK

MATCHING PIECES AND PARTS

LearningExpress Mechanical & Spatial Aptitude • CHAPTER 4

LEARNINGEXPRESS MECHANICAL/SPATIAL EXAM ANSWER SHEET

SPATIAL ANALYSIS

1. ⓐ ⓑ ⓒ ⓓ ⓔ
2. ⓐ ⓑ ⓒ ⓓ ⓔ
3. ⓐ ⓑ ⓒ ⓓ ⓔ
4. ⓐ ⓑ ⓒ ⓓ ⓔ
5. ⓐ ⓑ ⓒ ⓓ ⓔ
6. ⓐ ⓑ ⓒ ⓓ ⓔ
7. ⓐ ⓑ ⓒ ⓓ ⓔ
8. ⓐ ⓑ ⓒ ⓓ ⓔ
9. ⓐ ⓑ ⓒ ⓓ ⓔ
10. ⓐ ⓑ ⓒ ⓓ ⓔ
11. ⓐ ⓑ ⓒ ⓓ ⓔ
12. ⓐ ⓑ ⓒ ⓓ ⓔ
13. ⓐ ⓑ ⓒ ⓓ ⓔ
14. ⓐ ⓑ ⓒ ⓓ ⓔ
15. ⓐ ⓑ ⓒ ⓓ ⓔ
16. ⓐ ⓑ ⓒ ⓓ ⓔ
17. ⓐ ⓑ ⓒ ⓓ ⓔ
18. ⓐ ⓑ ⓒ ⓓ ⓔ
19. ⓐ ⓑ ⓒ ⓓ ⓔ
20. ⓐ ⓑ ⓒ ⓓ ⓔ
21. ⓐ ⓑ ⓒ ⓓ ⓔ
22. ⓐ ⓑ ⓒ ⓓ ⓔ
23. ⓐ ⓑ ⓒ ⓓ ⓔ
24. ⓐ ⓑ ⓒ ⓓ ⓔ
25. ⓐ ⓑ ⓒ ⓓ ⓔ
26. ⓐ ⓑ ⓒ ⓓ ⓔ
27. ⓐ ⓑ ⓒ ⓓ ⓔ
28. ⓐ ⓑ ⓒ ⓓ ⓔ
29. ⓐ ⓑ ⓒ ⓓ ⓔ
30. ⓐ ⓑ ⓒ ⓓ ⓔ

UNDERSTANDING PATTERNS

1. ⓐ ⓑ ⓒ ⓓ ⓔ
2. ⓐ ⓑ ⓒ ⓓ ⓔ
3. ⓐ ⓑ ⓒ ⓓ ⓔ
4. ⓐ ⓑ ⓒ ⓓ ⓔ
5. ⓐ ⓑ ⓒ ⓓ ⓔ
6. ⓐ ⓑ ⓒ ⓓ ⓔ
7. ⓐ ⓑ ⓒ ⓓ ⓔ
8. ⓐ ⓑ ⓒ ⓓ ⓔ
9. ⓐ ⓑ ⓒ ⓓ ⓔ
10. ⓐ ⓑ ⓒ ⓓ ⓔ
11. ⓐ ⓑ ⓒ ⓓ ⓔ
12. ⓐ ⓑ ⓒ ⓓ ⓔ
13. ⓐ ⓑ ⓒ ⓓ ⓔ
14. ⓐ ⓑ ⓒ ⓓ ⓔ
15. ⓐ ⓑ ⓒ ⓓ ⓔ
16. ⓐ ⓑ ⓒ ⓓ ⓔ
17. ⓐ ⓑ ⓒ ⓓ ⓔ
18. ⓐ ⓑ ⓒ ⓓ ⓔ
19. ⓐ ⓑ ⓒ ⓓ ⓔ
20. ⓐ ⓑ ⓒ ⓓ ⓔ
21. ⓐ ⓑ ⓒ ⓓ ⓔ
22. ⓐ ⓑ ⓒ ⓓ ⓔ
23. ⓐ ⓑ ⓒ ⓓ ⓔ
24. ⓐ ⓑ ⓒ ⓓ ⓔ
25. ⓐ ⓑ ⓒ ⓓ ⓔ
26. ⓐ ⓑ ⓒ ⓓ ⓔ
27. ⓐ ⓑ ⓒ ⓓ ⓔ
28. ⓐ ⓑ ⓒ ⓓ ⓔ
29. ⓐ ⓑ ⓒ ⓓ ⓔ
30. ⓐ ⓑ ⓒ ⓓ ⓔ

EYE-HAND COORDINATION

1. ⓐ ⓑ ⓒ ⓓ ⓔ
2. ⓐ ⓑ ⓒ ⓓ ⓔ
3. ⓐ ⓑ ⓒ ⓓ ⓔ
4. ⓐ ⓑ ⓒ ⓓ ⓔ
5. ⓐ ⓑ ⓒ ⓓ ⓔ
6. ⓐ ⓑ ⓒ ⓓ ⓔ
7. ⓐ ⓑ ⓒ ⓓ ⓔ
8. ⓐ ⓑ ⓒ ⓓ ⓔ
9. ⓐ ⓑ ⓒ ⓓ ⓔ
10. ⓐ ⓑ ⓒ ⓓ ⓔ
11. ⓐ ⓑ ⓒ ⓓ ⓔ
12. ⓐ ⓑ ⓒ ⓓ ⓔ
13. ⓐ ⓑ ⓒ ⓓ ⓔ
14. ⓐ ⓑ ⓒ ⓓ ⓔ
15. ⓐ ⓑ ⓒ ⓓ ⓔ
16. ⓐ ⓑ ⓒ ⓓ ⓔ
17. ⓐ ⓑ ⓒ ⓓ ⓔ
18. ⓐ ⓑ ⓒ ⓓ ⓔ
19. ⓐ ⓑ ⓒ ⓓ ⓔ
20. ⓐ ⓑ ⓒ ⓓ ⓔ
21. ⓐ ⓑ ⓒ ⓓ ⓔ
22. ⓐ ⓑ ⓒ ⓓ ⓔ
23. ⓐ ⓑ ⓒ ⓓ ⓔ
24. ⓐ ⓑ ⓒ ⓓ ⓔ
25. ⓐ ⓑ ⓒ ⓓ ⓔ
26. ⓐ ⓑ ⓒ ⓓ ⓔ
27. ⓐ ⓑ ⓒ ⓓ ⓔ
28. ⓐ ⓑ ⓒ ⓓ ⓔ
29. ⓐ ⓑ ⓒ ⓓ ⓔ
30. ⓐ ⓑ ⓒ ⓓ ⓔ
31. ⓐ ⓑ ⓒ ⓓ ⓔ
32. ⓐ ⓑ ⓒ ⓓ ⓔ

READING MAPS

1. ⓐ ⓑ ⓒ ⓓ ⓔ
2. ⓐ ⓑ ⓒ ⓓ ⓔ
3. ⓐ ⓑ ⓒ ⓓ ⓔ
4. ⓐ ⓑ ⓒ ⓓ ⓔ
5. ⓐ ⓑ ⓒ ⓓ ⓔ
6. ⓐ ⓑ ⓒ ⓓ ⓔ
7. ⓐ ⓑ ⓒ ⓓ ⓔ
8. ⓐ ⓑ ⓒ ⓓ ⓔ
9. ⓐ ⓑ ⓒ ⓓ ⓔ
10. ⓐ ⓑ ⓒ ⓓ ⓔ
11. ⓐ ⓑ ⓒ ⓓ ⓔ
12. ⓐ ⓑ ⓒ ⓓ ⓔ
13. ⓐ ⓑ ⓒ ⓓ ⓔ
14. ⓐ ⓑ ⓒ ⓓ ⓔ
15. ⓐ ⓑ ⓒ ⓓ ⓔ
16. ⓐ ⓑ ⓒ ⓓ ⓔ
17. ⓐ ⓑ ⓒ ⓓ ⓔ
18. ⓐ ⓑ ⓒ ⓓ ⓔ
19. ⓐ ⓑ ⓒ ⓓ ⓔ
20. ⓐ ⓑ ⓒ ⓓ ⓔ

SPATIAL CONCEPTS

HIDDEN FIGURES

Hidden figures questions require you to find given geometric shapes inside more elaborate and complicated figures. Sometimes the answers will literally pop out at you. Other times, you might be left scratching your head without an answer, or worse yet—you might be falling into a trap laid out by those sinister Hidden Figures question designers.

In the sample questions below, these are the basic figures you will be looking for:

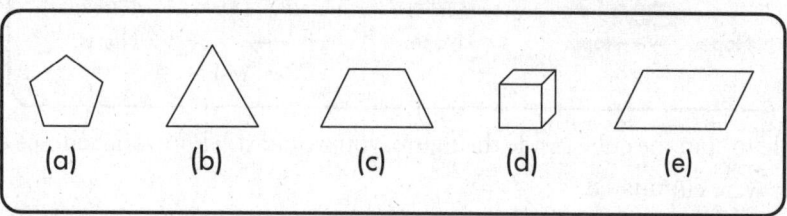

Question 1: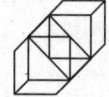

If nothing "pops out at you," a good strategy is to analyze each given shape to see if it could possibly be hiding inside the figure above.

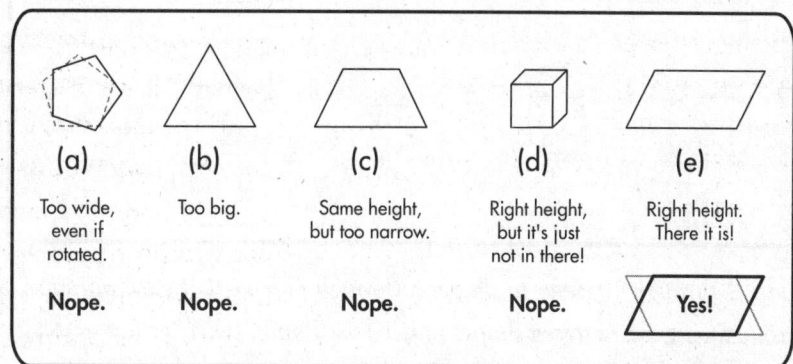

Notice how the figure in question looks like two trapezoids reflected over each other. This would tempt some unsuspecting test takers into picking choice **c**. However upon closer inspection, you can see that trapezoid **c** is narrower than the trapezoids in the question. Always be careful to pick the shape that is the exact size. Also, when dealing with polygons, make sure you are picking the figure with the correct number of sides.

Question 2:

Even if the question seems funky, run through your choices and reject all impossible answers.

LearningExpress Mechanical & Spatial Aptitude • CHAPTER 4

SPATIAL CONCEPTS

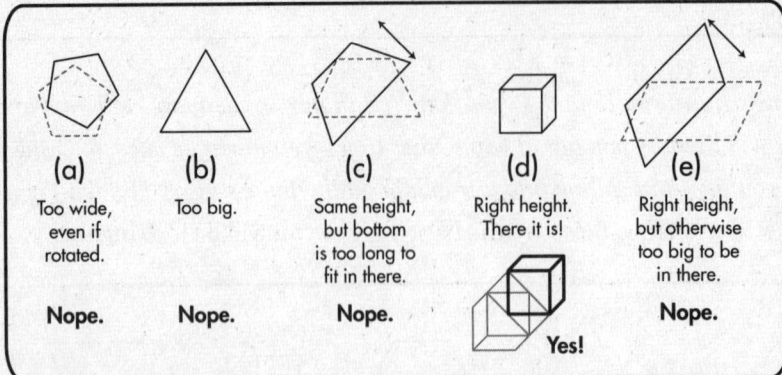

If you weren't able to spot the cube inside the figure, you would still know that choice **d** was correct because all of the other choices were eliminated.

20 PRACTICE QUESTIONS

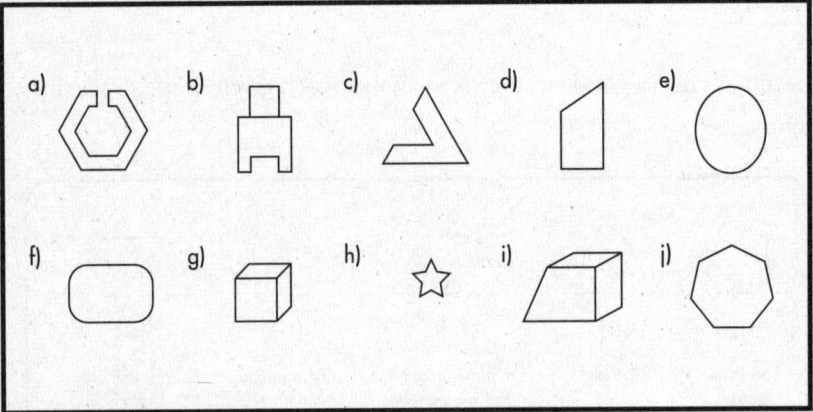

When answering questions 1 through 10, refer to shapes a through j above. For each question, determine which lettered shape is hidden inside the figure. Lettered shapes may be used once, twice, or not at all.

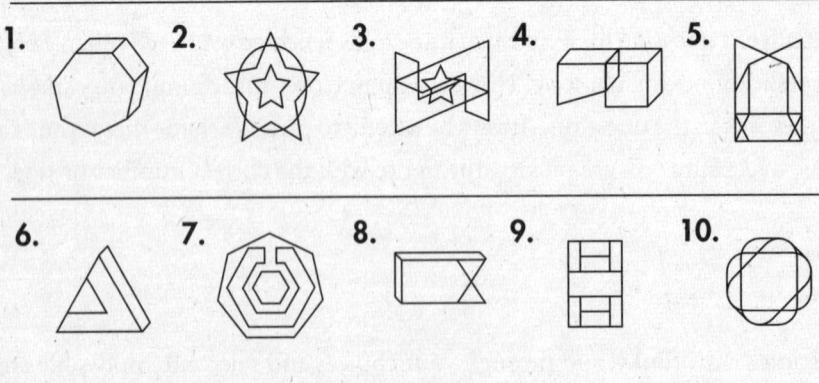

SPATIAL CONCEPTS

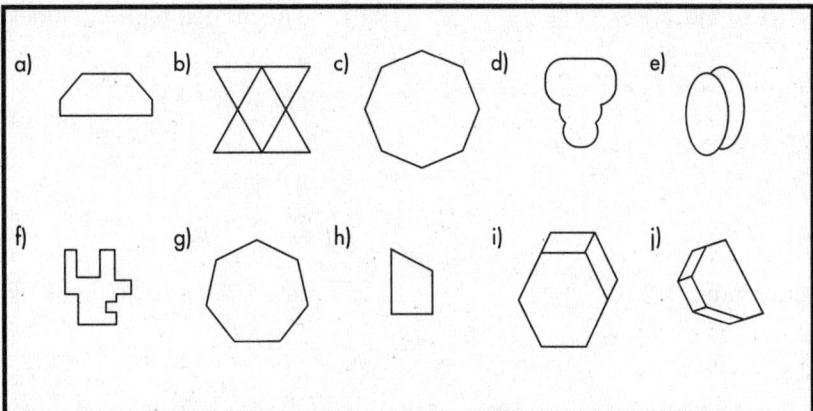

When answering questions 11 through 20, refer to shapes a through j above. For each question, determine which lettered shape is hidden inside the figure. Lettered shapes may be used once, twice, or not at all.

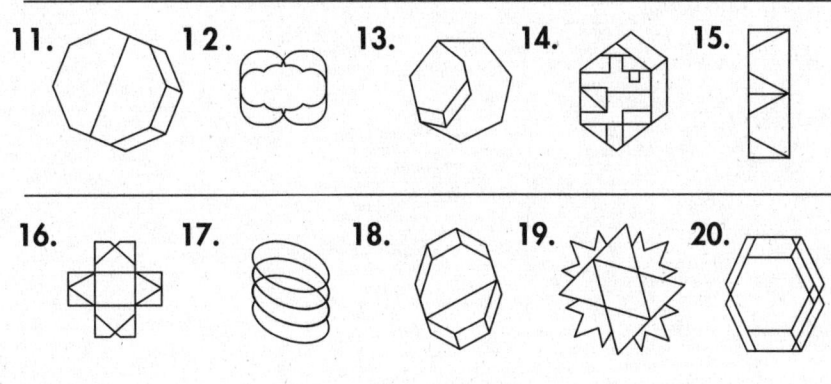

Use Figure J-1 for questions 21–25:

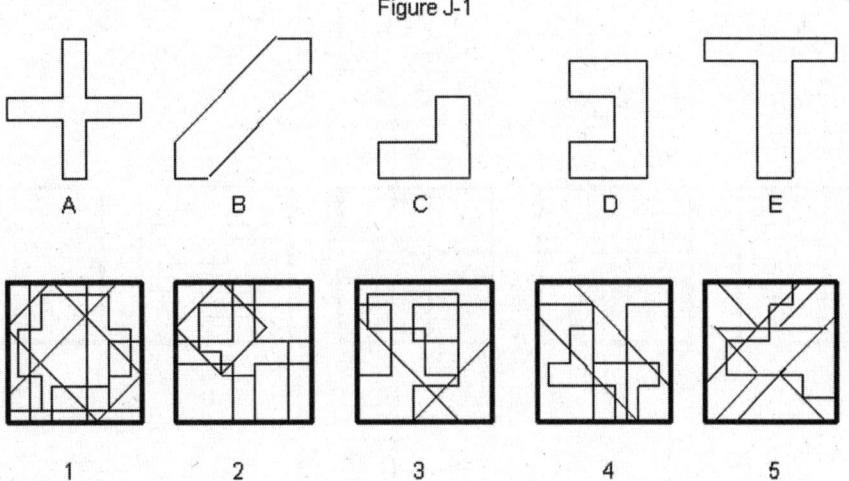

LearningExpress Mechanical & Spatial Aptitude • CHAPTER 4

SPATIAL CONCEPTS

21. The hidden figure in block 1 is _____.
  a. A
  b. B
  c. C
  d. D
  e. E

22. The hidden figure in block 2 is _____.
  a. A
  b. B
  c. C
  d. D
  e. E

23. The hidden figure in block 3 is _____.
  a. A
  b. B
  c. C
  d. D
  e. E

24. The hidden figure in block 4 is _____.
  a. A
  b. B
  c. C
  d. D
  e. E

25. The hidden figure in block 5 is _____.
  a. A
  b. B
  c. C
  d. D
  e. E

Use Figure J-2 for questions 26–30:

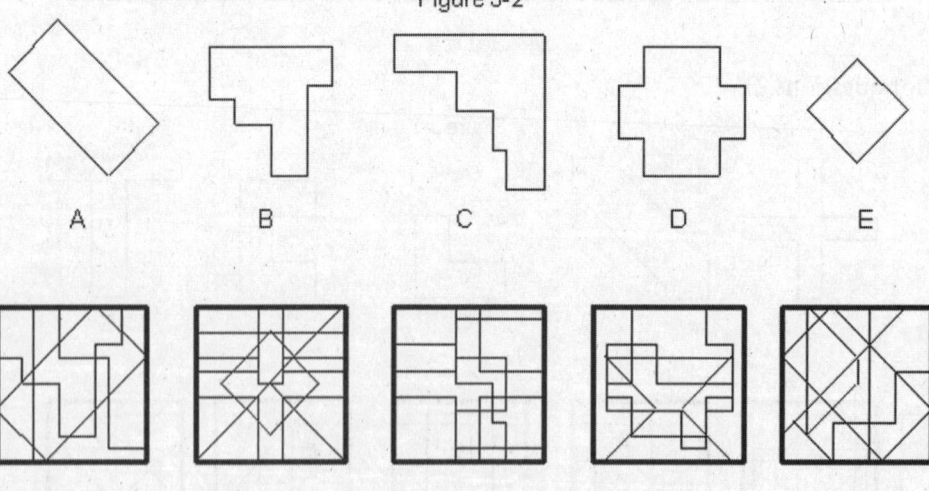

SPATIAL CONCEPTS

26. The hidden figure in block 6 is _____.
  a. A
  b. B
  c. C
  d. D
  e. E

27. The hidden figure in block 7 is _____.
  a. A
  b. B
  c. C
  d. D
  e. E

28. The hidden figure in block 8 is _____.
  a. A
  b. B
  c. C
  d. D
  e. E

29. The hidden figure in block 9 is _____.
  a. A
  b. B
  c. C
  d. D
  e. E

30. The hidden figure in block 10 is _____.
  a. A
  b. B
  c. C
  d. D
  e. E

HIDDEN FIGURES ANSWER EXPLANATIONS

1. j

2. e

3. h

4. g

5. i

6. c

7. a

8. d

9. b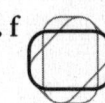

10. f

11. c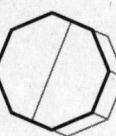

12. d

13. g

14. f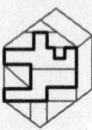

15. h

16. a

17. e

18. j

19. b

20. i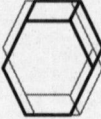

21. c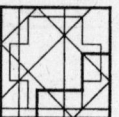

22. a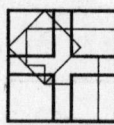

23. d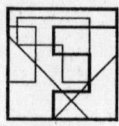

24. e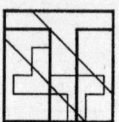

25. b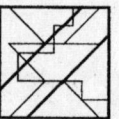

26. b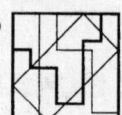

27. e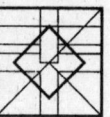

28. c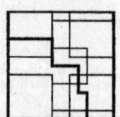

29. d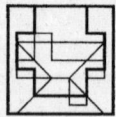

30. a

SPATIAL CONCEPTS

BLOCK COUNTING

These 3-D–based questions have you counting lots and lots of blocks: some that you can see, and other hidden blocks that you need to assume are present. Start at the bottom level, counting each block, one at a time. It is helpful to make a note in the margin, such as "Level 1 = 23." Next, check out the second level up, again counting each box, one at a time. Record a value for "Level 2 = _____" in the margin. Work your way upward to the topmost layer. Finally, tally up all of your numbers. Keeping track of each level in an organized manner will help you feel secure about your answer so you won't have to re-do the question. Face it, you're not going to want to do these questions twice!

The second sample is a rectangle three blocks wide, four blocks deep, and two blocks high with a hollow center. This one is fairly simple to count, and you should have counted 20 blocks easily. Though this one was fairly simple, the questions ahead may get a lot more complicated, so remember to count the blocks one at a time to avoid simple miscalculations.

30 PRACTICE QUESTIONS

1.

This first sample question has a pyramid-like structure with one center column four blocks high (that center block isn't resting on the edges of the surrounding columns) and four symmetrical sides, consisting of six blocks each, that gradually step down one block at a time giving you a total of 28 blocks. A good way to attack this problem would be to start at the outside where you can see that there is only one block resting on the plane and work your way inward counting the columns as they step up.

SPATIAL CONCEPTS

2.

3.
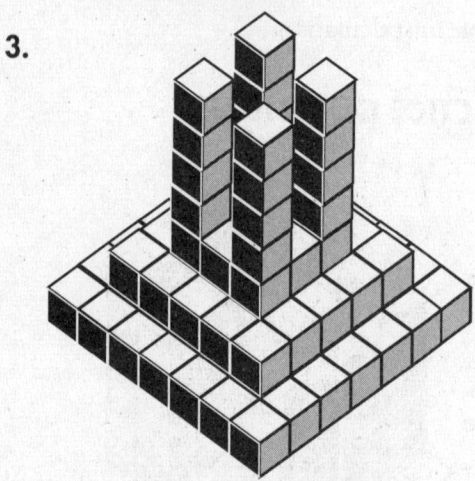

4.

5.

6.

7.

CHAPTER 4 • *LearningExpress Mechanical & Spatial Aptitude*

SPATIAL CONCEPTS

8.

9.
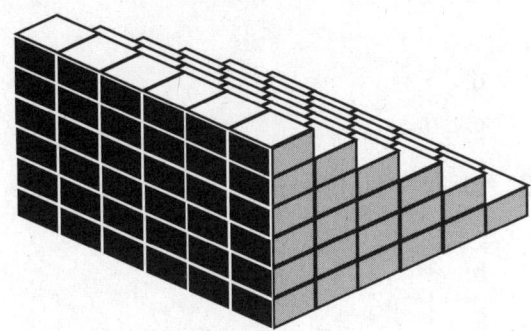

10.

11.

12.

13.

14.

15.

For questions 16–20, refer to Figure I-1

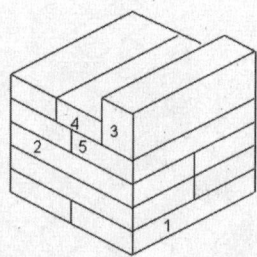

Figure I-1

16. Block 1 is touched by _____ other blocks.
   a. 2
   b. 3
   c. 4
   d. 5
   e. 6

17. Block 2 is touched by _____ other blocks.
   a. 2
   b. 3
   c. 4
   d. 5
   e. 6

18. Block 3 is touched by _____ other blocks.
   a. 2
   b. 3
   c. 4
   d. 5
   e. 6

19. Block 4 is touched by _____ other blocks.
   a. 2
   b. 3
   c. 4
   d. 5
   e. 6

20. Block 5 is touched by _____ other blocks.
   a. 2
   b. 3
   c. 4
   d. 5
   e. 6

For questions 21–25, refer to Figure I-2

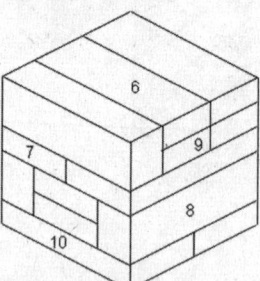

Figure I-2

21. Block 6 is touched by _____ other blocks.
   a. 2
   b. 3
   c. 4
   d. 5
   e. 6

22. Block 7 is touched by _____ other blocks.
   a. 2
   b. 3
   c. 4
   d. 5
   e. 6

23. Block 8 is touched by _____ other blocks.
   a. 2
   b. 3
   c. 4
   d. 5
   e. 6

24. Block 9 is touched by _____ other blocks.
   a. 2
   b. 3
   c. 4
   d. 5
   e. 6

25. Block 10 is touched by _____ other blocks.
   a. 2
   b. 3
   c. 4
   d. 5
   e. 6

For questions 26–30, refer to Figure I-3

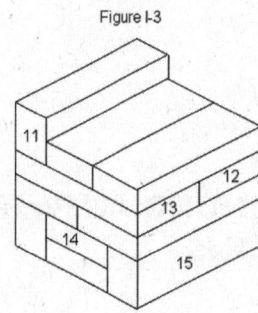

26. Block 11 is touched by _____ other blocks.
   a. 2
   b. 3
   c. 4
   d. 5
   e. 6

27. Block 12 is touched by _____ other blocks.
   a. 2
   b. 3
   c. 4
   d. 5
   e. 6

28. Block 13 is touched by _____ other blocks.
   a. 2
   b. 3
   c. 4
   d. 5
   e. 6

29. Block 14 is touched by _____ other blocks.
   a. 2
   b. 3
   c. 4
   d. 5
   e. 6

30. Block 15 is touched by _____ other blocks.
   a. 2
   b. 3
   c. 4
   d. 5

BLOCK COUNTING ANSWER EXPLANATIONS

1. 154
2. 141
3. 99
4. 48
5. 98
6. 132
7. 100
8. 52
9. 126
10. 81
11. 68
12. 141
13. 296
14. 70
15. 124
16. b. Block 1 touches two blocks above and one block to the left.
17. c. Block 2 touches one block below, one block to the right, and two blocks above.
18. a. Block 3 touches one block to the left and one block below.
19. c. Block 4 touches one block to the left, one block to the right, and two blocks below.
20. d. Block 5 touches two blocks above, one block to the left, and two blocks below.
21. b. Block 6 touches one block to the left, one block to the right, and one block below.
22. e. Block 7 touches two blocks below, one block to the right, and three blocks above.
23. d. Block 8 touches two blocks below, two blocks to the left, and one block above.
24. d. Block 9 touches two blocks below, one block to the left, one block to the right, and one block above.
25. c. Block 10 touches three blocks above and one block to the right.
26. b. Block 11 touches two blocks below and one block to the right.
27. e. Block 12 touches three blocks above, one block to the left, and two blocks below.
28. e. Block 13 touches three blocks above, one block to the right, and two blocks below.
29. d. Block 14 touches two blocks above, one block below, one block to the right, and one block to the left.
30. b. Block 15 touches one block above and two blocks to the left.

SPATIAL CONCEPTS

ROTATED BLOCKS

Rotated Blocks questions require the ability to mentally spin a 3-D figure around and envision what it will look like from this new angle. Since each face of the cube is labeled with a particular figure, sometimes it's easier to spot a wrong answer by focusing on the relative positions of these figures. The remaining choices will give you an idea of which way to rotate the original block.

ROTATED BLOCKS INSTRUCTIONS
Solid
In this first set of exercises, you will be rotating solid three-dimensional blocks of various shapes in order to enhance your ability to think in three-dimensions. For each numbered shape you will find four possible answers which may represent that numbered shape rotated 360 degrees in any direction. Your task is to determine which of the four choices is the only one that could be the original shape, rotated. You'll want to pay close attention to detail here in order to catch some of the small differences that may lead you to an incorrect answer. Some of the most common mistakes are made when you overlook subtly placed extra lines or mirror images. They may appear correct at a glance but under closer examination are wrong. Study the images carefully and the answers will become obvious.

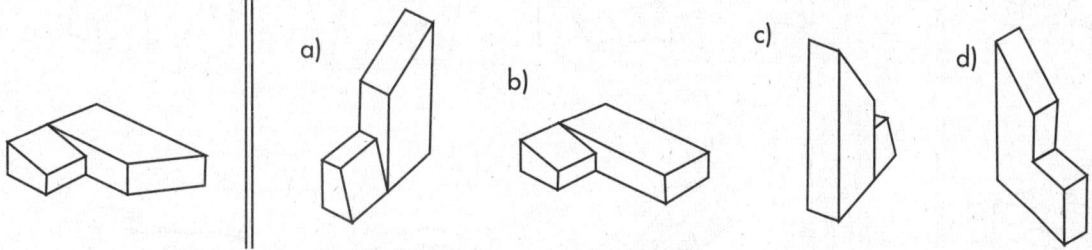

If you observed closely and looked for common mistakes, you should have found the correct answer to be **c**.

Patterned
In this set of exercises, there are numbered cubes with patterned faces and no pattern appears on more than one side of the cube. For each numbered cube there are four possible answers that represent the cube turned in a different direction. Your task is to decide which of the answer cubes is the original cube rotated in any direction. On this one you'll need to be aware of tricky mirrored patterns and pay close attention to the position of the patterns in relation to their adjacent faces. Then the answers will become clear.

LearningExpress Mechanical & Spatial Aptitude • CHAPTER 4

SPATIAL CONCEPTS

                        a.   b.   c.   d.

If you have figured correctly, you'll see the answer is **d**. It is the original block turned once clockwise. Then the circle faces forward. Next, it is turned on its side so that the diamond moves from the top to the right side.

30 PRACTICE QUESTIONS

1. 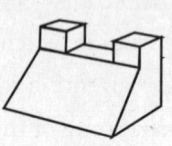 a) 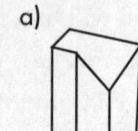 b) 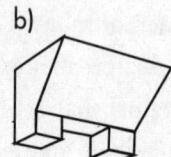 c) 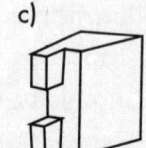 d)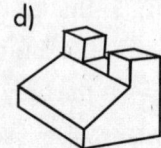

2.  a) 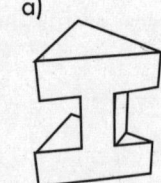 b) 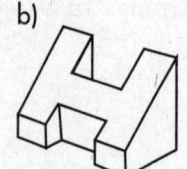 c) 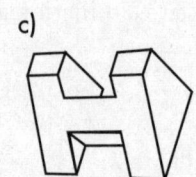 d)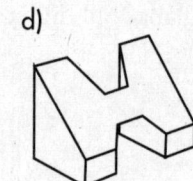

3. 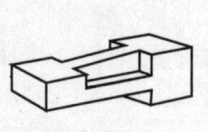 a) 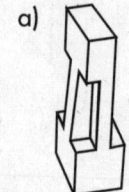 b) 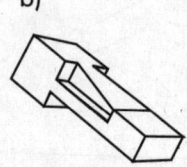 c) 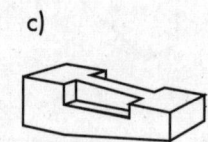 d)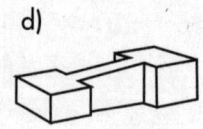

4. 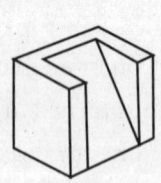 a) 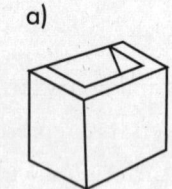 b) 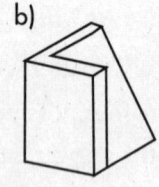 c)  d)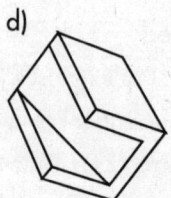

5. 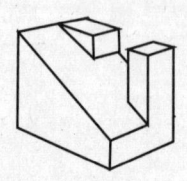 a)  b) 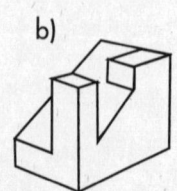 c) 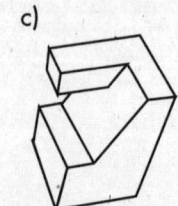 d)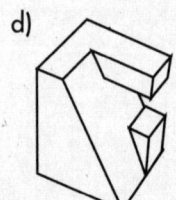

SPATIAL CONCEPTS

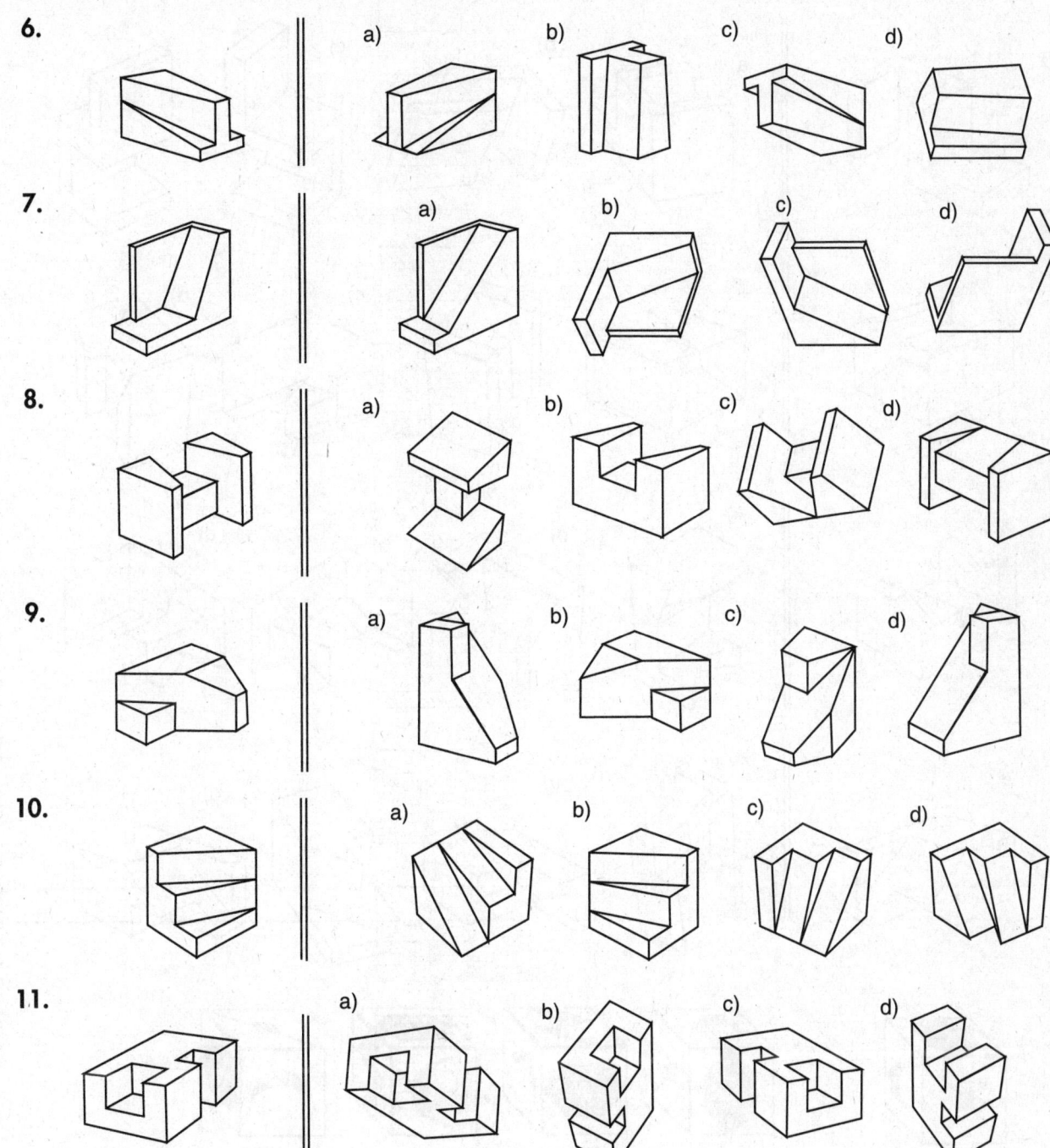

SPATIAL CONCEPTS

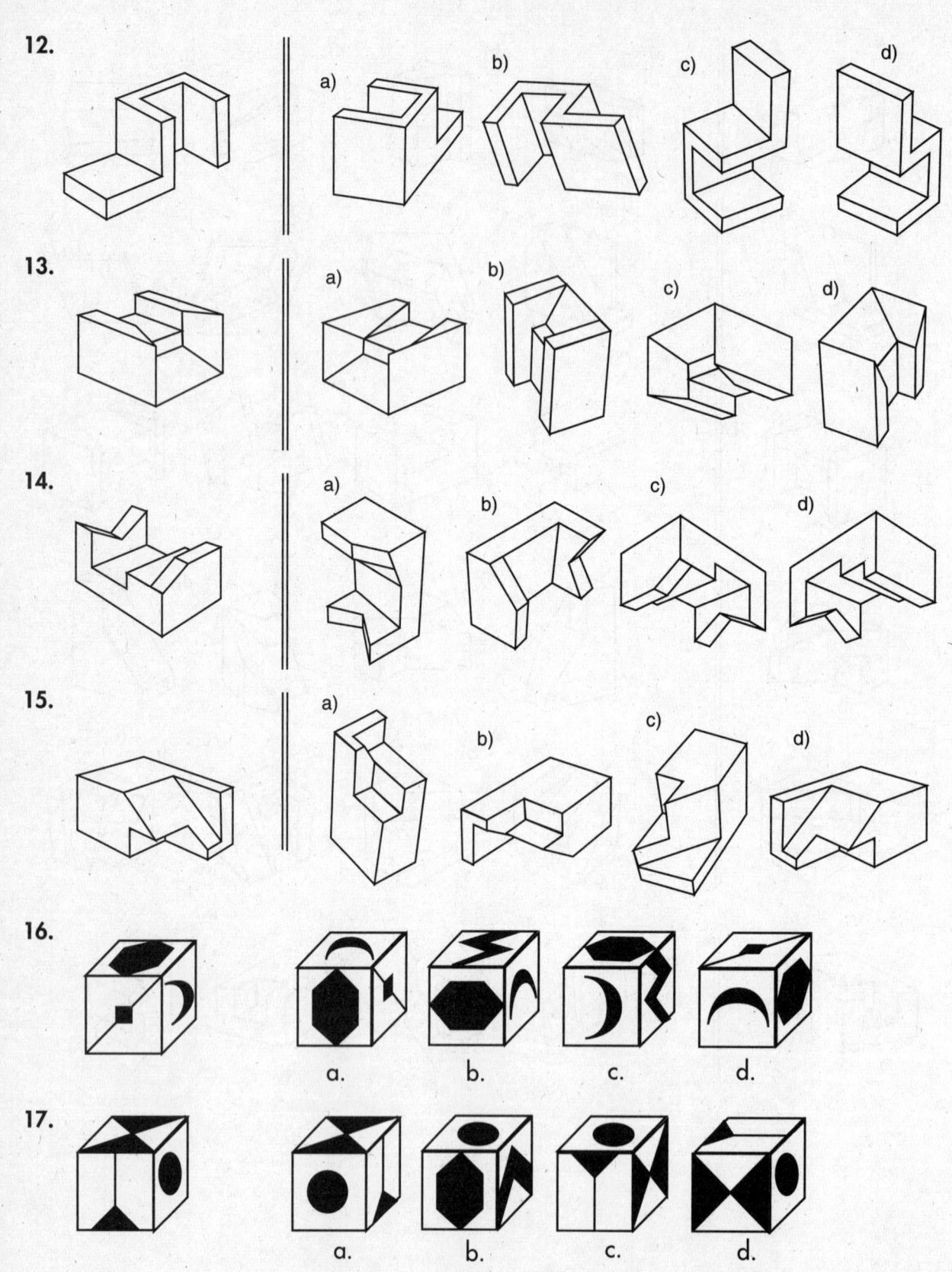

SPATIAL CONCEPTS

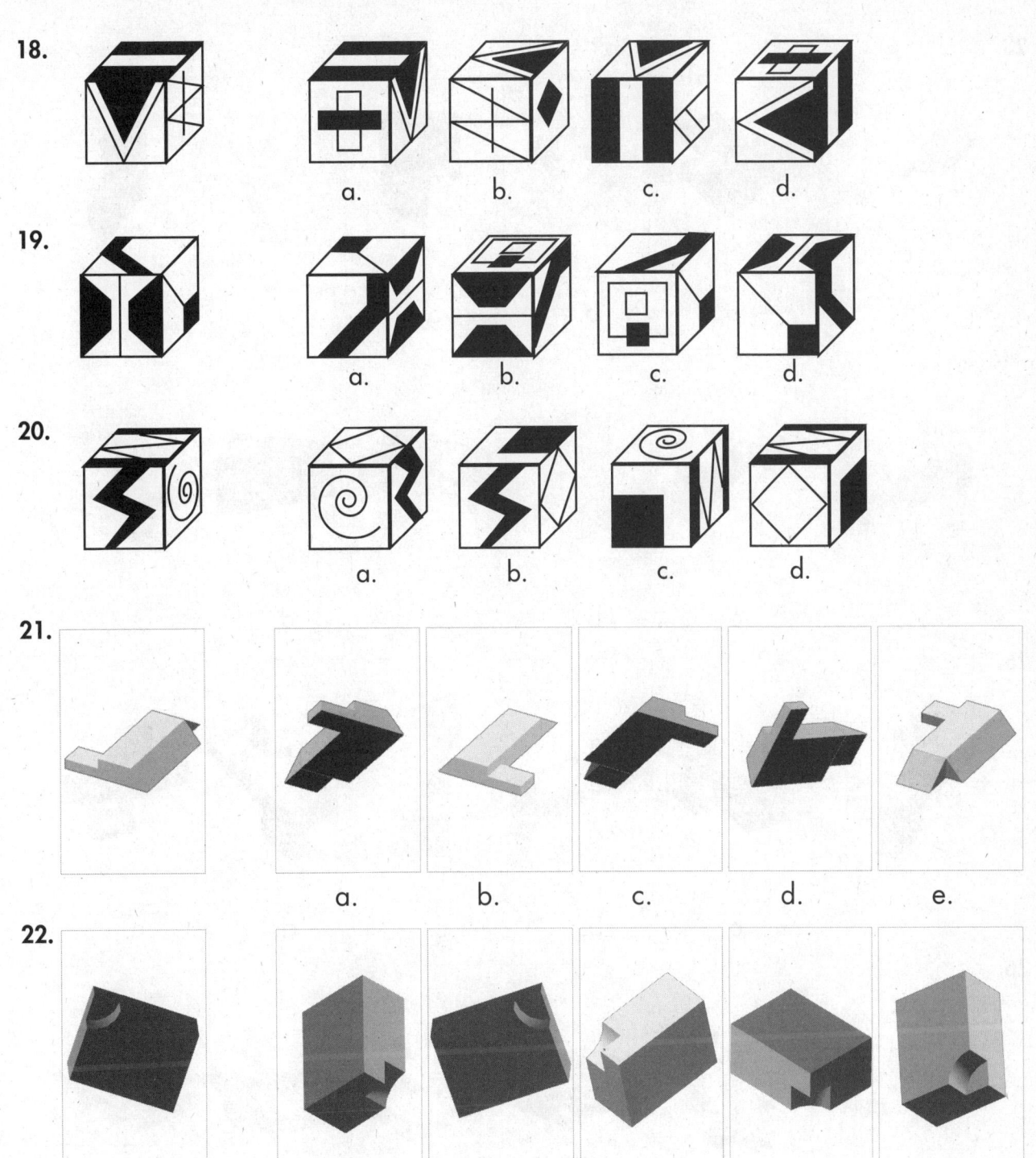

SPATIAL CONCEPTS

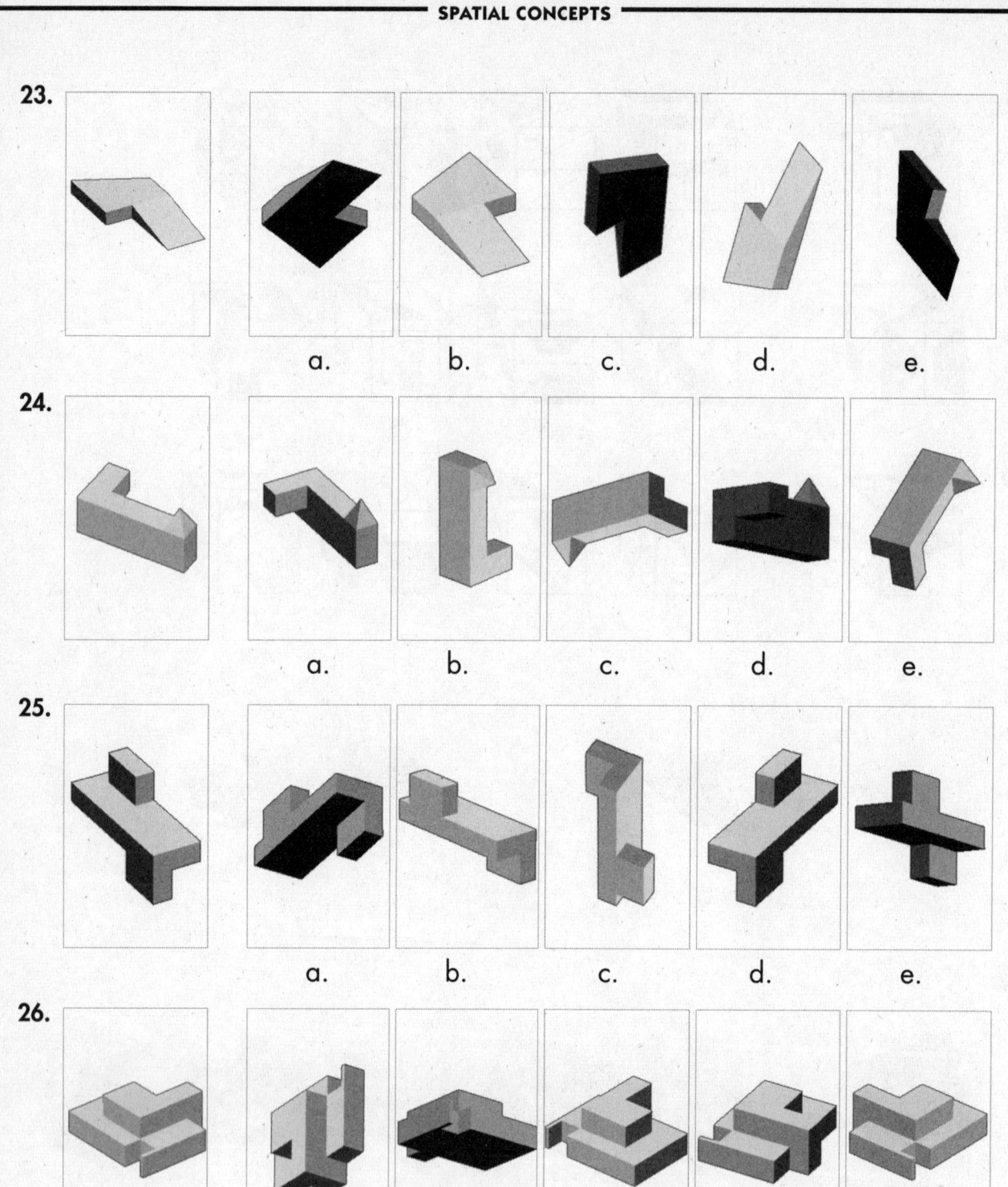

22 CHAPTER 4 • LearningExpress Mechanical & Spatial Aptitude

SPATIAL CONCEPTS

27.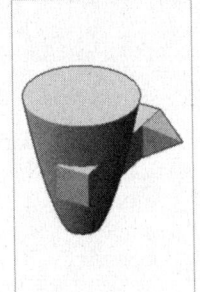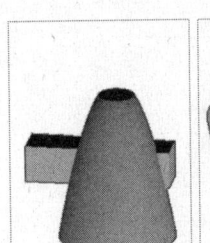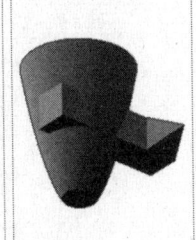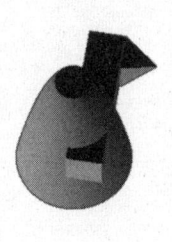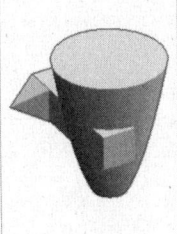
a.   b.   c.   d.   e.

28.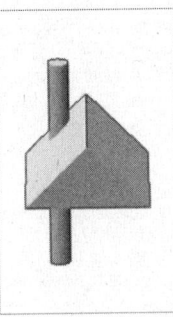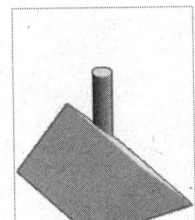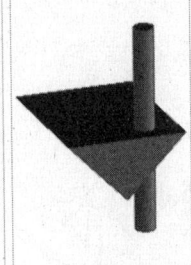
a.   b.   c.   d.   e.

29.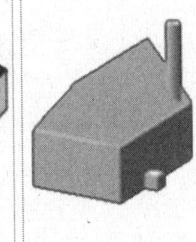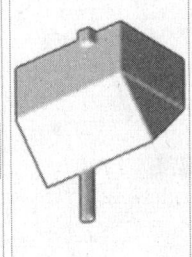
a.   b.   c.   d.   e.

30.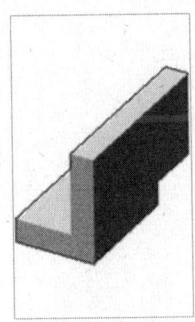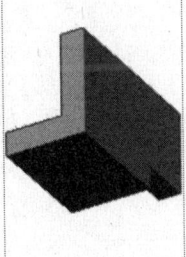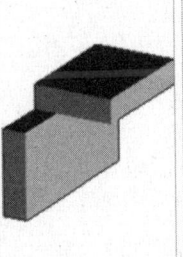
a.   b.   c.   d.   e.

ROTATED BLOCKS ANSWER EXPLANATIONS

1. b
2. c
3. a
4. d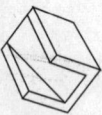
5. b
6. c
7. d
8. b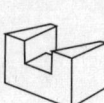

9. a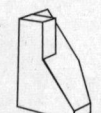
10. c
11. b
12. a
13. c
14. c
15. b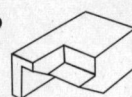

SPATIAL CONCEPTS

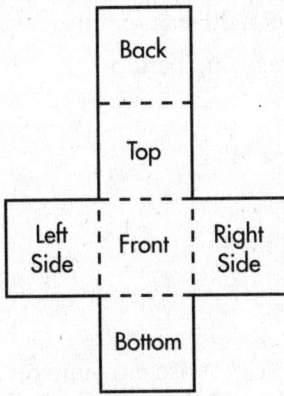

16. c. The original cube has been turned once clockwise to move the crescent-moon shape to the front and reveal a new right side.

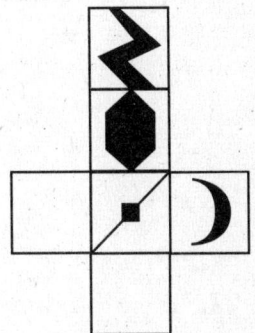

17. b. The original cube has been turned clockwise once to move the circle pattern to the front and reveal a new right side, then turned once away to move the circle to the top and reveal the bottom as the new front.

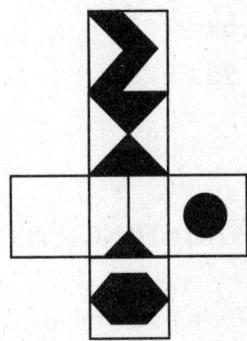

18. d. The original cube has been turned once onto its right side to move the top to the right side and reveal a new top pattern.

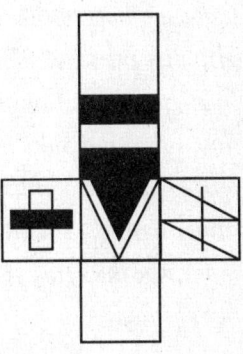

SPATIAL CONCEPTS

19. b. The original cube has been turned once onto its right side to move what was the top to the right side and reveal a new top pattern.

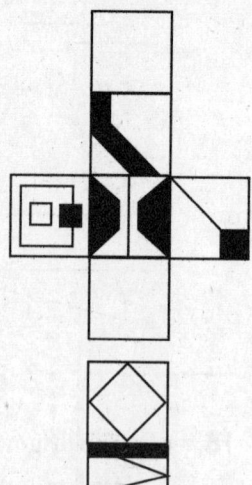

20. d. The original cube has been turned 180 degrees (clockwise or counter-clockwise).

21. a	**26.** d
22. a	**27.** b
23. e	**28.** c
24. c	**29.** a
25. c	**30.** b

MATCHING PIECES AND PARTS

There are several styles of Matching Pieces and Parts questions, but the underlying concept is the same. Some questions require the test-taker to visualize the parts that form a given whole. Other questions require the test-taker to visualize the whole that is made up of the given parts. All in all, these questions require the ability to mentally flip-flop, turn, and piece together shapes. To add to the challenge, you also must be on guard for pieces whose dimensions are slightly off. When dealing with polygons, make sure the figure you end up with has the correct number of sides.

In the first question below, you must decide which two lettered pieces will come together to make the parallelogram shown. Pieces may be rotated (turned) or reflected (flipped over).

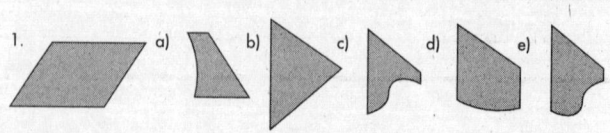

CHAPTER 4 • LearningExpress Mechanical & Spatial Aptitude

SPATIAL CONCEPTS

Initially, you should eliminate any choices that obviously could not make up the whole in question.

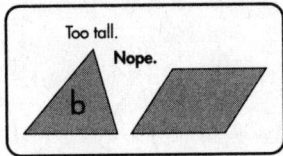

It would be impossible for choice **b** to be a part of the figure, as it is too large. Similarly, **c** and **e** would be too short:

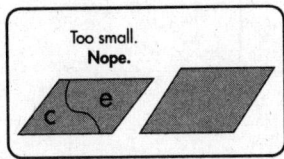

Now you should focus on **a** and **d**. Although they do not look very compatible at this point, remember that you are allowed to rotate and reflect these pieces. Let's flip **a** over as you would a piece of paper. And let's turn **d** on its side:

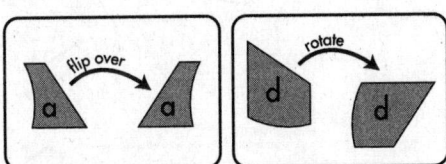

Now, we can fit them together:

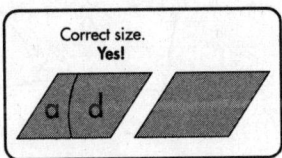

Sometimes you will be surprised which pieces turn out to be the right parts. The more choices you can eliminate off the bat, the easier your task will be.

In the next question, you are given 4 pieces. You must choose which answer choice represents a figure comprised of all four pieces. Pieces may be rotated and/or reflected.

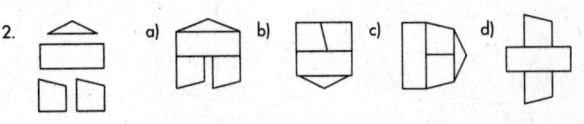

We will analyze each choice:

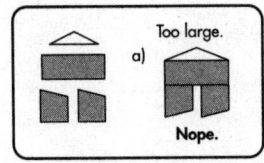

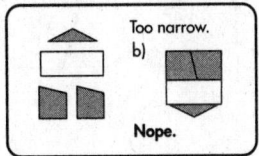

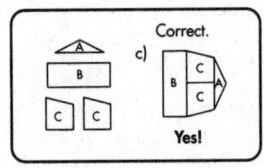

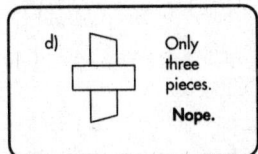

SPATIAL CONCEPTS

30 PRACTICE QUESTIONS

In questions 1–10 below, pick the TWO answer choices that will come together to make the figure shown. Pieces may be reflected and/or rotated.

1. 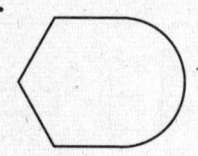 a)  b)  c)  d)  e)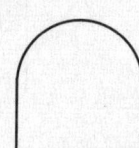

2. 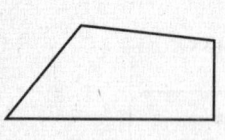 a) 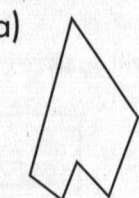 b) 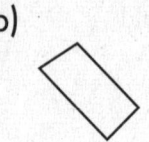 c)  d)  e)

3. 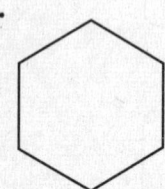 a) 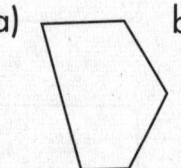 b)  c)  d)  e)

4.  a)  b)  c)  d)  e)

5. 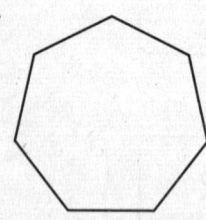 a)  b)  c)  d)  e)

6. 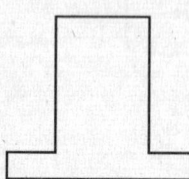 a) 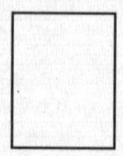 b) 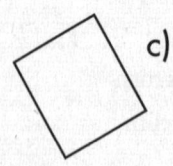 c) d) 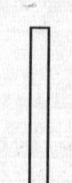 e)

SPATIAL CONCEPTS

7. a) b) c) d) e)

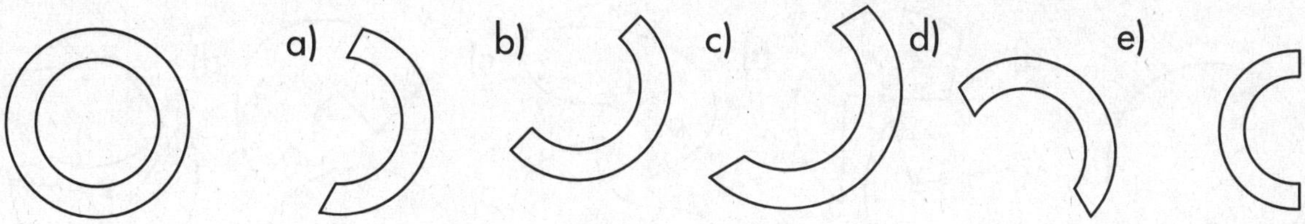

8. a) b) c) d) e)

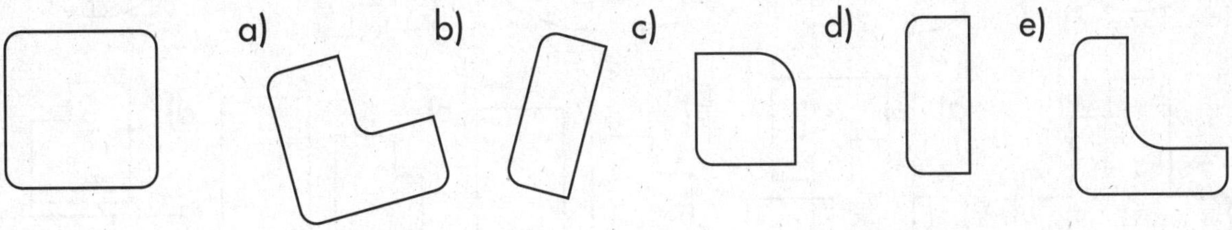

9. a) b) c) d) e)

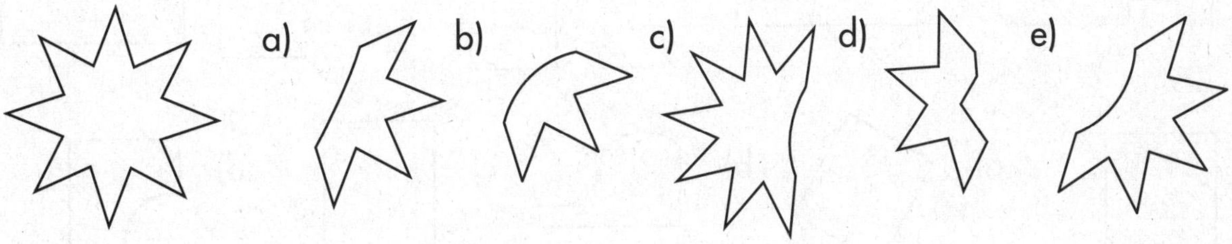

10. a) b) c) d) e)

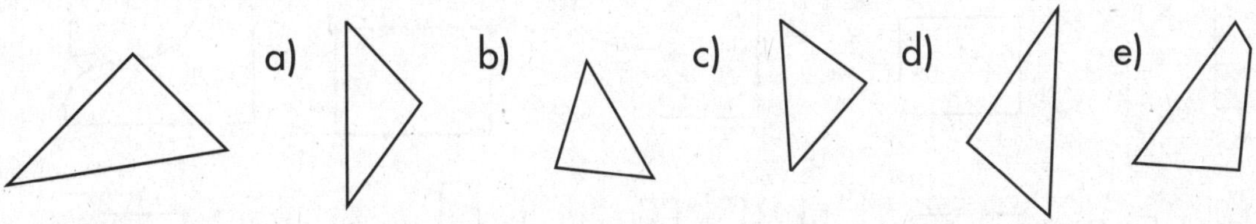

In questions 11–20 below, select the SINGLE answer choice that represents the two parts that join together to make the given whole. Pieces may be reflected and/or rotated.

11. a) b) c) d)

12. a) b) c) d)

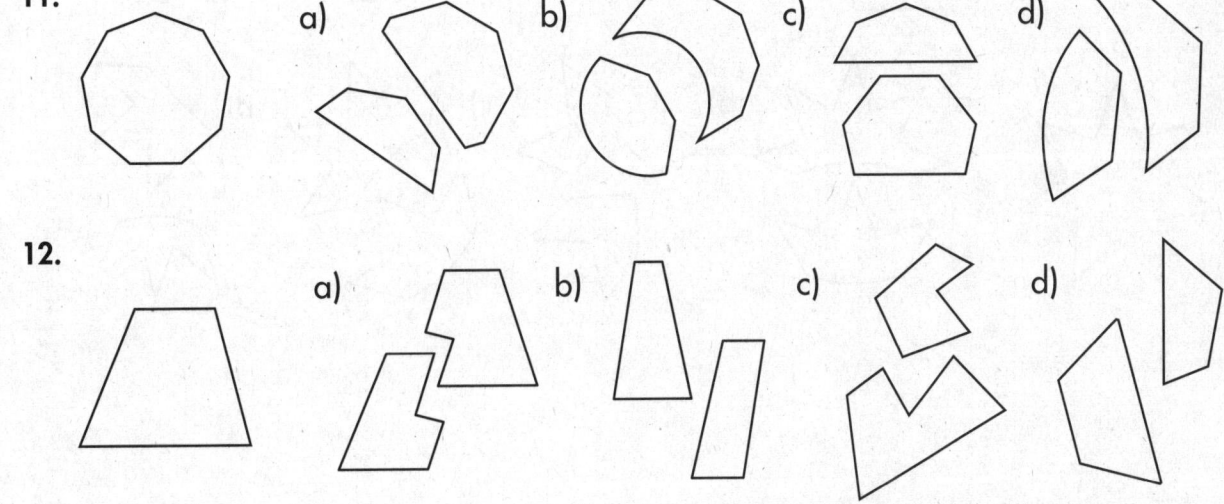

SPATIAL CONCEPTS

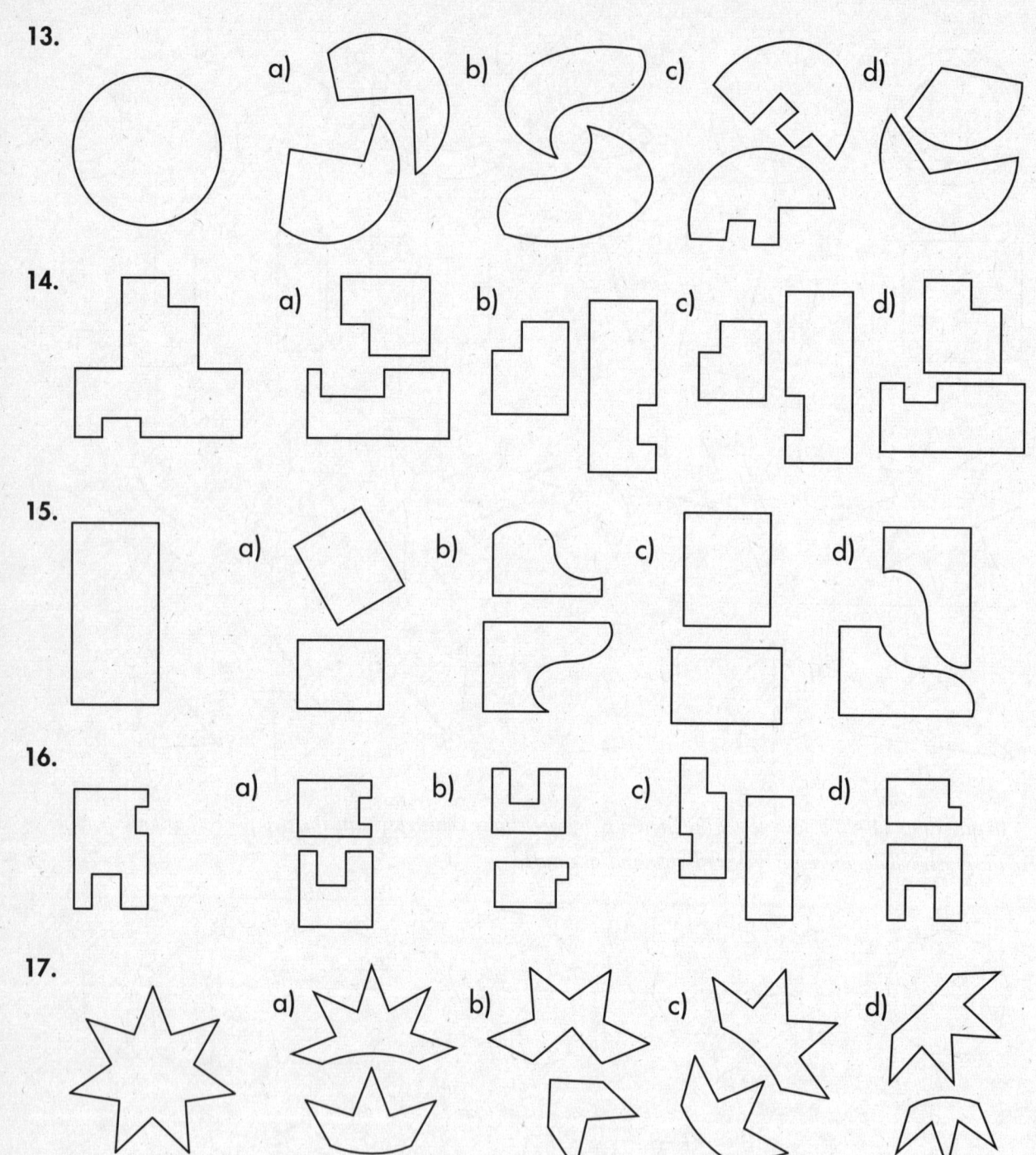

SPATIAL CONCEPTS

18. 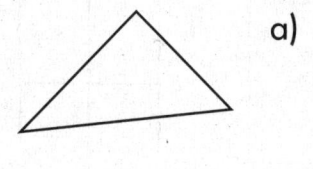 a)  b) 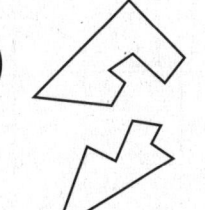 c) 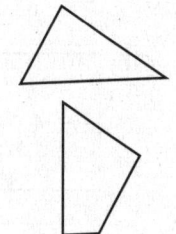 d)

19.  a) 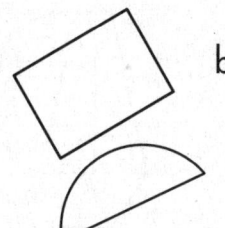 b) 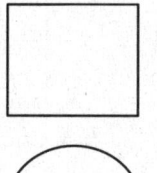 c) 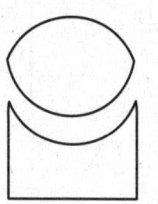 d)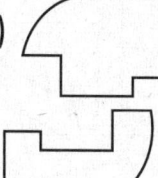

20.  a) 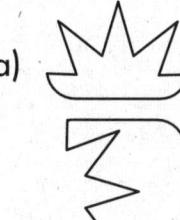 b) 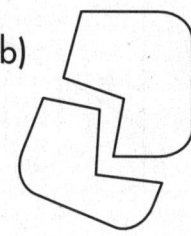 c) 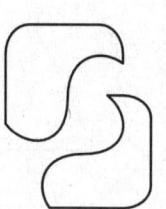 d)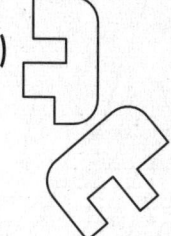

In questions 21–30 below, 4–5 pieces are given. Choose the answer choice that represents a figure comprised of ALL pieces. Pieces may be rotated and/or reflected.

21.  a) 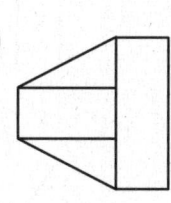 b) 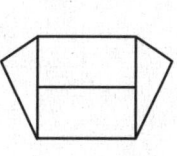 c) 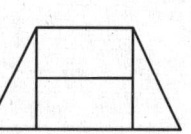 d)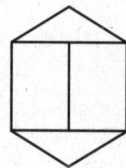

22. 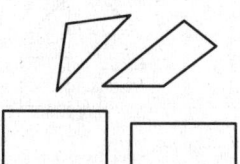 a) 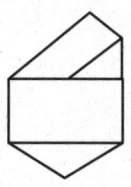 b) 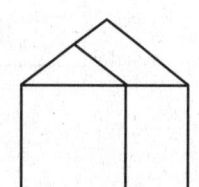 c) 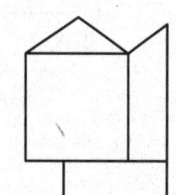 d)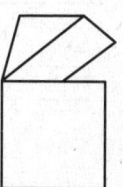

LearningExpress Mechanical & Spatial Aptitude • CHAPTER 4

SPATIAL CONCEPTS

23. 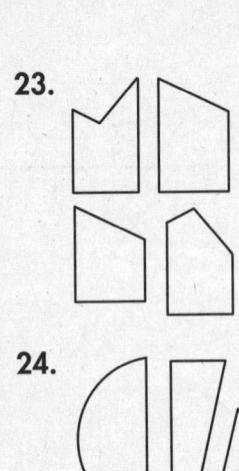 a) 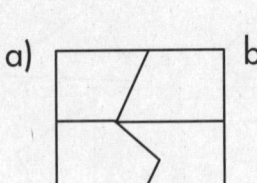 b) 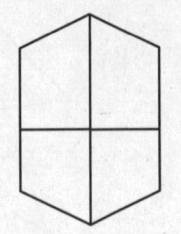 c) 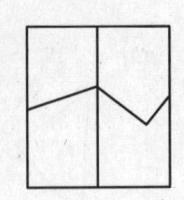 d)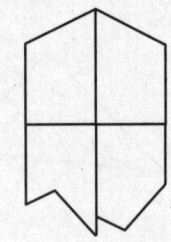

24.  a) 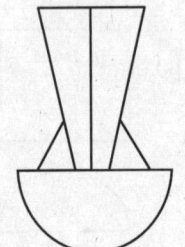 b) 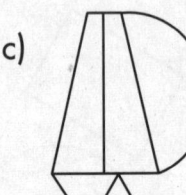 c) 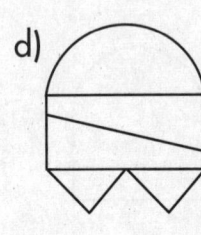 d)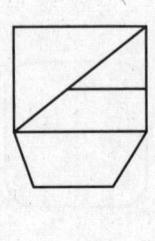

25.  a)  b) 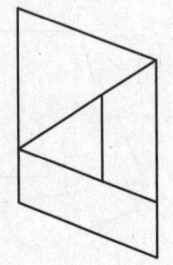 c) 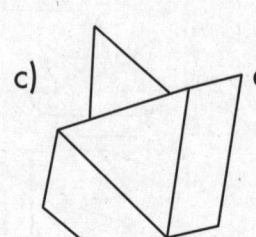 d)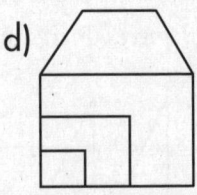

26. 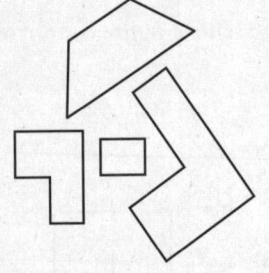 a) 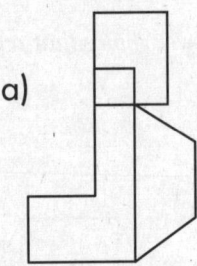 b) 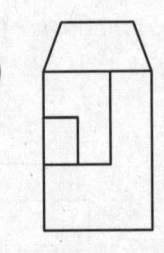 c) 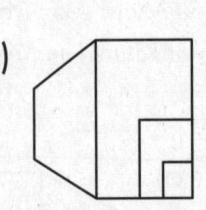 d)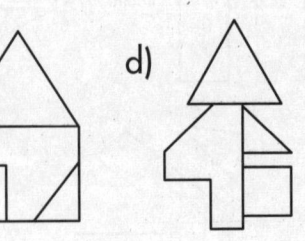

27.  a) 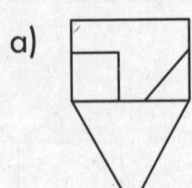 b) 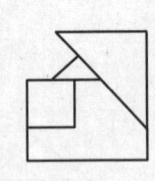 c) 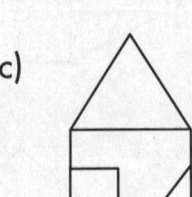 d)

CHAPTER 4 • *LearningExpress Mechanical & Spatial Aptitude*

SPATIAL CONCEPTS

28. 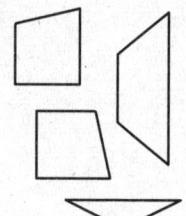 a) 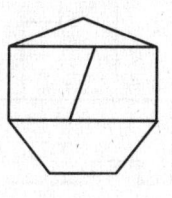 b) 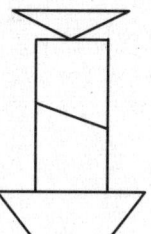 c) 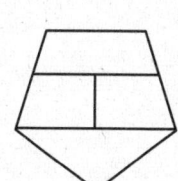 d)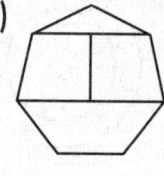

29. 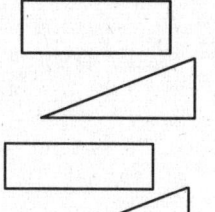 a)  b) 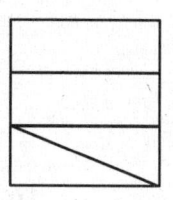 c) 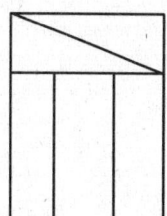 d)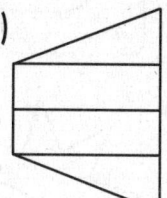

30. 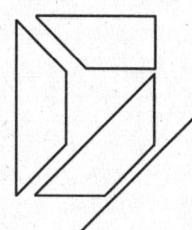 a) 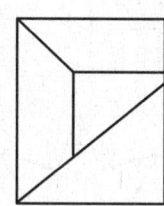 b) 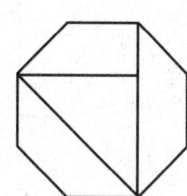 c) 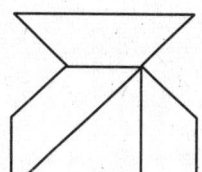 d)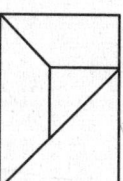

MATCHING PIECES AND PARTS ANSWER EXPLANATIONS

1. b+e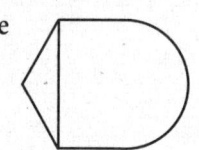

2. a+d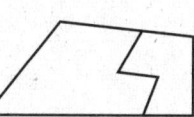

3. a+c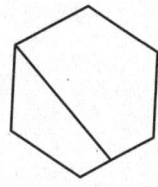

4. b+d

5. c+e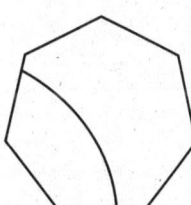

6. c+e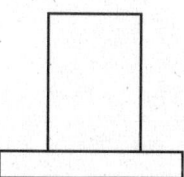

SPATIAL CONCEPTS

7. a+d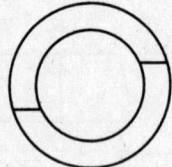

8. c+e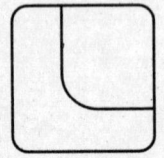

9. b+e

10. a+b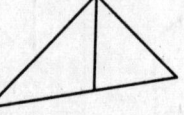

11. b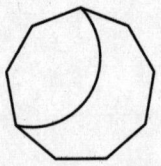

12. c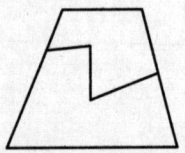

13. a

14. b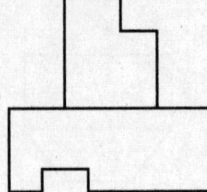

15. d

16. d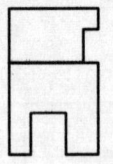

17. c

18. b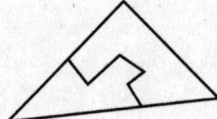

19. c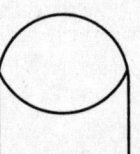

20. a

SPATIAL CONCEPTS

21. c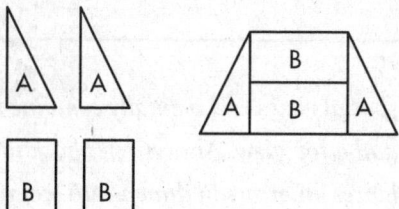

22. b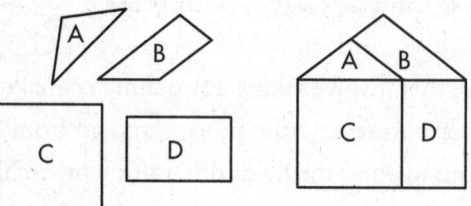

23. a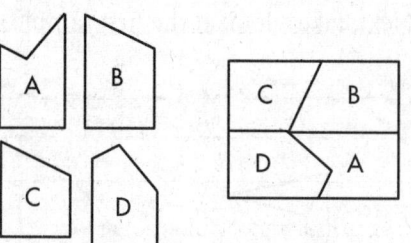

24. d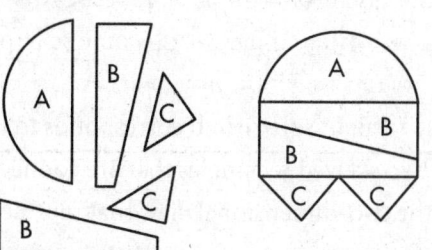

25. b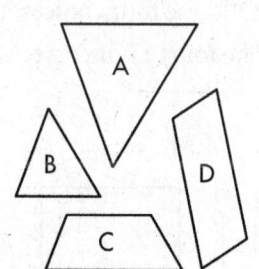

26. d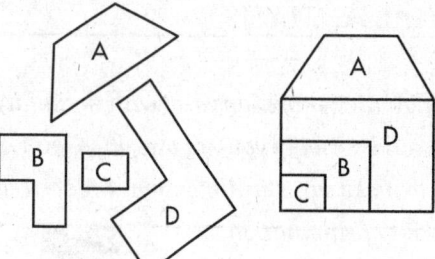

27. a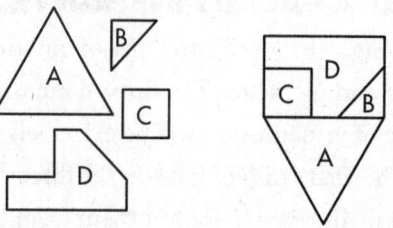

28. d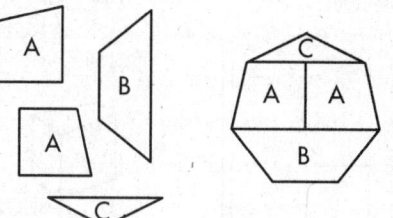

29. c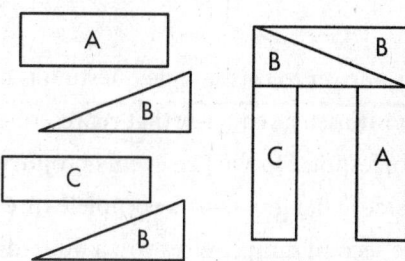

30. b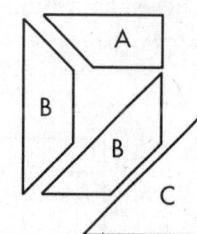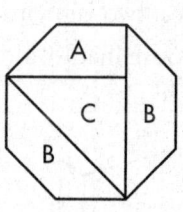

SPATIAL CONCEPTS

SPATIAL ANALYSIS

Spatial Analysis questions deal with the ability to take several separate spatial views and mentally combine them into a 3-D solid. Usually you are presented with a front view, a side view, and a top view. Always refer back to the three views to make sure the dimensions are correct. Scrutinize the answer choices for errors in dimensions when resorting to process of elimination.

SPATIAL ANALYSIS INSTRUCTIONS

You're going to be given two types of questions in this exercise that involve taking a two dimensional diagram of an object and picturing it in three dimensions. Then you'll have to reverse the process and go from 3D to 2D. This type of visualization will be extremely useful if you intend to enter the fields of Drafting or Architecture.

In this first sample you'll see the three views of a three-dimensional object (top, front, and side) as you would see them if you were to look at them from the top, front, or side. Next, take a look at the first sample and try to find the answer.

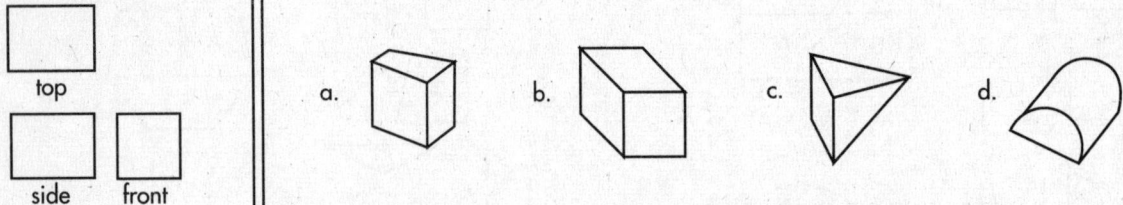

The answer to this sample question is **b**, and here's why. The straight square in **b** corresponds to the square in the two-dimensional view that represents the front. Then the two skewed rectangles that are connected to the square correspond to the two evenly proportioned rectangles in the two-dimensional view that represent the top and the side. That gives you a complete three-dimensional object.

The second sample gives you a three-dimensional object with four choices. Of these four choices, three are the correct two-dimensional views that would represent the top, front, and side. The fourth is incorrect. Identify the response that would be INCORRECT.

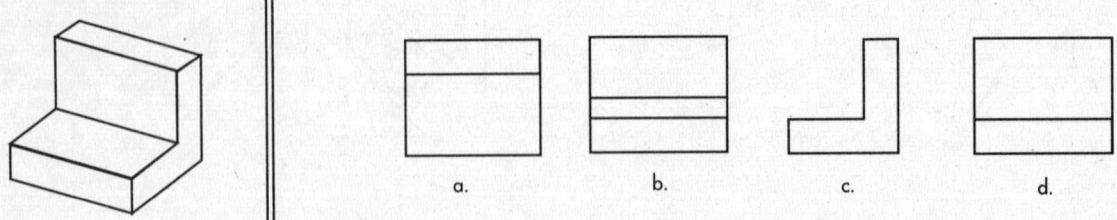

If you figured correctly, your answer should be **b**. The reason is simple. This answer choice adds an extra line that would not be visible in 2-D. Most spatial analysis questions are tricky, so take your time and make careful observations.

SPATIAL CONCEPTS

30 PRACTICE QUESTIONS

1.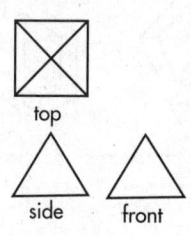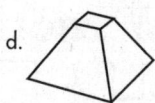
a. b. c. d.

2.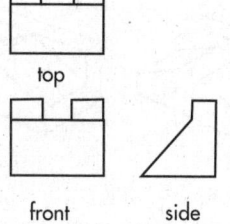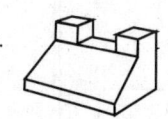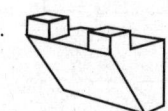
a. b. c. d.

3.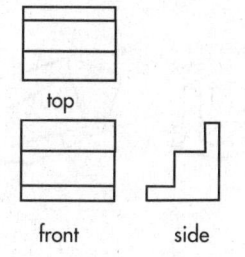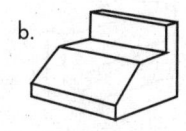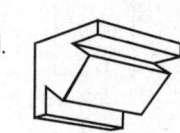
a. b. c. d.

4.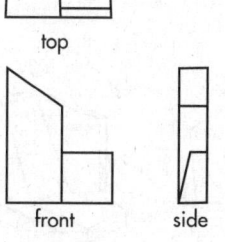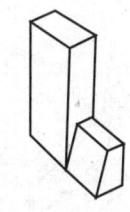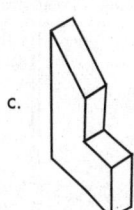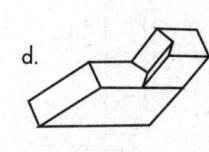
a. b. c. d.

5.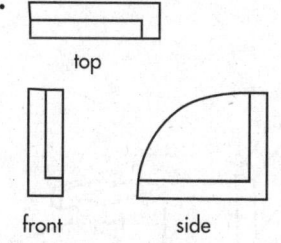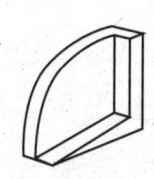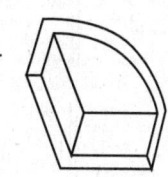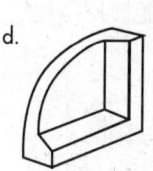
a. b. c. d.

LearningExpress Mechanical & Spatial Aptitude • CHAPTER 4

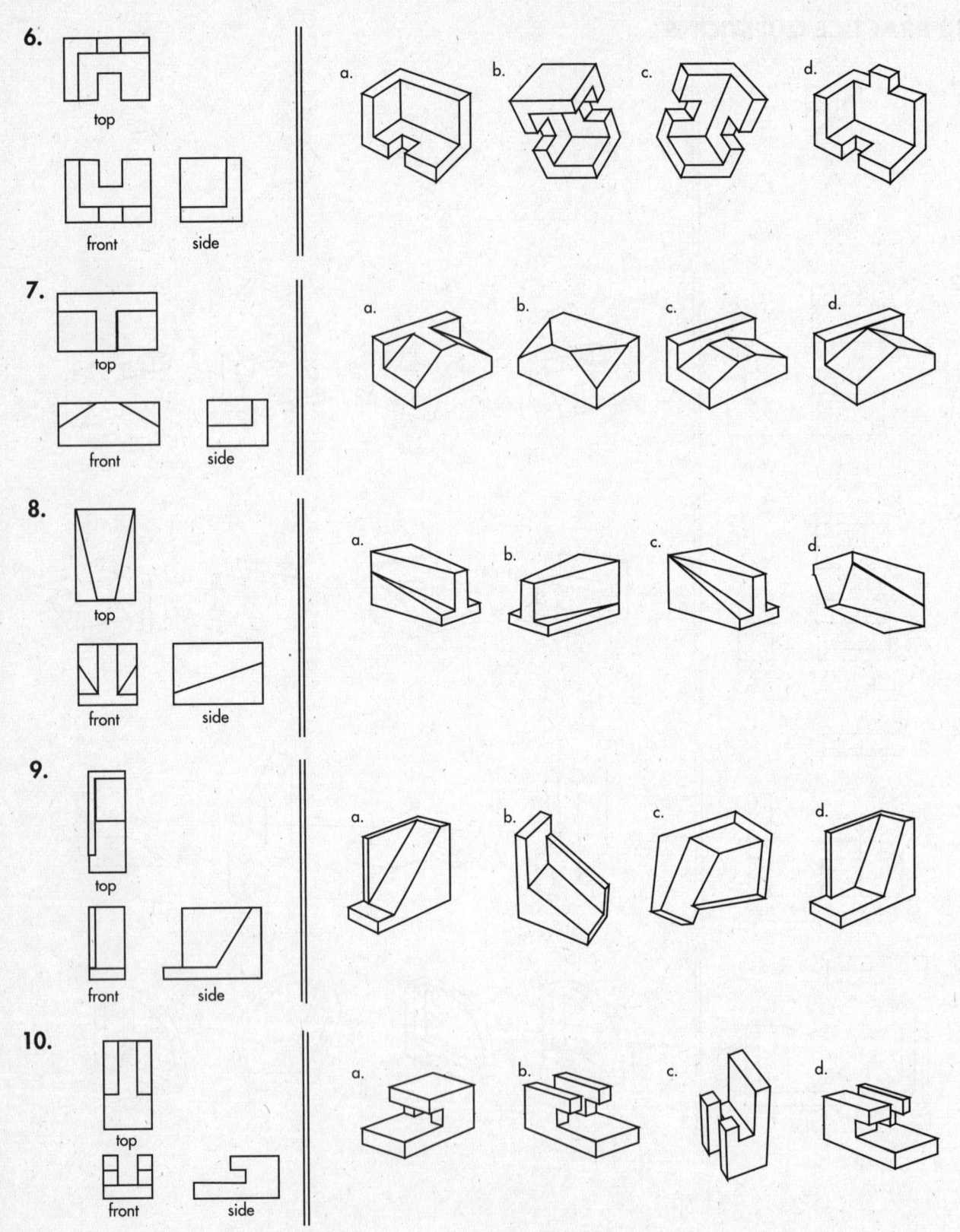

SPATIAL CONCEPTS

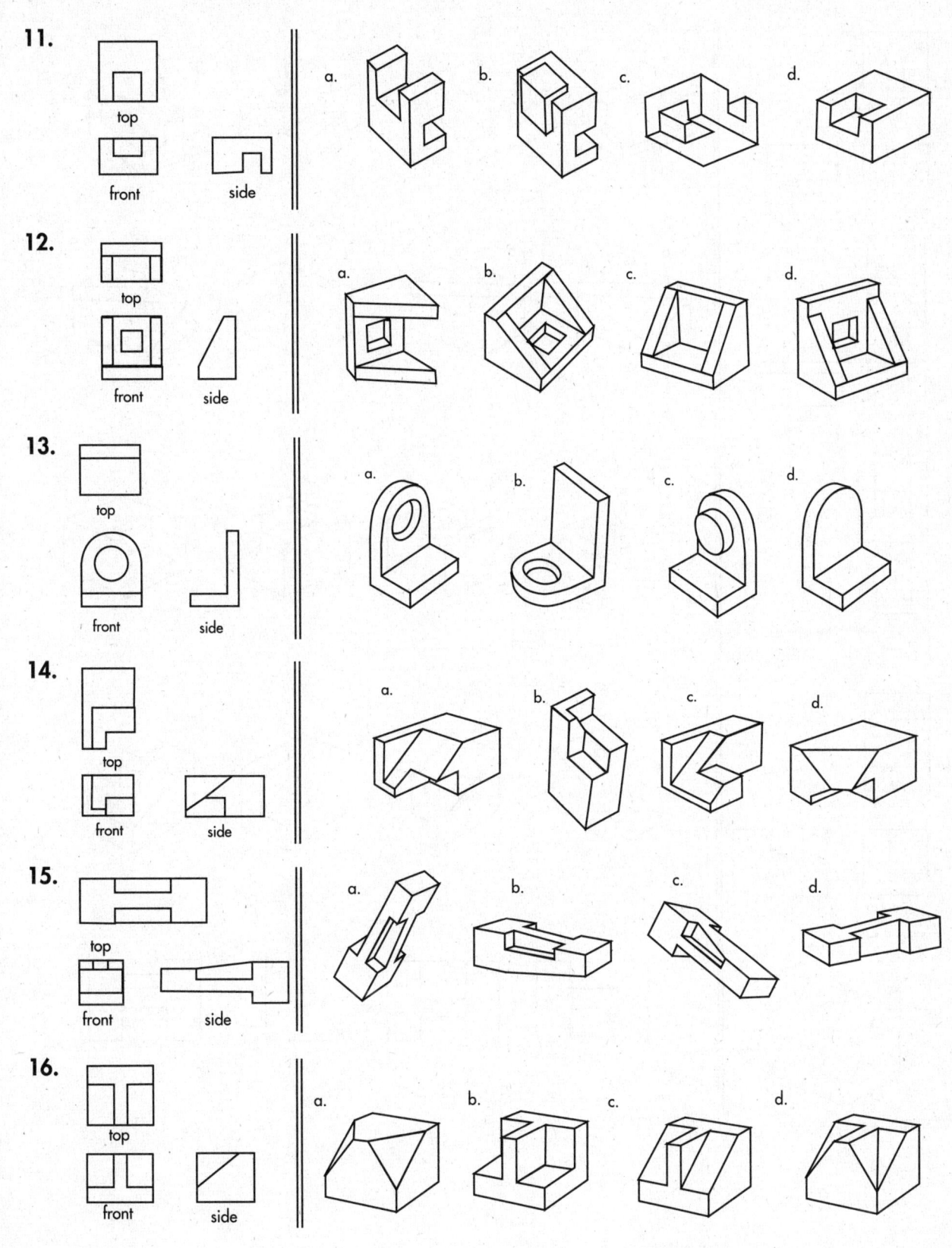

SPATIAL CONCEPTS

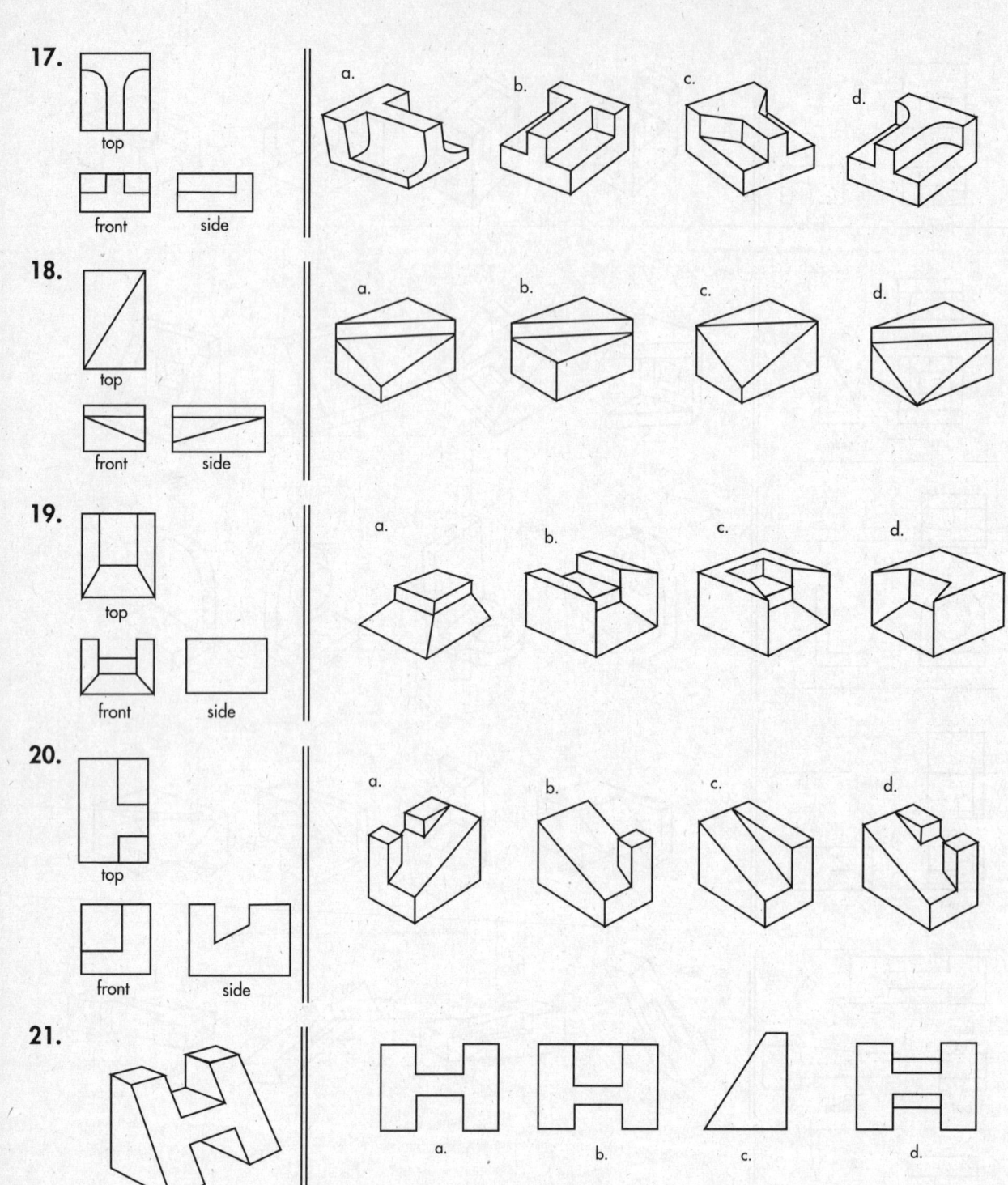

22.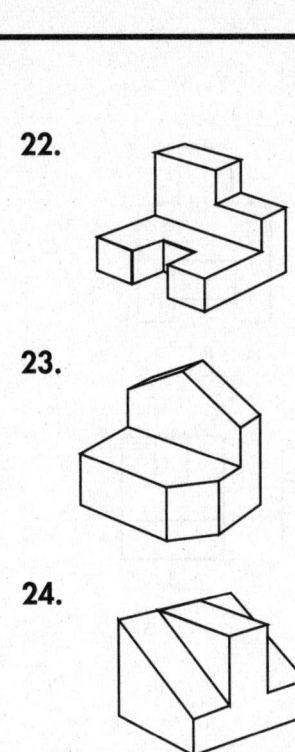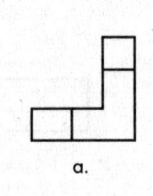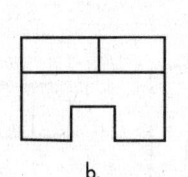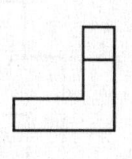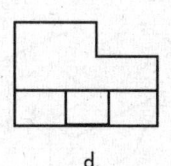
a. b. c. d.

23.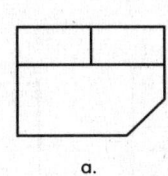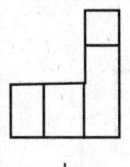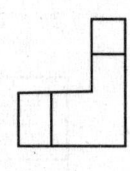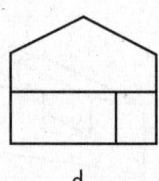
a. b. c. d.

24.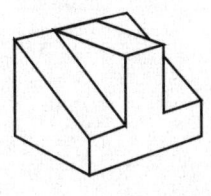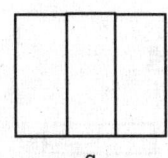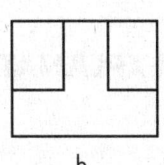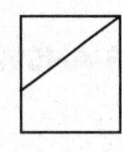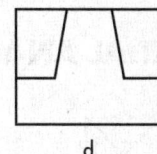
a. b. c. d.

25.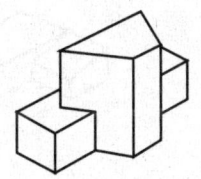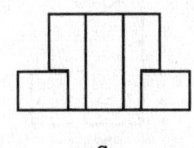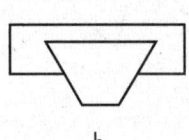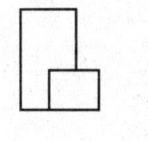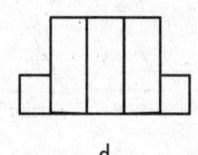
a. b. c. d.

26.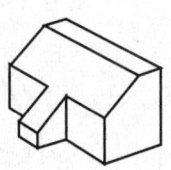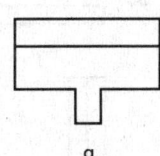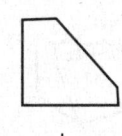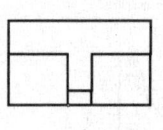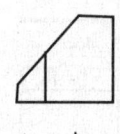
a. b. c. d.

27.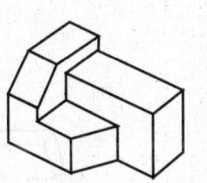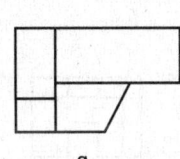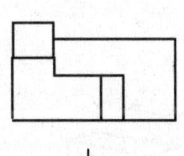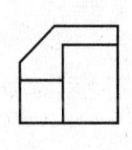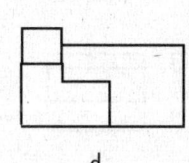
a. b. c. d.

28.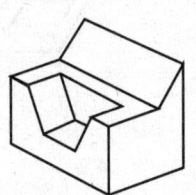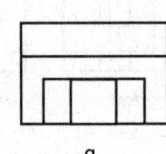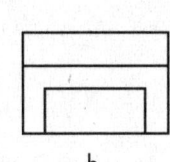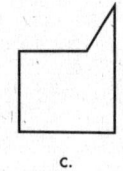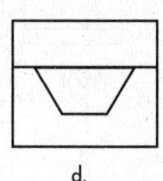
a. b. c. d.

LearningExpress Mechanical & Spatial Aptitude • CHAPTER 4

SPATIAL CONCEPTS

29.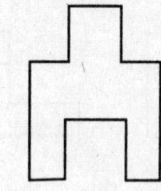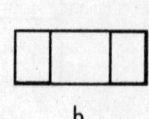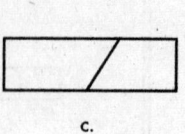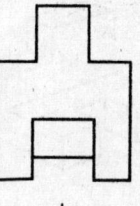

a. b. c. d.

30.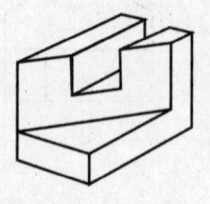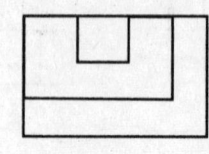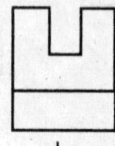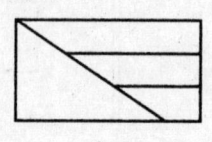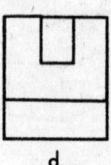

a. b. c. d.

SPATIAL ANALYSIS ANSWER EXPLANATIONS

1. 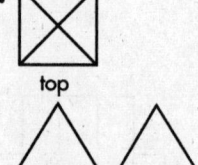 c.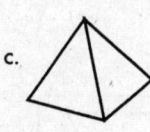

2. 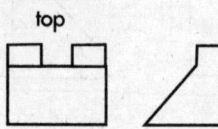 a.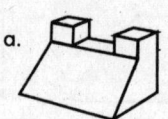

3. 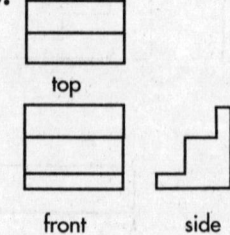 a.

4. 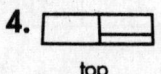 b.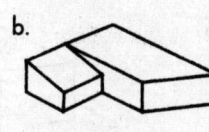

5. 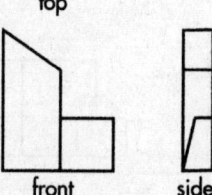 b.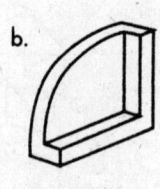

6. 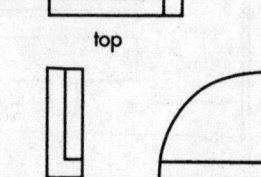 c.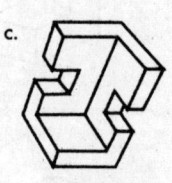

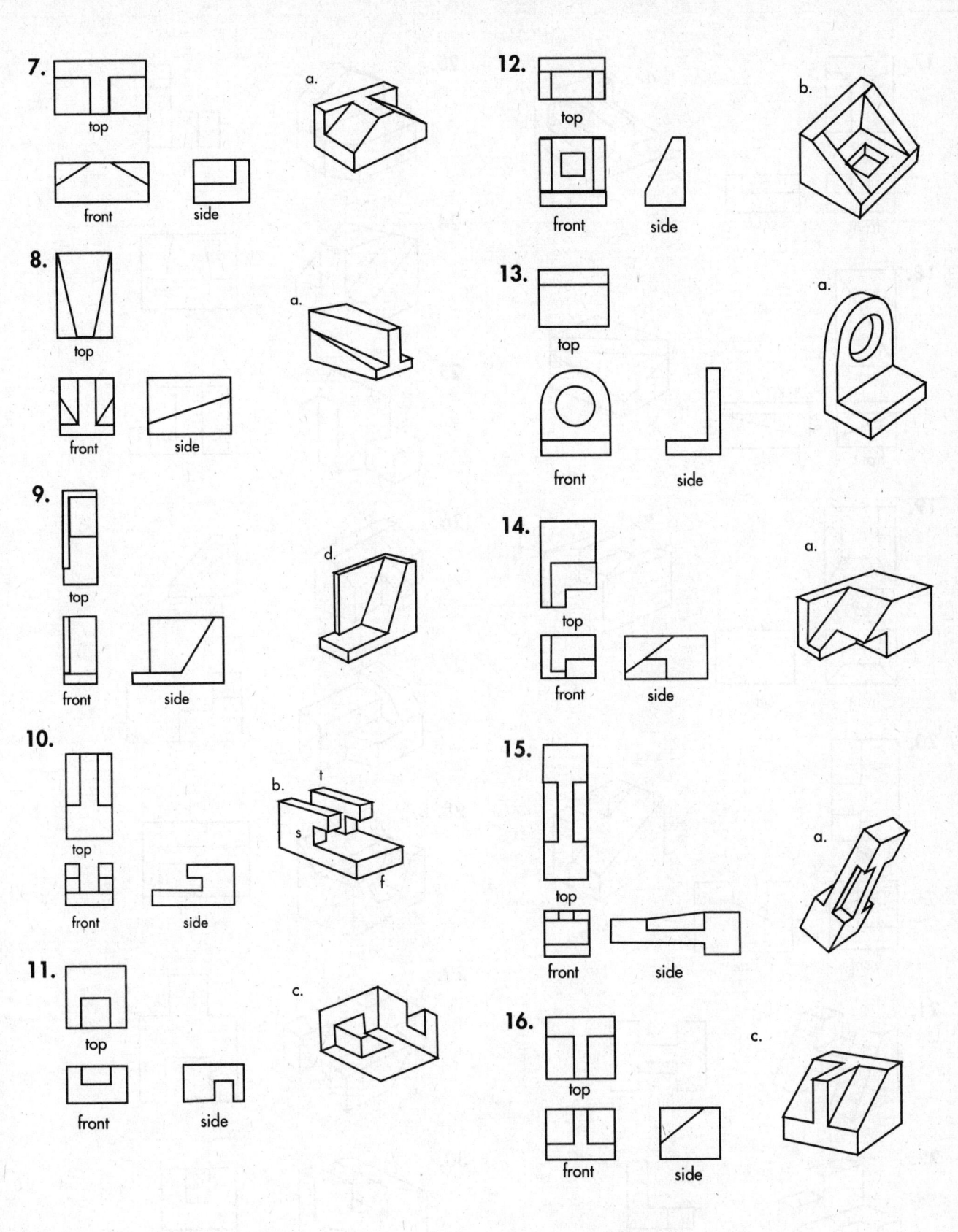

SPATIAL CONCEPTS

UNDERSTANDING PATTERNS

These pattern questions are designed to test your capacity to transform 2-D into 3-D and vice versa. You should be able to mentally fold up a 2-dimensional pattern into a 3-dimensional solid. Sometimes this is trickier than others. In such cases, process of elimination is your best friend. Figure out how many faces will be present in the folded product, and cross off inappropriate answers accordingly. Next, analyze the shape and placement of each face.

Other questions will present you with a patterned 3-D figure and ask you to mentally squash it flat into a 2-D representation. Again, counting up the number of faces can help you eliminate wrong answers. Next, look at the relative positions of the patterned shapes upon folding. Let's look at some examples below.

UNDERSTANDING PATTERNS INSTRUCTIONS

In this first sample question you will see an unfolded cardboard pattern. The solid lines represent the shape of the different parts and the dashed lines represent fold lines. For each unfolded pattern there are four choices that could possibly represent the pattern folded into a three-dimensional shape.

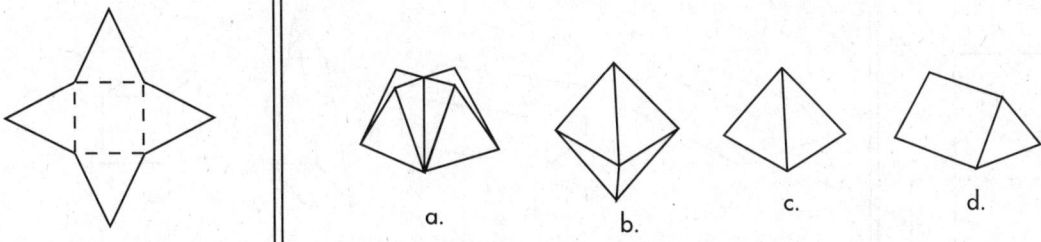

Here's a brief description of what the sample question would look like in three dimensions. Picture the image as it might look folded up to visualize the answer. The square in the center of the unfolded pattern represents the base of the pyramid with the four surrounding triangles representing the four sides of the pyramid. Since there are no other lines to represent any shapes, other than the ones described, then **c** can be the only possible answer.

The second sample uses the reverse of the principle set up in the first sample and uses cubes with patterned sides instead of solid shapes as a starting point. In this exercise you will take a three-dimensional cube with patterned faces (not necessarily every side will have a pattern on it) and decide which of the four possible answers represents an unfolded cube. To find the answer to this question, it is a good idea to first study the cube and observe the shape of the patterns and their placement on the face of the cube. Once you feel you have a good grasp of the cube, compare it to the possible answers. Look for the position of the symbols and where they would sit if the pattern were folded up.

LearningExpress Mechanical & Spatial Aptitude • CHAPTER 4

SPATIAL CONCEPTS

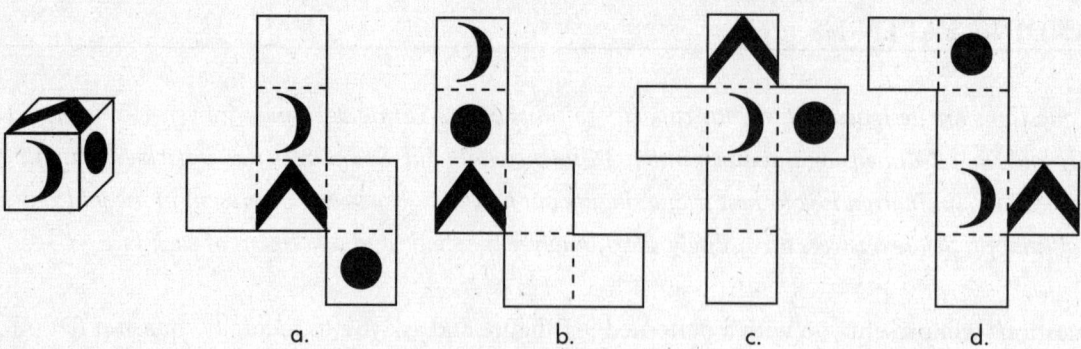

If you study the cube carefully you should see that **c** is the only possible answer. The front of the cube bears a crescent-moon shape, the top bears an upside down v-shape and the side bears a black circle. Answer choice **c** uses the crescent-moon shape as its front. If you fold all the other sides around it, they fall into place and give you the original cube.

30 PRACTICE QUESTIONS

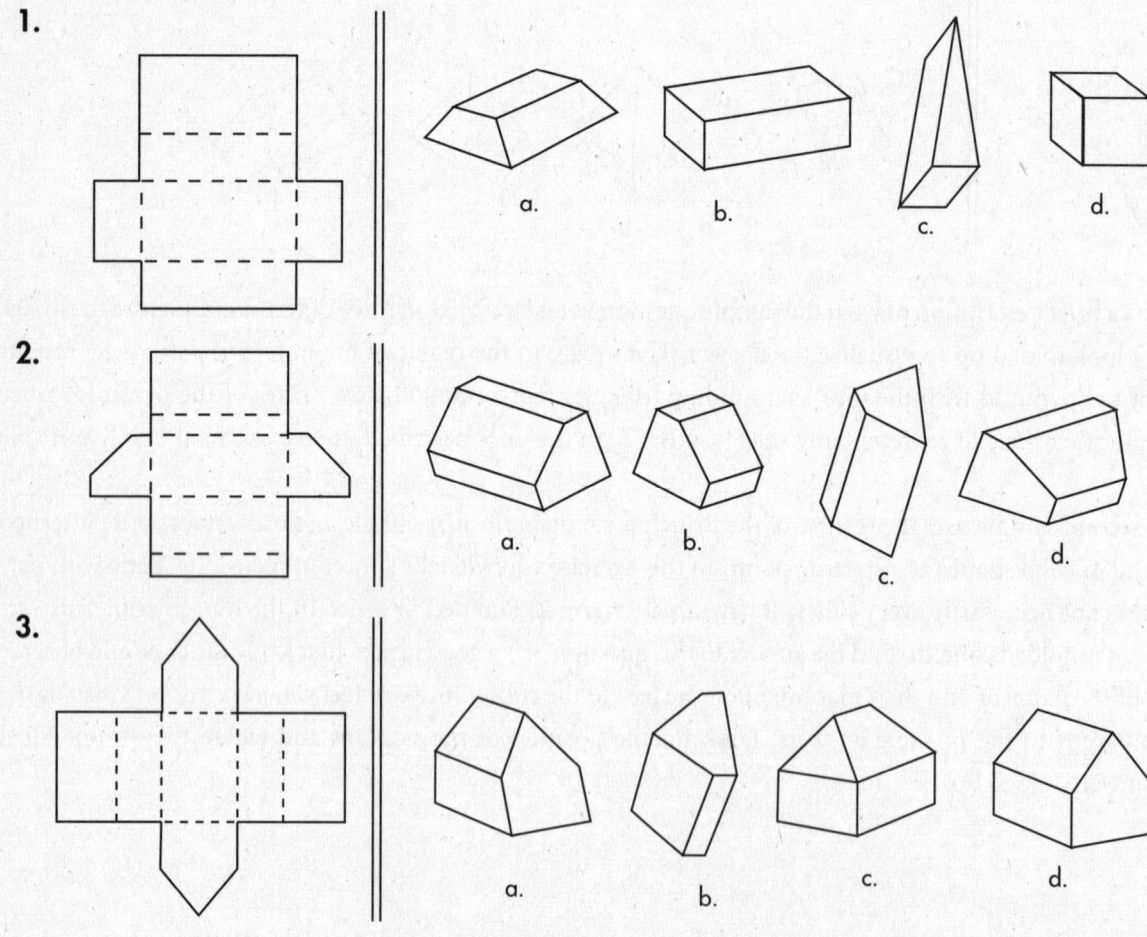

SPATIAL CONCEPTS

4.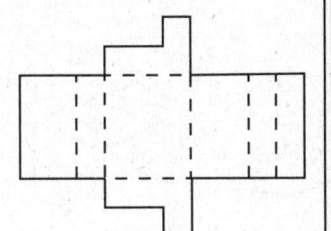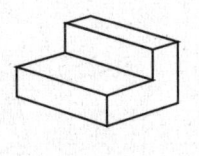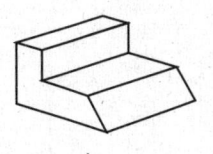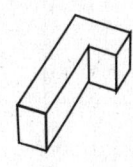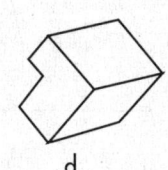
  a. b. c. d.

5.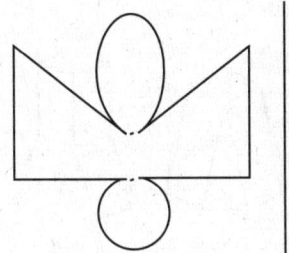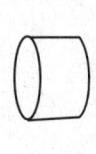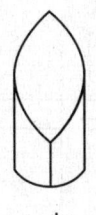
  a. b. c. d.

6.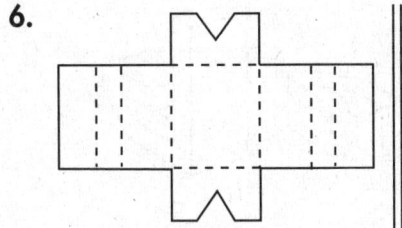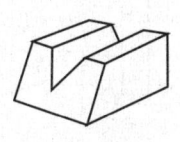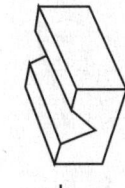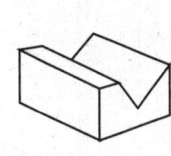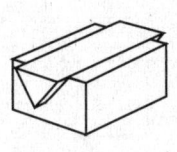
  a. b. c. d.

7.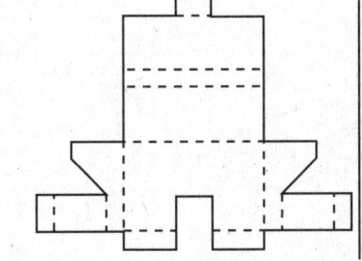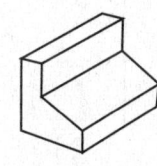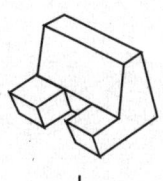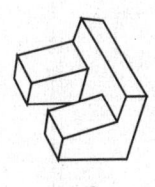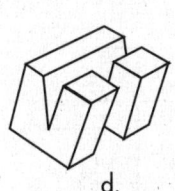
  a. b. c. d.

8.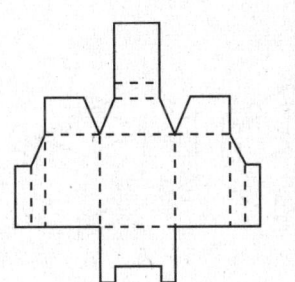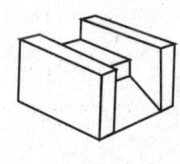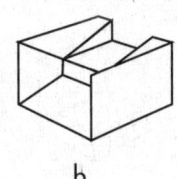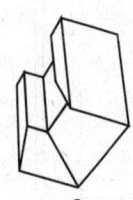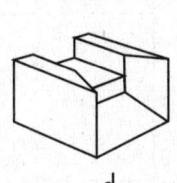
  a. b. c. d.

SPATIAL CONCEPTS

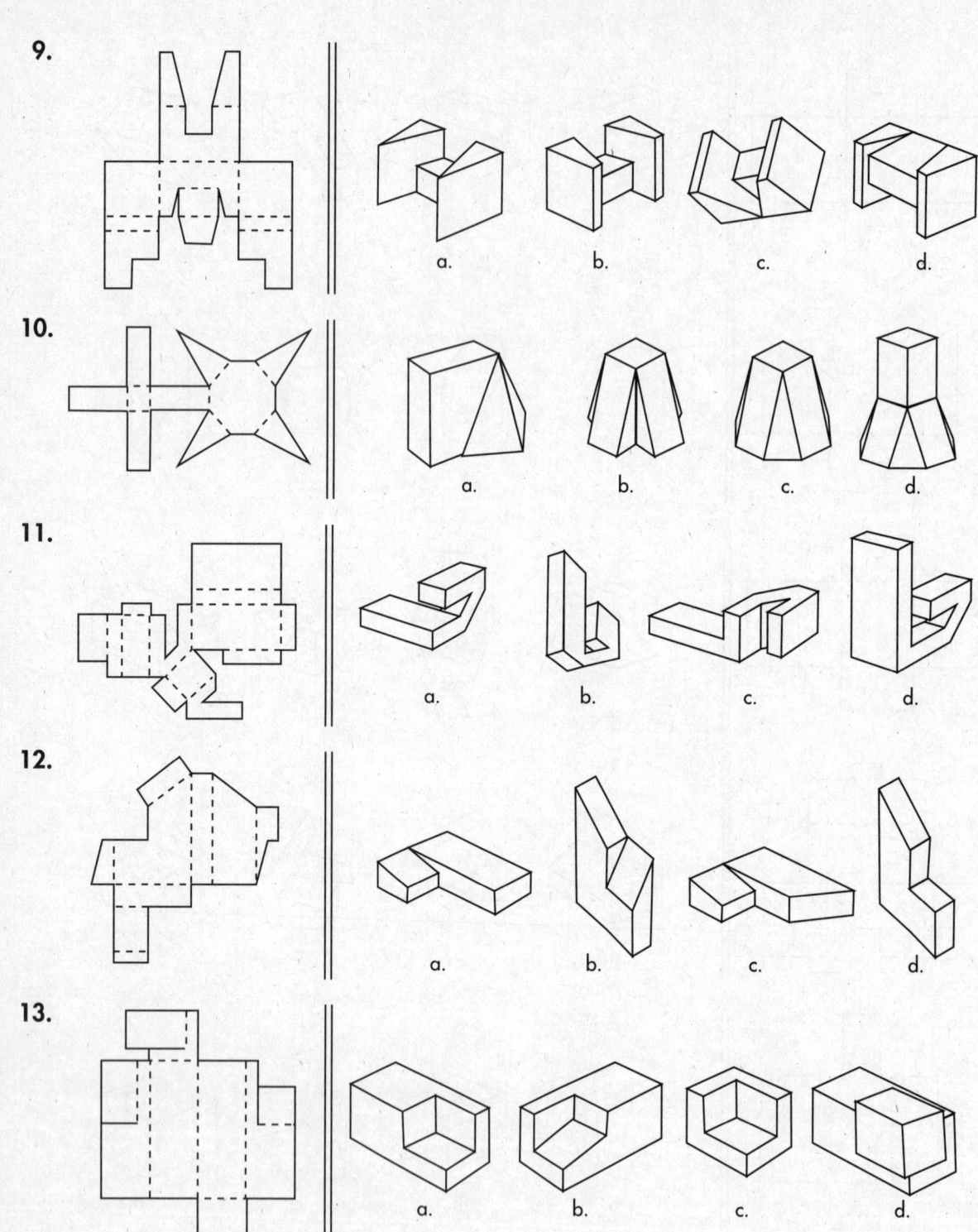

SPATIAL CONCEPTS

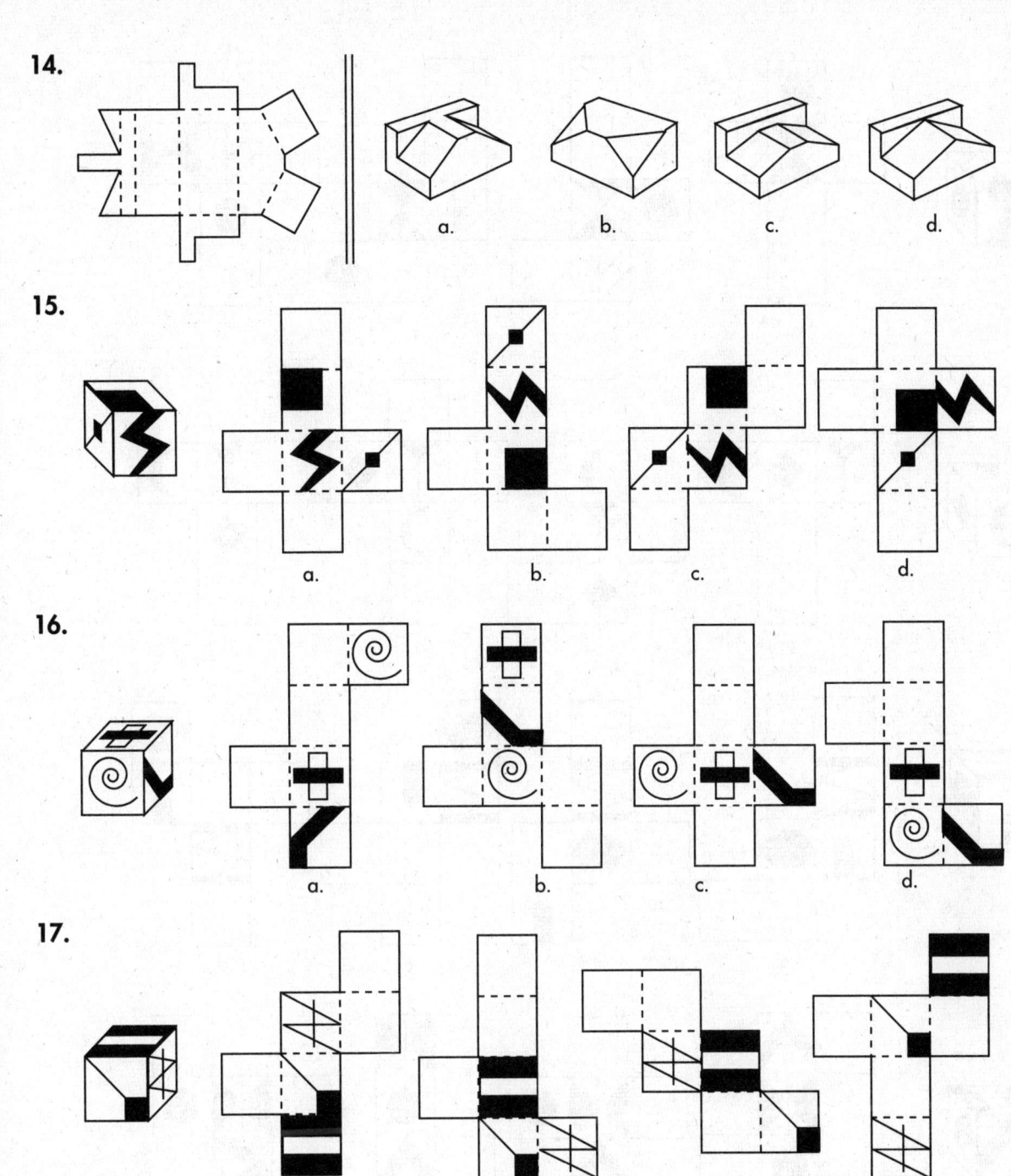

SPATIAL CONCEPTS

18.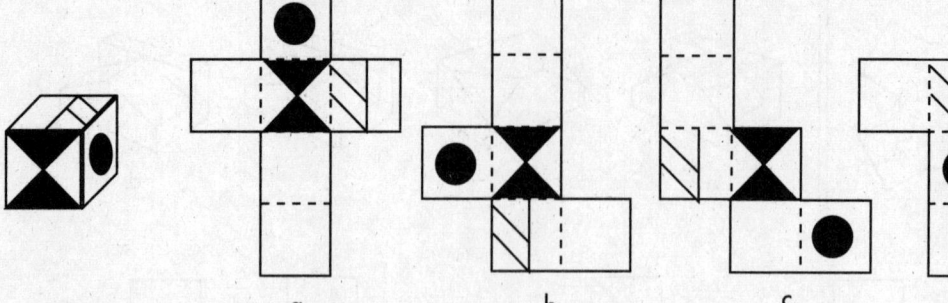

19.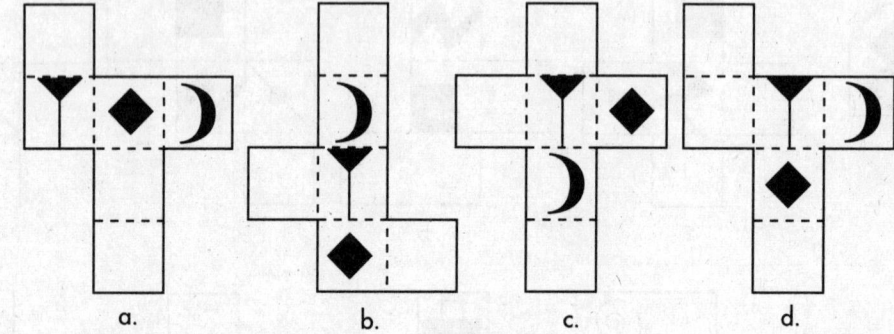

20.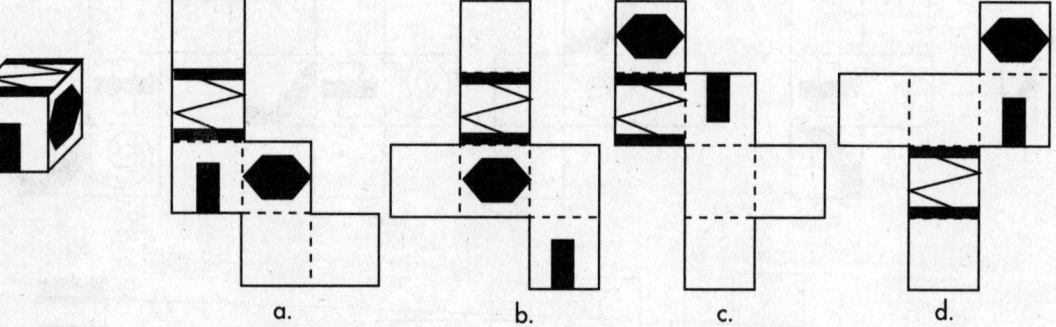

21.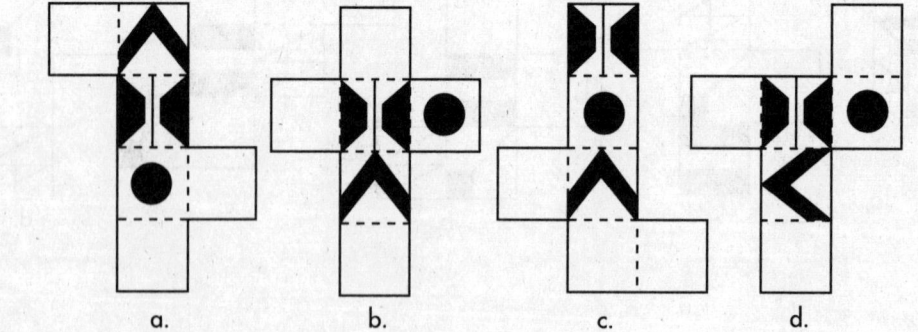

22.

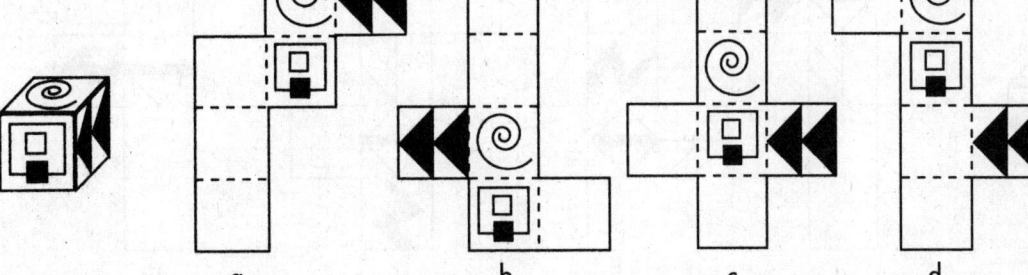

23.

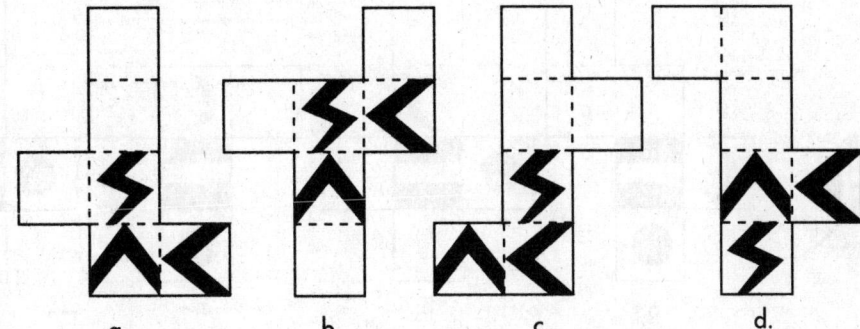

24.

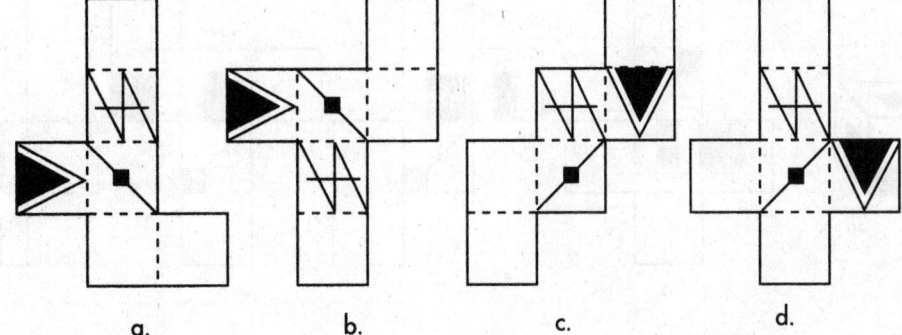

25.

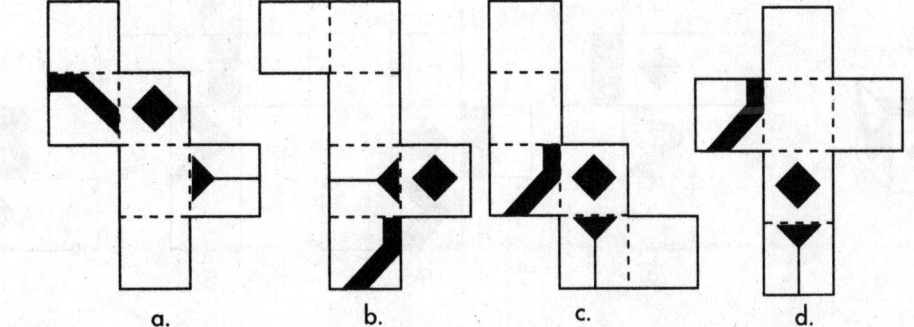

SPATIAL CONCEPTS

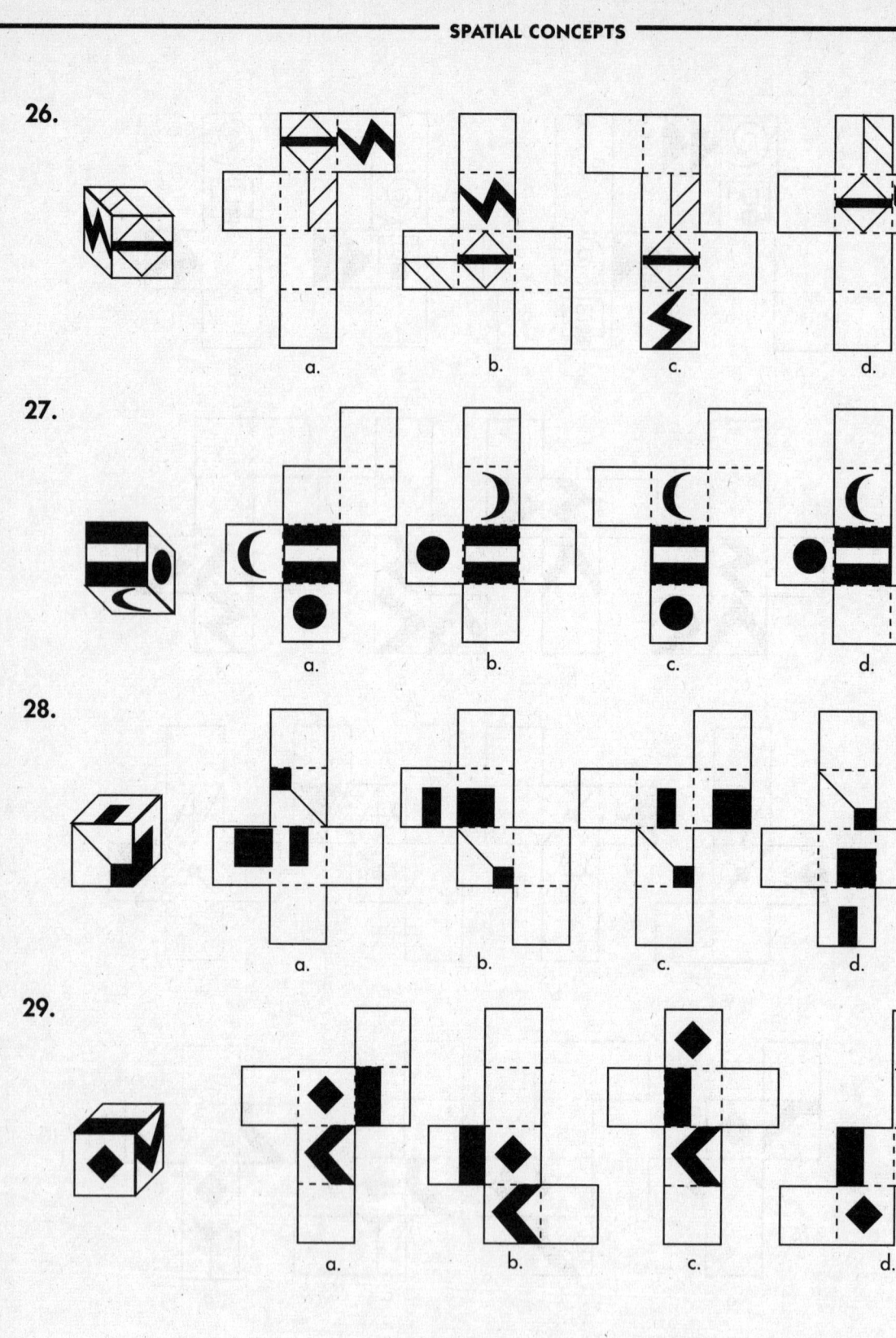

SPATIAL CONCEPTS

30.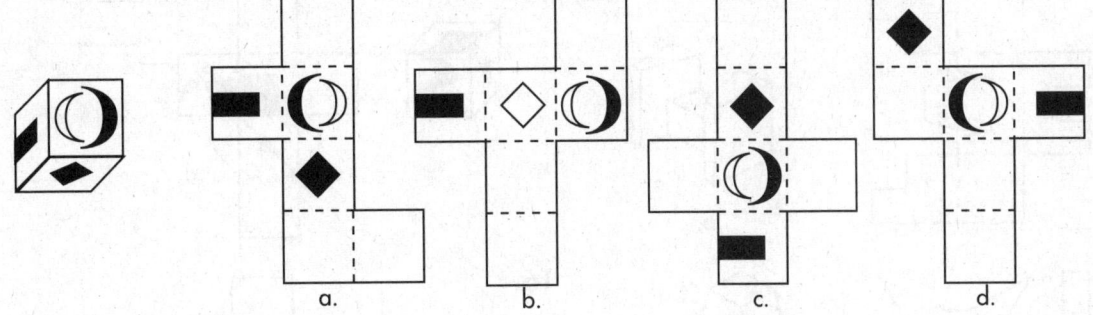

a.   b.   c.   d.

UNDERSTANDING PATTERNS ANSWER EXPLANATIONS

1.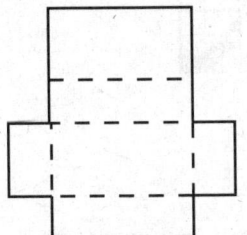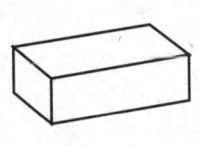
b.

5.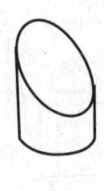
b.

2.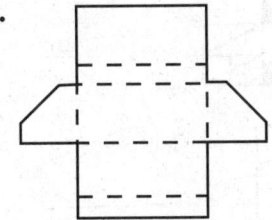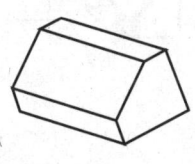
a.

6.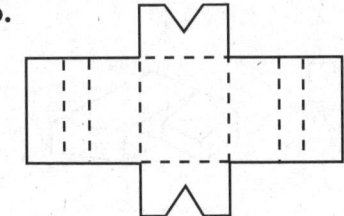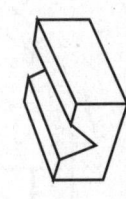
b.

3.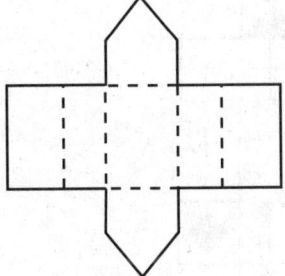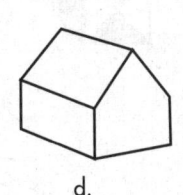
d.

7.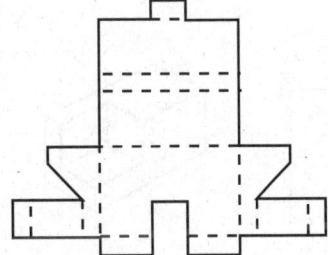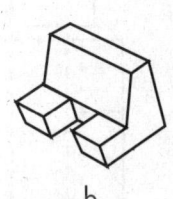
b.

4.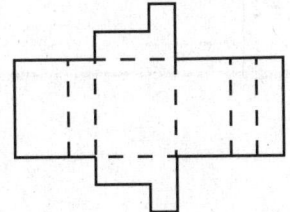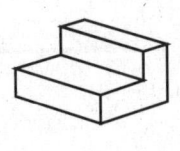
a.

8.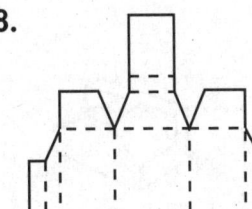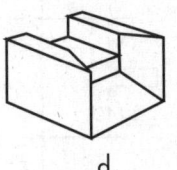
d.

LearningExpress Mechanical & Spatial Aptitude • CHAPTER 4

SPATIAL CONCEPTS

9.
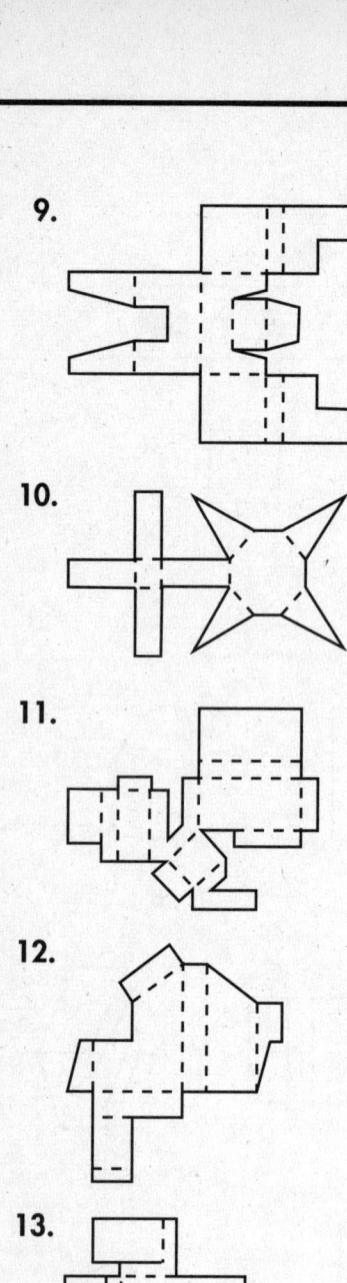
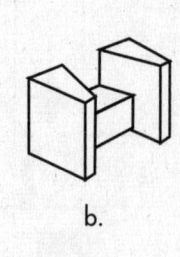
b.

10.

c.

11.
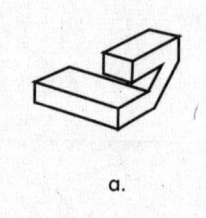
a.

12.
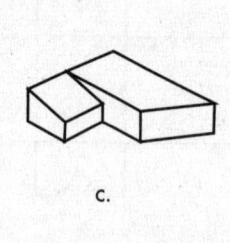
c.

13.
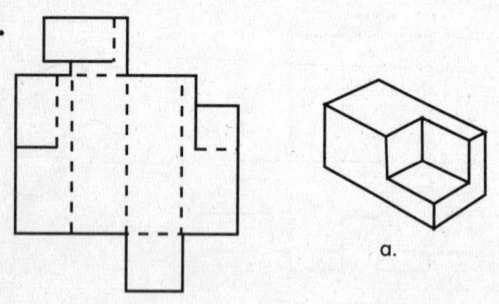
a.

14.
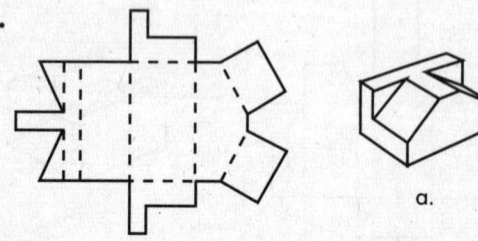
a.

15.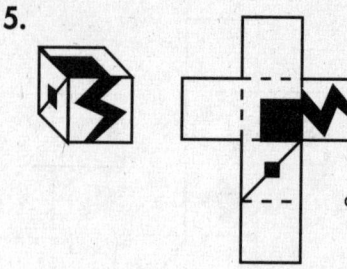
d.

16.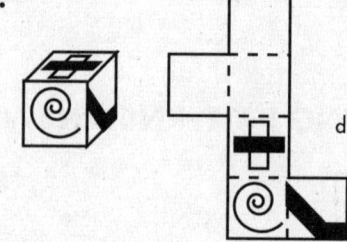
d.

17.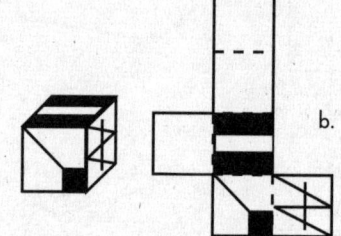
b.

18.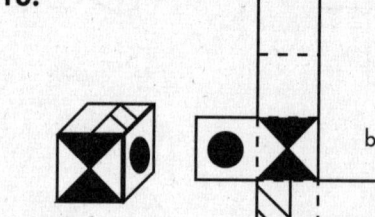
b.

19.
c.

SPATIAL CONCEPTS

20.  a.

21. 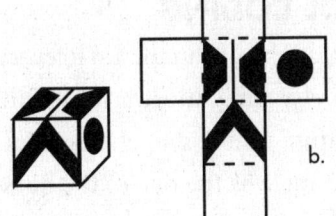 b.

22. 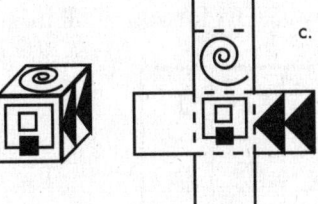 c.

23. 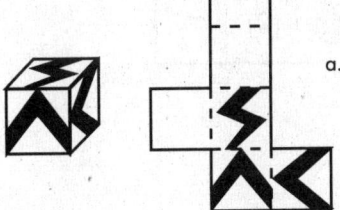 a.

24. 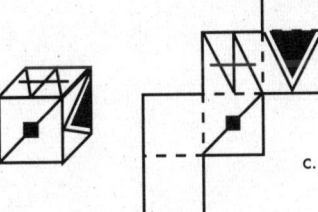 c.

25. 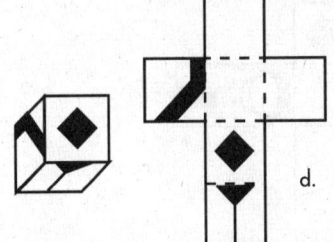 d.

26. 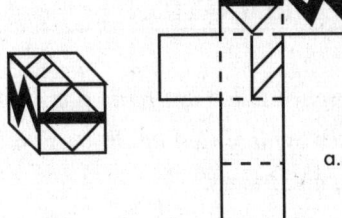 a.

27. 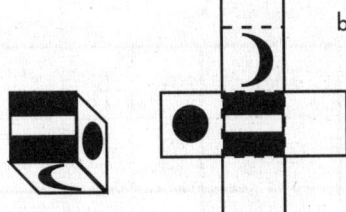 b.

28. 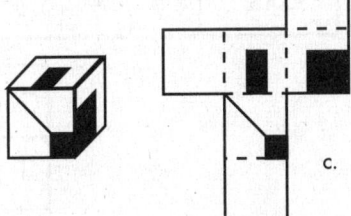 c.

29. 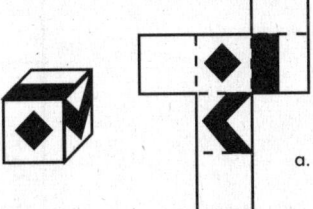 a.

SPATIAL CONCEPTS

30.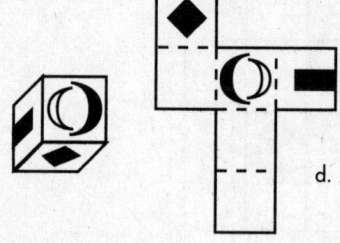
d.

EYE-HAND COORDINATION

Several tests are designed to test eye-hand coordination. These include: Letter-Symbol Coding, Inspection Tests, Examining Objects, and Mazes.

LETTER-SYMBOL CODING

These types of questions bring out the kid in everyone. Although they are pretty straightforward and fun, just be careful not to confuse similar shapes. Make sure the shape is at the same angle as the one in the question. If the shape is a polygon, make sure it has the correct number of sides. Below is an example of a Letter-Symbol Code followed by a chart for you to fill in.

Letter	A	B	C	D	E	F	G	H	I	J
Code	⊙	☆	▼	▽	▣	★	⬠	▲	■	△
Letter	K	L	M	N	O	P	Q	R	S	T
Code	⬢	▽	⬡	⬟	☆	▲	⬠	⬢	⊙	⬡

Question	Answer
1. ⬠	
2. ⬡	
3. ▼	
4. ⊙	
5. ⬢	
6. ▣	
7. ▽	
8. ⬟	

SPATIAL CONCEPTS

You can check your answers against this key.

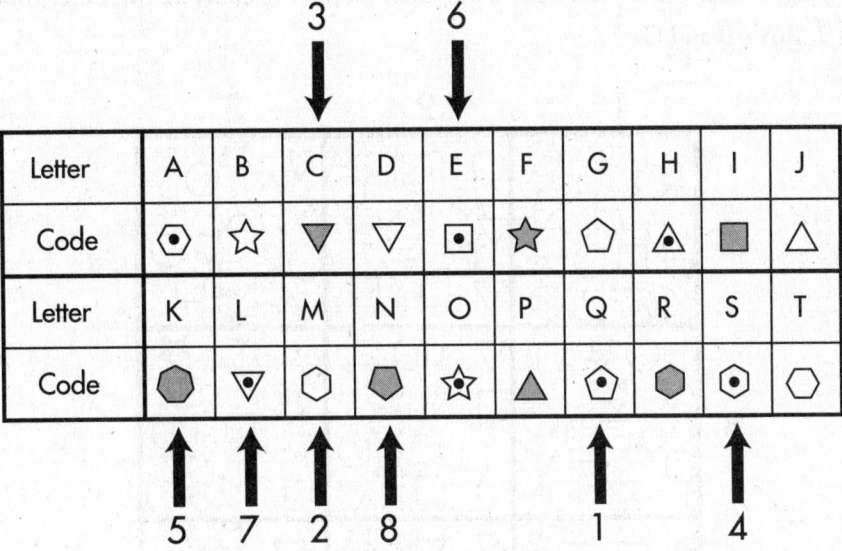

If you missed any of the above questions, *slow down* and take care to compare all of the aspects of the given symbol and the choice you are about to pick.

SPATIAL CONCEPTS

INSPECTION TESTS

These tests require you to closely analyze a figure. For example, in the chart below, determine how many triangles are in Column 2, Rows B and C.

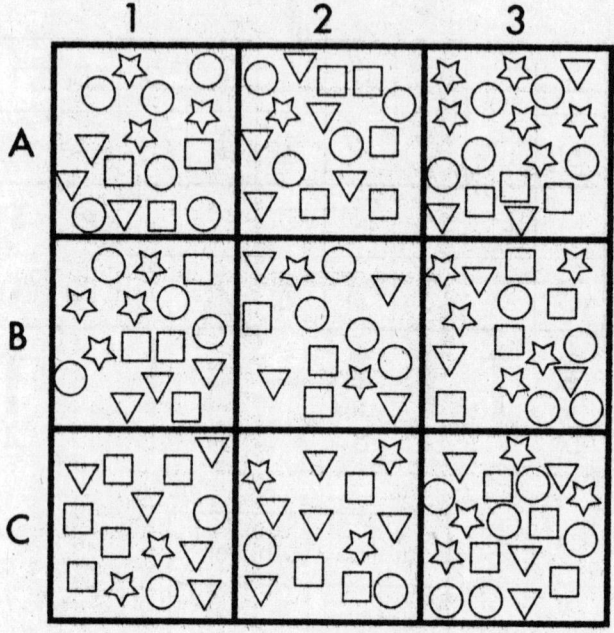

Did you count nine? The key below shows all the triangles.

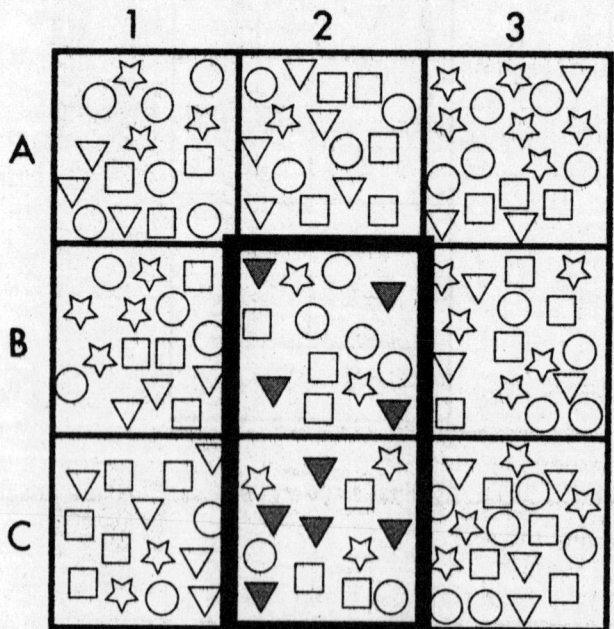

These questions tend to get pretty tedious. Be *extremely* careful.

EXAMINING OBJECTS

In these questions you must examine objects and classify them according to a given set of rules or codes. Read the instructions carefully and underline anything that you think is important. Otherwise, jot down some quick notes next to the graphic sorting code.

The Sorting Code above is a graphical summary for the following Sorting Code. Read the code carefully.
Sorting Code for Boxes 1 through 4:

Box 1: Ship

Both pieces are not defective and are the same size.

Box 2: Trash

Both pieces are defective.
　　Note: A "defect" is displayed as a dashed line going across the piece. See the graphic code above.

Box 3: Resize

Both pieces are not defective but the sizes do not match.

Box 4: Recycle

Anytime one piece is defective, place the package into Box 4.

SPATIAL CONCEPTS

In the question below, you are presented with a package containing two pieces. Use the above sorting code to determine which box the package needs to be placed in.

1.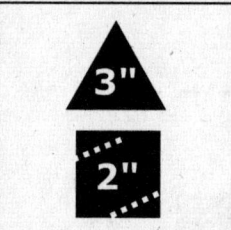
   a. Box 1
   b. Box 2
   c. Box 3
   d. Box 4

Answer: **d.** Although you may have been tempted to put this package into Box 3 (Resize), notice that the criteria for Box 3 states: *Both pieces are not defective but the sizes do not match*. In this example we do have *one* defective piece. According to the Sorting Code, we see that this package belongs in Box 4: *Anytime one piece is defective, place the package into Box 4*.

MAZES

As you wind your way through a maze, pretend the solid lines are walls that you cannot cross. Try the sample maze below.

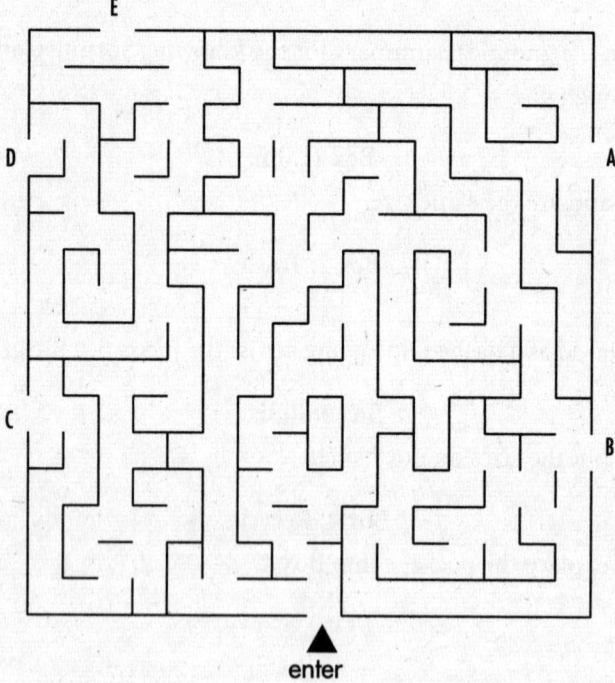

Did you come out at **B**? Following is the answer key.

SPATIAL CONCEPTS

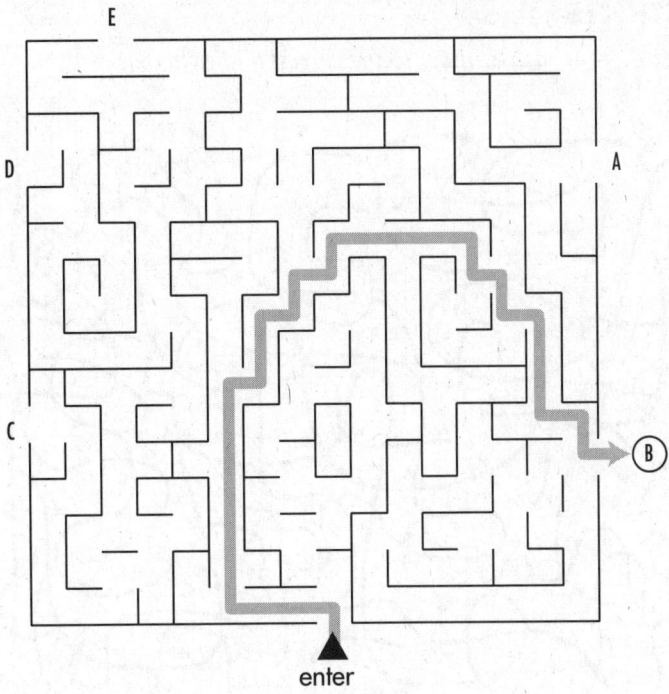

Notice that if you tried to go backward and entered through A, C, D, or E, you would soon hit a wall. If you are having trouble going forward, you can always eliminate answers by going backward.

SPATIAL CONCEPTS

32 PRACTICE QUESTIONS

In questions 1–8, trace the path from each number to the corresponding letter.

1. ____
2. ____
3. ____
4. ____
5. ____
6. ____
7. ____
8. ____

9. Follow the maze below and mark the letter that correctly represents the way out of the maze. _____

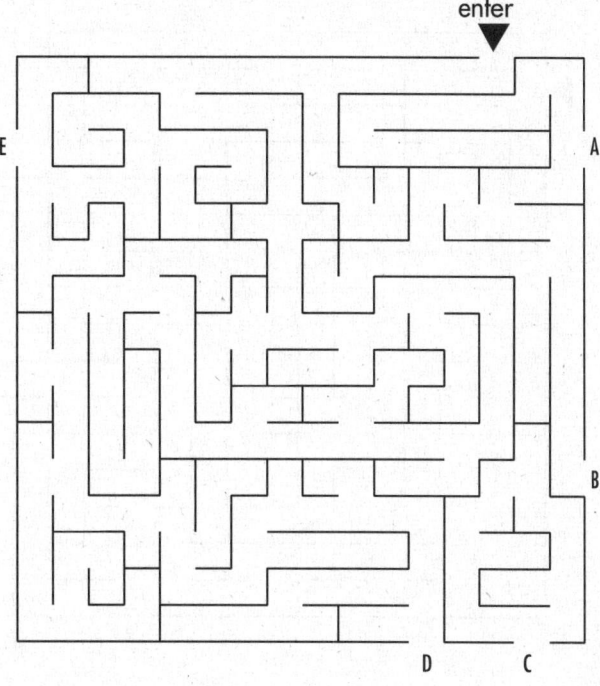

10. Follow the maze below and mark the letter that correctly represents the way out of the maze. _____

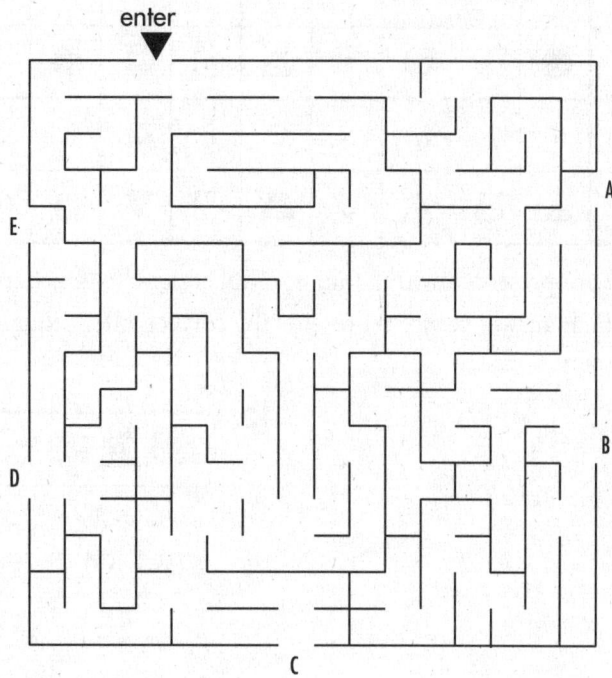

SPATIAL CONCEPTS

11. Follow the maze below and mark the letter that correctly represents the way out of the maze. _____

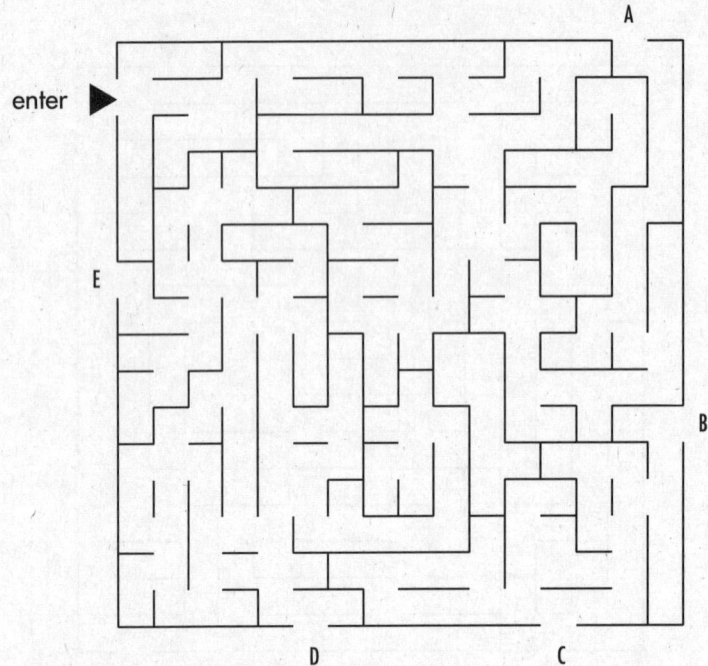

Letter	A	B	C	D	E	F	G	H	I	J
Code	⬣	⬠⊙	⬡	⬠⊙	▲	⬡⊙	⬠	⬣	▽	⬡
Letter	K	L	M	N	O	P	Q	R	S	T
Code	▲	■	△⊙	▽	▲	⊙	▼	⬟	⊙	⬟

In questions 12–19, you are presented with a four-symbol code. Use the chart above to translate the code into letters, and determine which answer choice represents the correct letter sequence.

12.

   a. FHME
   b. FAME
   c. SAME
   d. SHIN
   e. FAIN

13.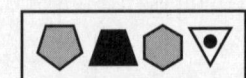

   a. GOCI
   b. CKGM
   c. GKCI
   d. COGM
   e. GKCI

14.
   a. OCBF
   b. RJPS
   c. OGPF
   d. RGPF
   e. OJPS

15.
   a. OMAN
   b. KMAN
   c. OITN
   d. KITN
   e. KITE

16.
   a. IDAF
   b. BDHF
   c. IFHD
   d. BFHD
   e. IDHF

17.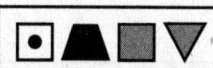
   a. BKRE
   b. POLE
   c. BKLN
   d. POLN
   e. PKRE

18.
   a. BACK
   b. IDHQ
   c. BFAQ
   d. IAHQ
   e. BHAQ

19.
   a. FKEN
   b. FOEN
   c. FKNE
   d. DOEN
   e. DONE

SPATIAL CONCEPTS

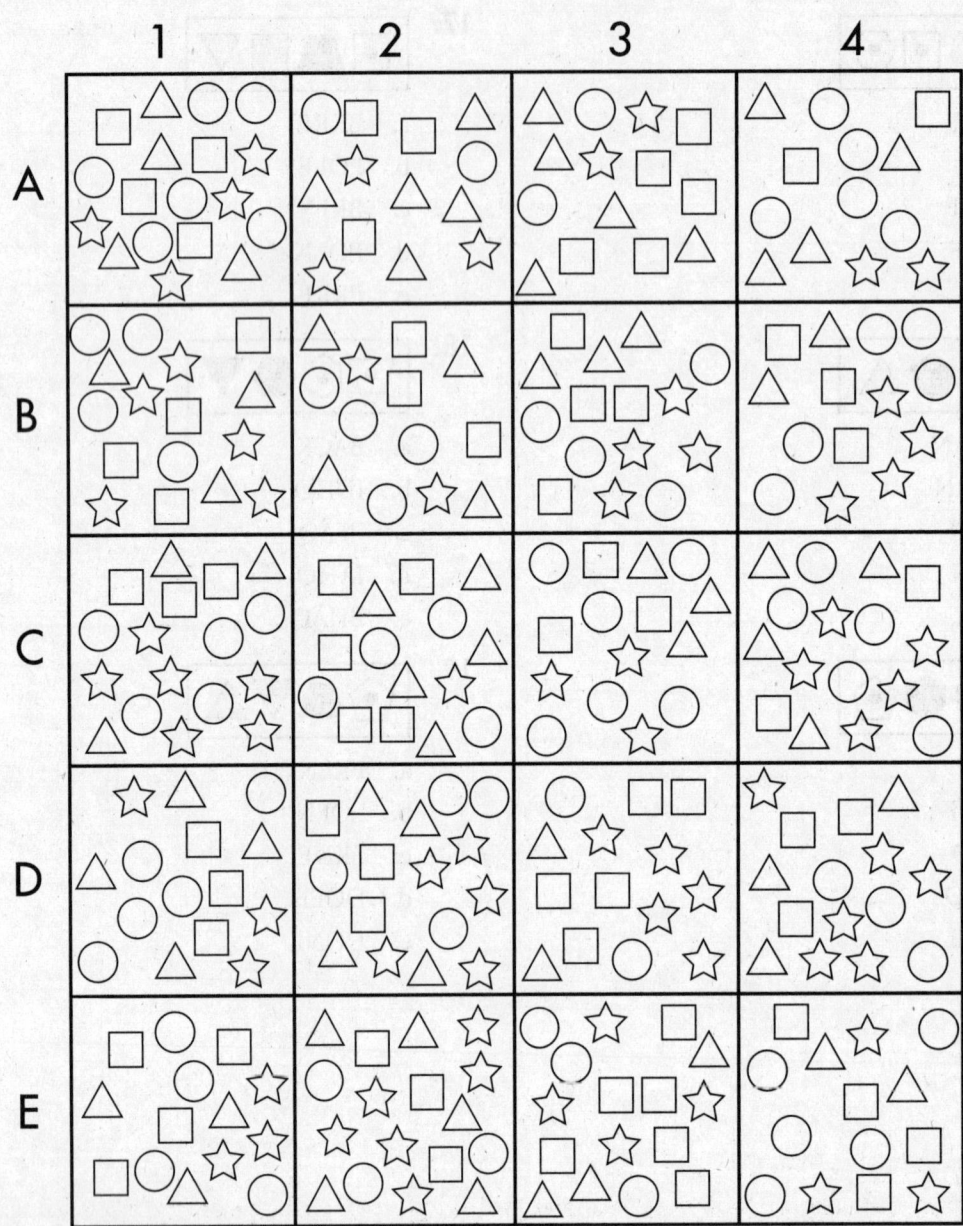

Use the chart above to determine the calculations required for questions 20–28.

20. Count the number of squares in Row C:
   a. 11
   b. 12
   c. 13
   d. 14
   e. none of the above

21. Count the number of triangles in Column 2, Rows B, C, and E:
   a. 11
   b. 12
   c. 13
   d. 14
   e. none of the above

CHAPTER 4 • *LearningExpress Mechanical & Spatial Aptitude*

SPATIAL CONCEPTS

22. Count the number of circles in Rows A, C, and E:
    a. 49
    b. 50
    c. 51
    d. 52
    e. none of the above

23. Count the number of stars in Column 1, Rows A, C, D, and E:
    a. 16
    b. 18
    c. 19
    d. 21
    e. none of the above

24. Count the number of squares in Columns 1 and 3.
    a. 37
    b. 38
    c. 39
    d. 40
    e. none of the above

25. Count the number of triangles in Columns 1 and 2, excluding Row B:
    a. 33
    b. 37
    c. 38
    d. 40
    e. none of the above

26. How many stars and circles are in Row C?
    a. 33
    b. 34
    c. 35
    d. 36
    e. none of the above

27. Count the number of stars, circles, squares, and triangles in Row A, in Columns 1 and 2:
    a. 28
    b. 29
    c. 30
    d. 31
    e. none of the above

28. Count the number of squares and stars in Columns 1 and 4:
    a. 69
    b. 70
    c. 71
    d. 72
    e. none of the above

SPATIAL CONCEPTS

The Sorting Code above is a graphical summary for the following Sorting Code. Read the code carefully.

Sorting Code for Boxes 1 through 5:

Box 1: Pass Box

All packages placed in this box must satisfy each of the following requirements:
- *The two pieces fit together properly.*
- *The two pieces are the same color.*
- *The two pieces are free from defects.*

Box 2: Fail Box

All packages placed in this box contain two defective pieces. Regardless of fit or color, if both pieces inside a package are defective, put them in the Fail Box.

Note: A "defect" is displayed as a dashed line going across the piece. See the graphic code above.

Box 3: Recycle Box

All packages placed in this box contain one defective piece. Regardless of fit or color, if one piece of the pair is defective, put the package in the Recycle Box.

Box 4: Color Box

All packages placed in this box contain pieces that do not match in color. This box takes priority over the Join Box: When examining mismatched pairs that will not fit together and have different colors, place the package in the Color Box.

Box 5: Join Box

All packages in this box do not fit together.

SPATIAL CONCEPTS

In questions 29–32 below, you are presented with a package containing two pieces. Use the sorting code on p. 68 to determine which box each package needs to be placed in.

29.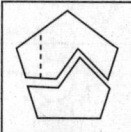

a. Box 1
b. Box 2
c. Box 3
d. Box 4
e. Box 5

30.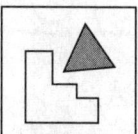

a. Box 1
b. Box 2
c. Box 3
d. Box 4
e. Box 5

31.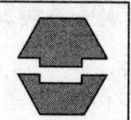

a. Box 1
b. Box 2
c. Box 3
d. Box 4
e. Box 5

32.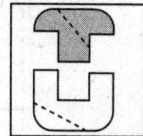

a. Box 1
b. Box 2
c. Box 3
d. Box 4
e. Box 5

SPATIAL CONCEPTS

EYE-HAND COORDINATION ANSWER EXPLANATIONS

1. e
2. h
3. c
4. b
5. g
6. a
7. d
8. f

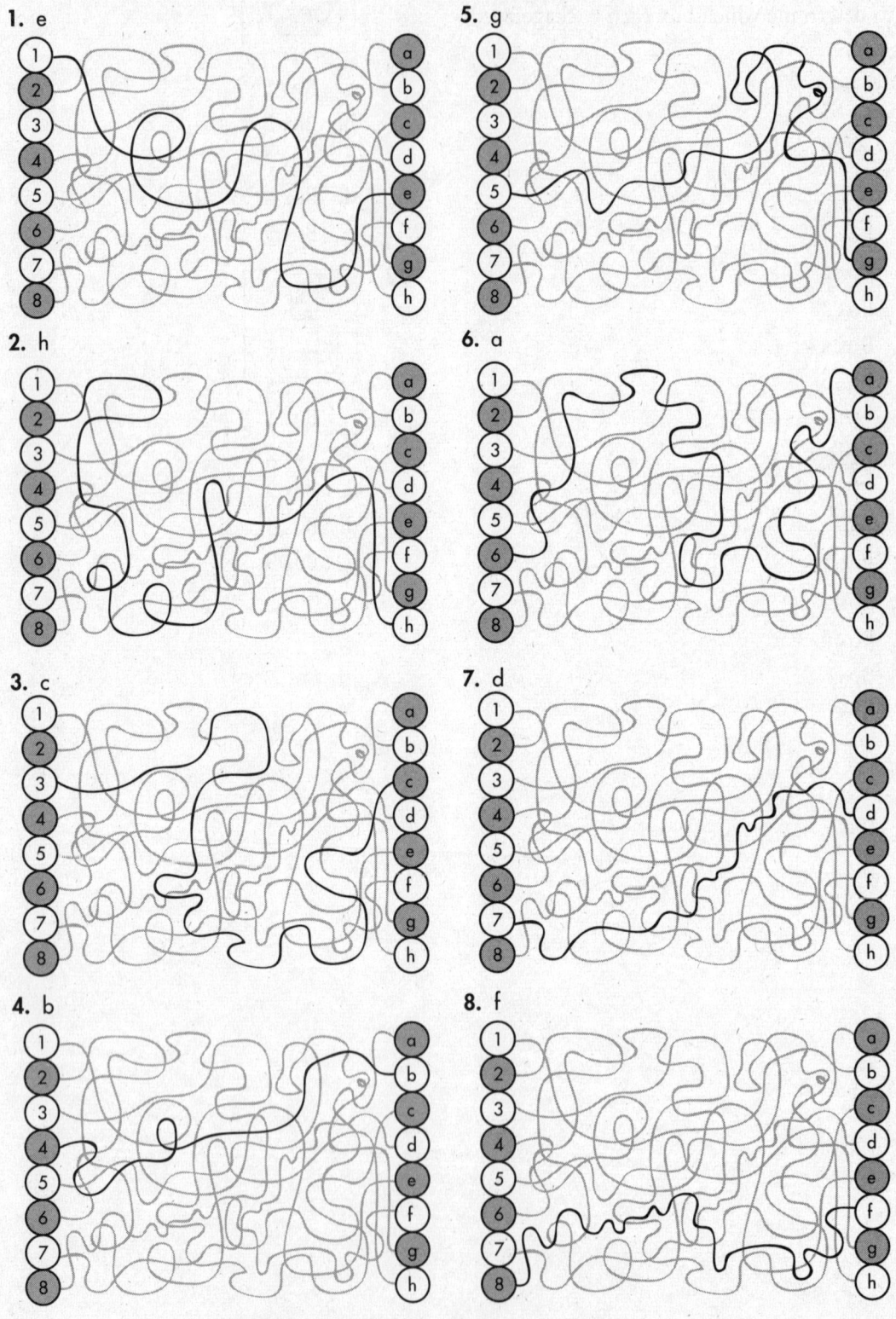

SPATIAL CONCEPTS

9.

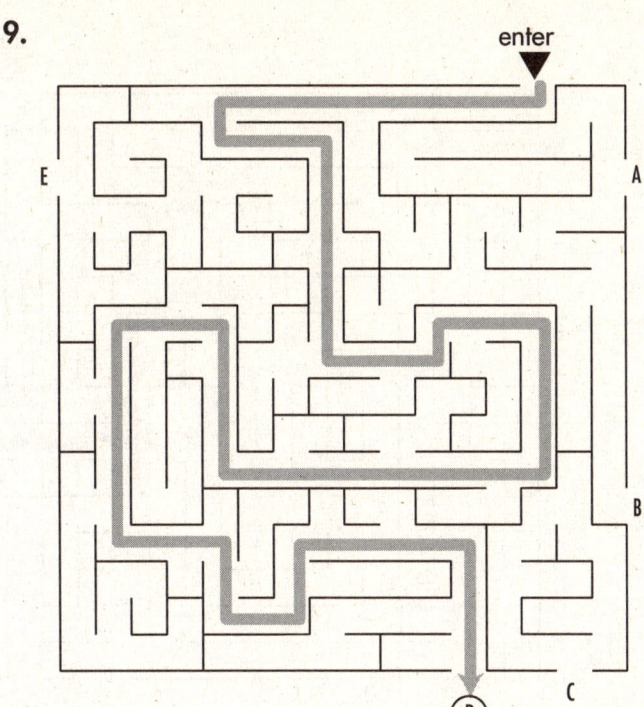

10.

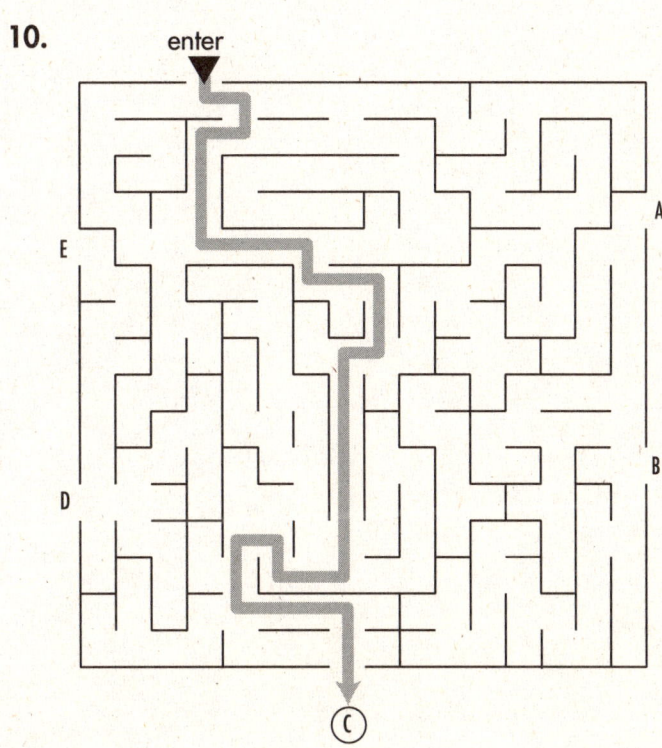

SPATIAL CONCEPTS

11.

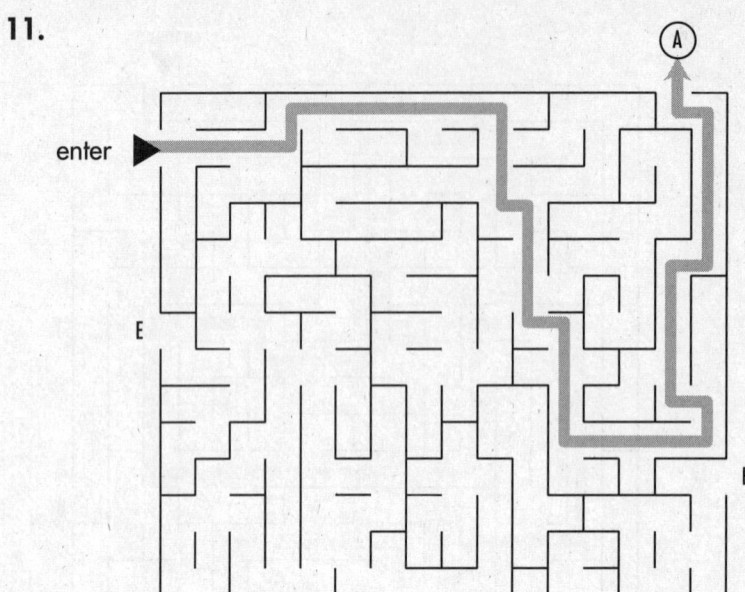

CHAPTER 4 • *LearningExpress Mechanical & Spatial Aptitude*

SPATIAL CONCEPTS

12. c. SAME

13. a. GOCI

14. b. RJPS

15. e. KITE

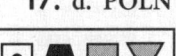

16. d. BFHD

17. d. POLN

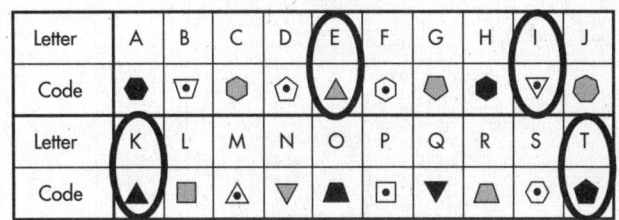

18. c. BFAQ

19. e. DONE

20. c. 13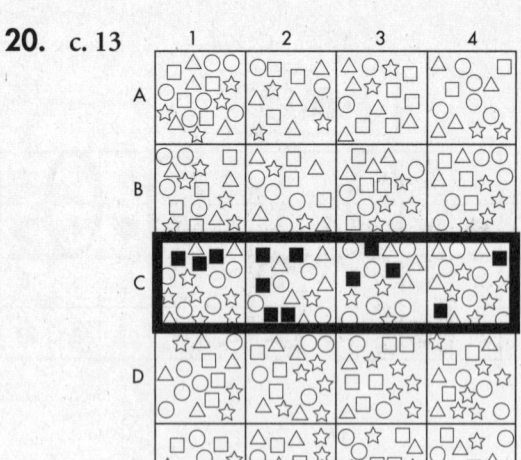

23. a. 16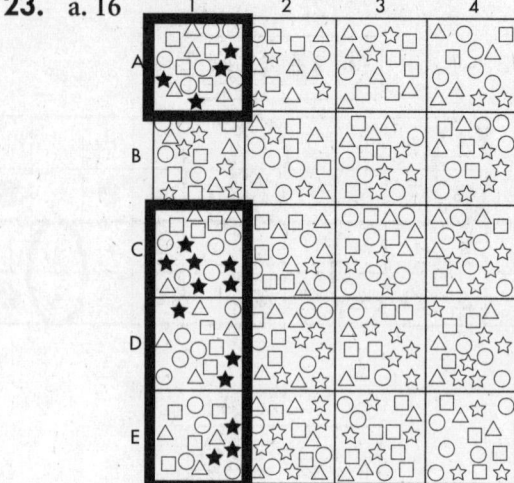

21. d. 14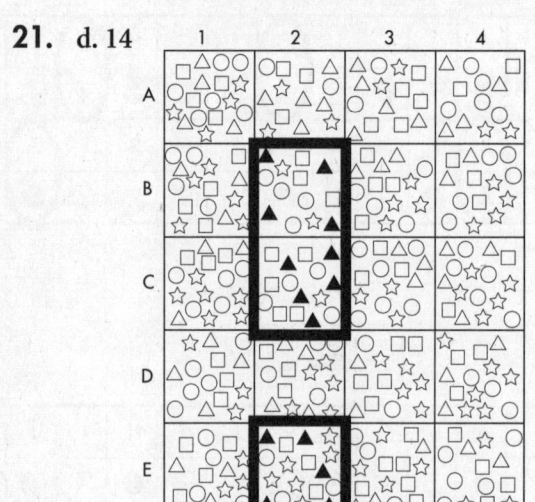

24. e. 41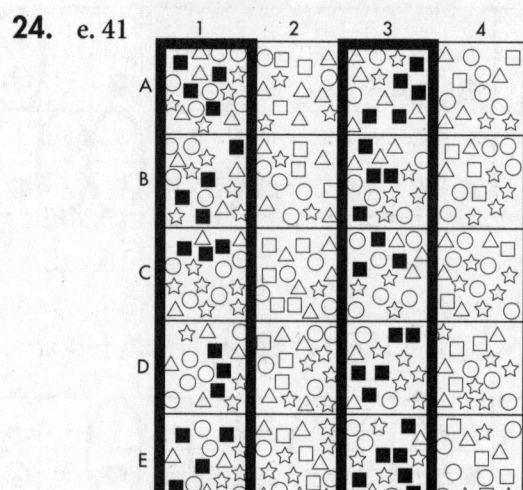

22. b. 50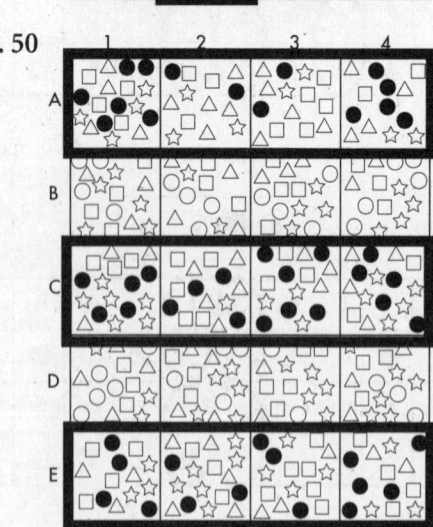

25. a. 33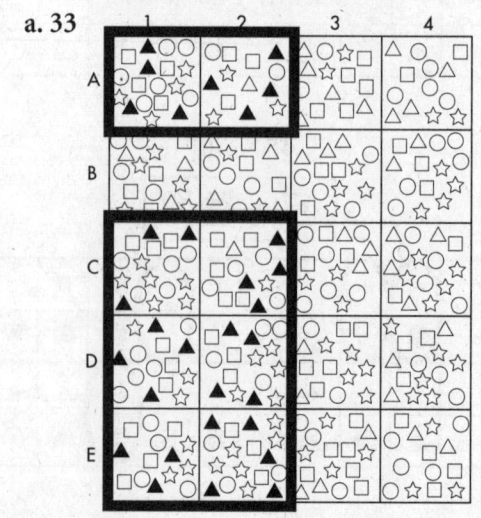

SPATIAL CONCEPTS

26. c. 35

20 circles + 15 stars

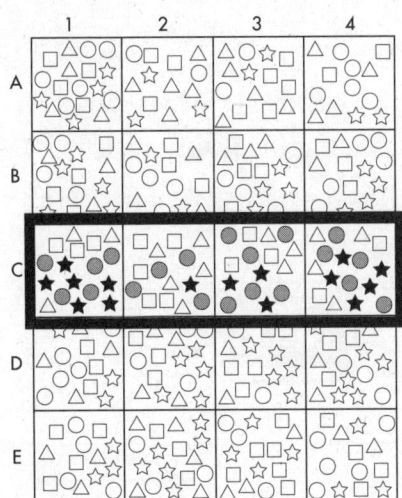

27. d. 31

Count all shapes in this region.

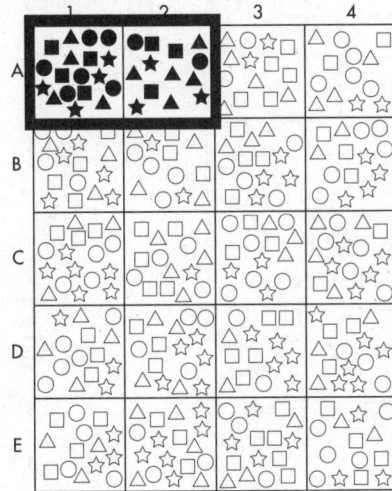

28. e. 73

32 squares + 41 stars

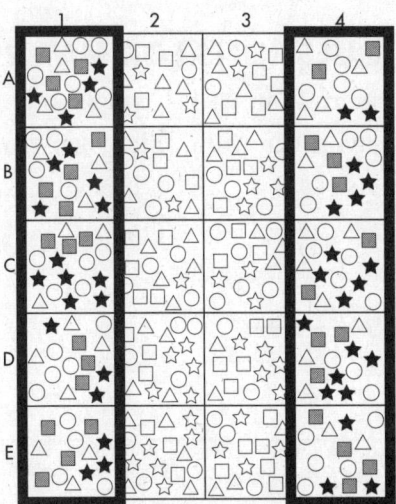

29. c. This package belongs in Box 3, the Recycle Box, because *one* piece is defective.

30. d. This package belongs in Box 4, the Color Box, because mismatched color takes priority over mismatched fit. The sorting code states: *When examining mismatched pairs that will not fit together and have different colors, place the package in the Color Box.*

31. a. This package passes inspection because the two pieces fit together properly, are the same color, and are free from defects.

32. b. This package contains *two* defective pieces and belongs in the Fail Box, which is Box 2. The Sorting Code states: *Regardless of fit or color, if both pieces inside a package are defective, put them in the Fail Box.*

READING MAPS

Some people seem to have a good "sense of direction" when it comes to finding an efficient way to their destination. Map Reading questions test your ability to imagine a 3D situation on a 2D piece of paper. Just put yourself into the map and follow the directions. It may help to physically rotate your test booklet as you imagine placing yourself inside the map. Once you have placed yourself at the right spot and are facing the correct direction, you can follow

SPATIAL CONCEPTS

instructions that tell you to "go right" or "go left." Questions dealing with absolute directions (north, south, east, and west) are easier because you can simply refer to the compass on the page.

SAMPLE QUESTIONS FOR MAP READING

Answer Questions 1 through 3 based solely on the following map. You are required to follow traffic laws and the flow of traffic. A single arrow depicts one-way streets and two arrows pointing in opposite directions represent two-way streets.

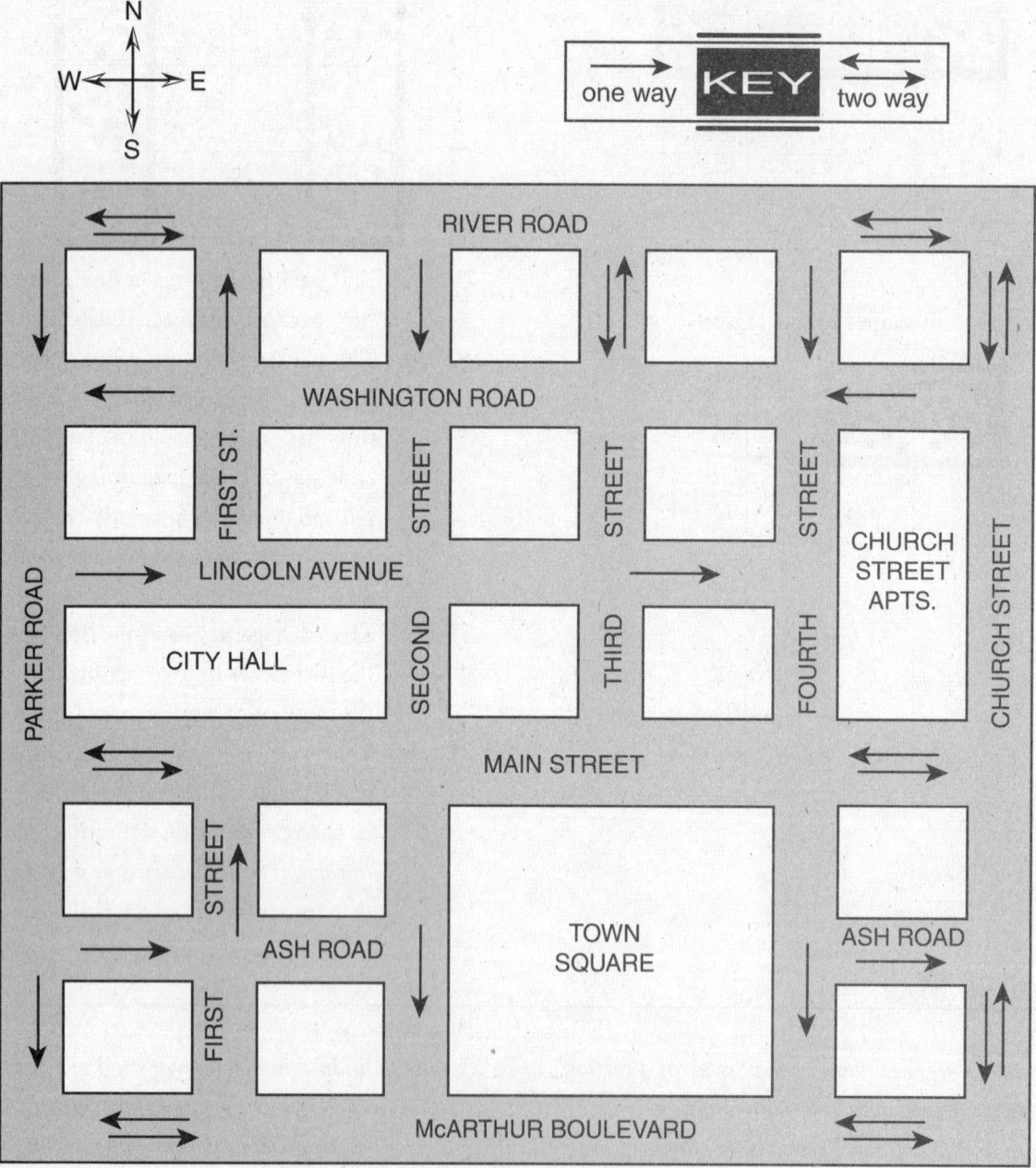

SPATIAL CONCEPTS

1. Officer Harolds is sitting at a red light at the intersection of Fourth Street and Washington Road facing southbound. The dispatcher sends him on a one-vehicle collision call. A motorist has run into the northwest corner of the City Hall building. What is the quickest route for Officer Harolds to take to get to City Hall?
    a. Turn west onto Washington Road, then south on Third Street, and then west on Main Street to Parker Road.
    b. Turn west onto Washington Road, then south onto Parker Road, and then east to Lincoln Avenue.
    c. Turn west onto Washington Road, south on Second Street, and then east onto Main Street to Parker Road.
    d. Turn west onto Washington Road, then south onto Parker Road, and then east onto Main Street.

Strategies for Map Reading

The situation tells you that Officer Harolds needs to answer a collision call. The dispatcher tells you the specific location, the northwest corner of City Hall. As you can see by the map, the City Hall building can be approached on four sides by four different streets. Since you'd like to be close to the northwest corner of the building, you should be considering a route that will put you on that side of City Hall.

Your first step will be to study the map and pick out the quickest legal route to the collision. The arrows show you that Washington Road is a one-way street. Since Officer Harolds is facing south on Fourth Street at Washington Road, his only option available is to turn west onto Washington Road. Notice that Washington Road runs parallel to Lincoln Avenue, the street where City Hall is located. Also notice that Lincoln Avenue runs to the east and you want to end up on the northwest corner of the building. Now look at City Hall. The northwest corner of this building is at the intersection of Parker Road and Lincoln Avenue. (To determine the northwest corner of the building, it may be a helpful trick to imagine that the north-south-east-west indicator is written in the middle of the word "City Hall." That makes it easy to see where the northwest corner would be for the building.) The quickest, easiest route appears to be west on Washington Road, south on Parker Road and east on Lincoln Avenue. You have your route, so now it's time to see if one of the multiple-choice options matches the route you determined.

When you first glance at the four options, it's fairly obvious that they all start with a west turn onto Washington Road. Starting with option **a**, we see that this option lists turning south onto Third Street and then west on Main Street. Main Street is one block south of the street you'd like to be on, so this option is not the most efficient route. Eliminate this option and go on to option **b**.

In option **b**, you see that the first turn after heading west on Washington Road is to turn south onto Parker Road, then east to Lincoln Avenue, which will put the officer at the scene of the collision. This option matches the route you figured out before reading the answers, so **b** is more than likely the right choice.

However, it's always best to continue reading the answers to make sure you don't pass up an option that turns out to be better than the one you originally figured. Option **c** has Officer Harolds turning east on Main Street, which is heading away from the call and does not end up at Parker Road. Option **d** is not the best answer because the corner of Parker Road and Main Street is one block too far to the south. The only reason you'd choose either of these options would be not knowing which was the northwest corner of City Hall.

LearningExpress Mechanical & Spatial Aptitude • CHAPTER 4

Remember, even when you feel like you already have the right answer, it is best to examine all the answer choices to be on the safe side.

Finding the Direction

Question 2 is based on the same map as Question 1, but it is different. The test maker wants to know if you can figure out which direction you are facing.

2. Officer Watson is driving eastbound on Main Street at Fourth Street. If he makes a U-turn on Main Street, turns onto Third Street and then makes another U-turn, what direction will he be facing?
   a. east
   b. west
   c. north
   d. south

Strategies for Direction Questions

The best strategy for solving this type of question is the same as Question 1. Trace your path after reading the question, then look through the answers until you find the one that matches your decision. Obviously, you don't have much reading to do to pick out the right answer. You'll mainly be looking to see which letter is in front of the answer you want.

In Question 2, the answer you want is **d**. When you traced your path on the map, you should have seen that if Officer Watson is heading east on Main Street and he makes a U-turn, he will be heading west. If he turns onto Third Street, the only way he can turn will be north on Third Street. If he makes a second U-turn, he will now be facing south.

MORE MAP-READING PRACTICE

The key to answering map-reading questions is to take your time. If you hurry through a question, you may misread the question or the answer choices, which will naturally cause you to choose the wrong answer.

Let's try a third question using the same sample map.

3. On a rainy, windy night Officers Epps and Burton are dispatched to a burglar alarm at a business on Ash Road and Church Street. They are driving north on First Street and have just passed Washington Road. What is the quickest route they can take?
   a. north on First Street, west on River Road, then south on Parker Road, then east on McArthur Boulevard, then north on Church Street to Ash Road
   b. north on First Street, then east on River Road, then south on Third Street, then east on Main Street, then north on Church Street to Ash Road
   c. north on First Street, then east on River Road, then south on Church Street to Ash Road
   d. north on First Street, then west on River Road, then south on Parker Road, then east on Lincoln Avenue, then south on Second Street, then east on McArthur Boulevard, then north on Church Street to Ash Road

After reading the question you are ready to trace your route. Keep in mind that you want to get to Ash Road and Church Street in the quickest, easiest manner without going the wrong way on any one-way streets. First Street is a one-way street going toward a two-way street, River Road. You have the option of heading east or west on River Road. East makes more sense because it is in the direction of Church Street. The most direct route appears to be east on River Road to

SPATIAL CONCEPTS

Church Street, then south on Church Street to Ash Road.

Now it's time to check your answer against the options. Option **a** has you turning west on First Street, and you've already determined that west is not the most efficient direction to turn. Option **b** suggests that you turn east on River Road, then south on Third Street, then east on Main Street, and then north on Church Street. You should turn South on Church Street to get to Ash Road, not north. You already have too many turns for this to be an efficient route. Time to look at option **c**. Option **c** directs you east on River Road, then south on Church Street—and there you are at Ash Road. This route matches the route we had in mind. Option **d** has too many turns (like option **b**). In addition, it involves a west turn onto River Road, which we already decided was inefficient.

30 PRACTICE QUESTIONS

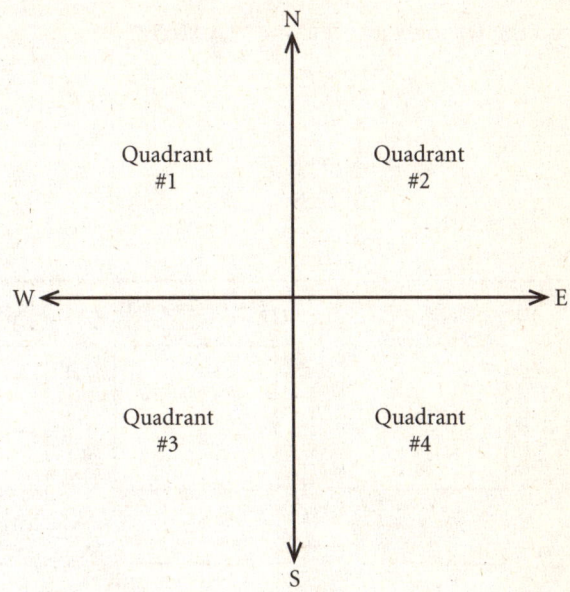

1. A messenger who delivers packages is standing at the intersection of the two lines shown above. If she travels north for two blocks, then west for three blocks, then south for four blocks, and then east for five blocks, in which quadrant will she be?
   a. Quadrant #1
   b. Quadrant #2
   c. Quadrant #3
   d. Quadrant #4

SPATIAL CONCEPTS

Answer questions 2–4 solely on the basis of the map below. The arrows indicate traffic flow; one arrow indicates a one-way street going in the direction of the arrow; two arrows represent a two-way street. You are not allowed to go the wrong way on a one-way street.

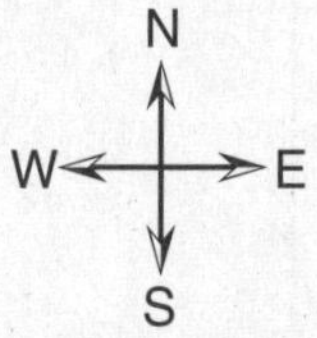

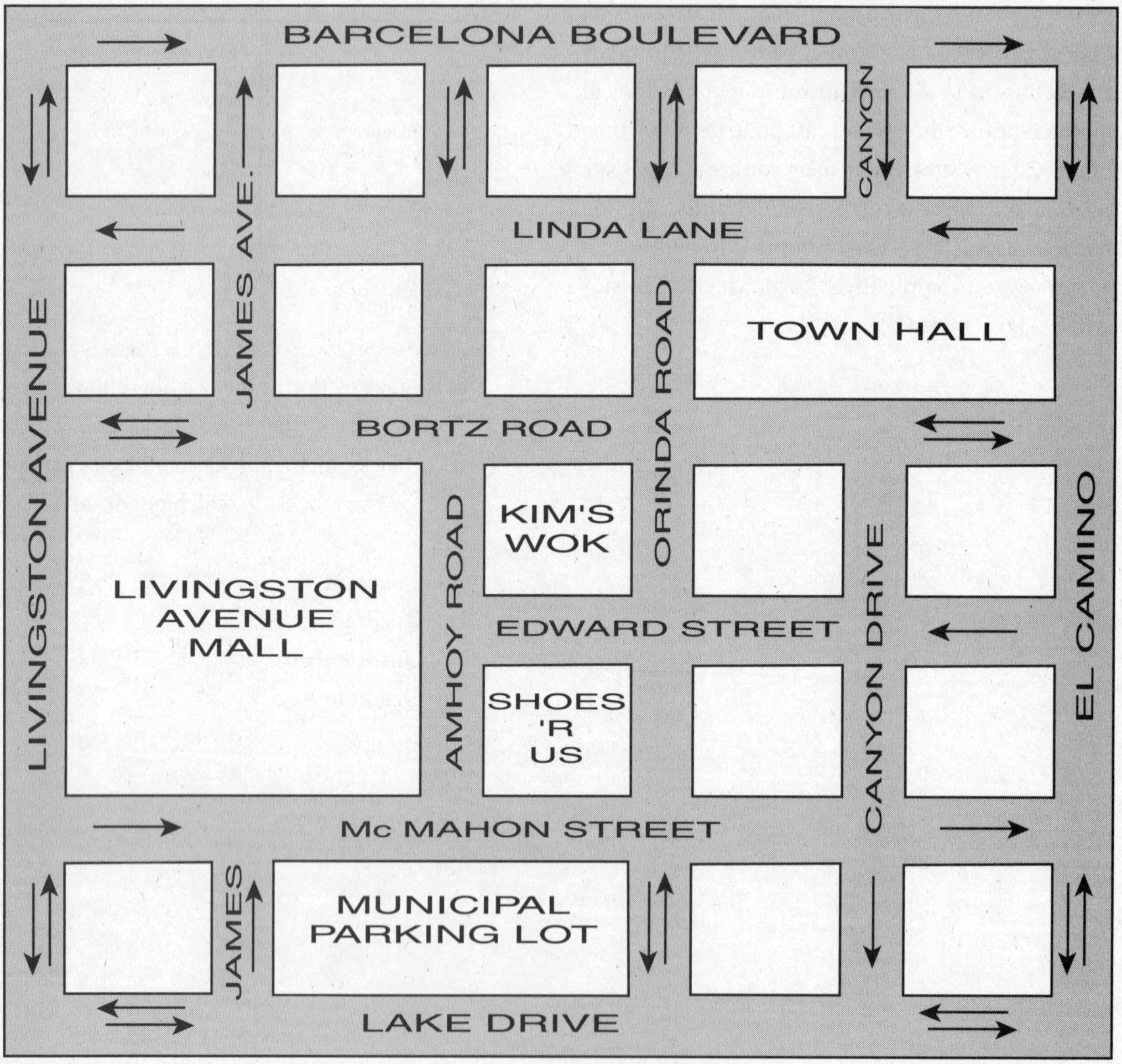

SPATIAL CONCEPTS

2. Sanitation Workers Kazinski and Benning are completing a routine pick-up at the Livingston Avenue Mall at the southeast corner of the building. Dispatch notifies them of a special pick-up at a residence located at the northwest corner of Canyon Drive and Linda Lane. What is the quickest route for Kazinski and Benning to take?
   a. turn north on Amhoy Road, then east on Linda Lane, and then north on Canyon Drive
   b. turn east on McMahon Street, then north on El Camino, then west on Linda Lane, then north on Orinda Road, and then east on Barcelona Boulevard to Canyon Drive
   c. turn north on Amhoy Road, then east on Barcelona Boulevard, and then south on Canyon Drive
   d. turn north on Amhoy Road, then east on Bortz Road, then north on Orinda Road, and then east on Barcelona Boulevard

3. Sanitation Workers Martini and Schmid are southbound on Canyon Drive and have just crossed Edward Street. They receive a call that a city collection truck has broken down, leaving one pick-up to be made near a bus stop located at Livingston Avenue and Bortz Road. They are asked to make the unscheduled pick-up. What is the quickest route for Sanitation Workers Martini and Schmid to take to the bus stop?
   a. continue south on Canyon Drive, then west on McMahon Street, then north on Orinda Road, then west on Edward Street, then north on Amhoy Road, and then west on Bortz Road to Livingston Avenue
   b. continue south on Canyon Drive, then west on Lake Drive, and then north on Livingston Avenue to Bortz Road
   c. make a U-turn on Canyon Drive, and then go west on Bortz Road to Livingston Avenue
   d. continue south on Canyon Drive, then east on Lake Drive, then north on El Camino, and then west on Bortz Road to Livingston Avenue

4. Sanitation Shift Supervisor Richfield is driving west on Bortz Road. She makes a right onto James Avenue, then a left onto Linda Lane, then a right onto Livingston Avenue, and then a right onto Barcelona Boulevard. What direction is she facing?
   a. east
   b. south
   c. west
   d. north

LearningExpress Mechanical & Spatial Aptitude • CHAPTER 4

SPATIAL CONCEPTS

Answer questions 5–7 solely on the basis of the map below. The arrows indicate traffic flow; one arrow indicates a one-way street going in the direction of the arrow; two arrows represent a two-way street. You are not allowed to go the wrong way on a one-way street.

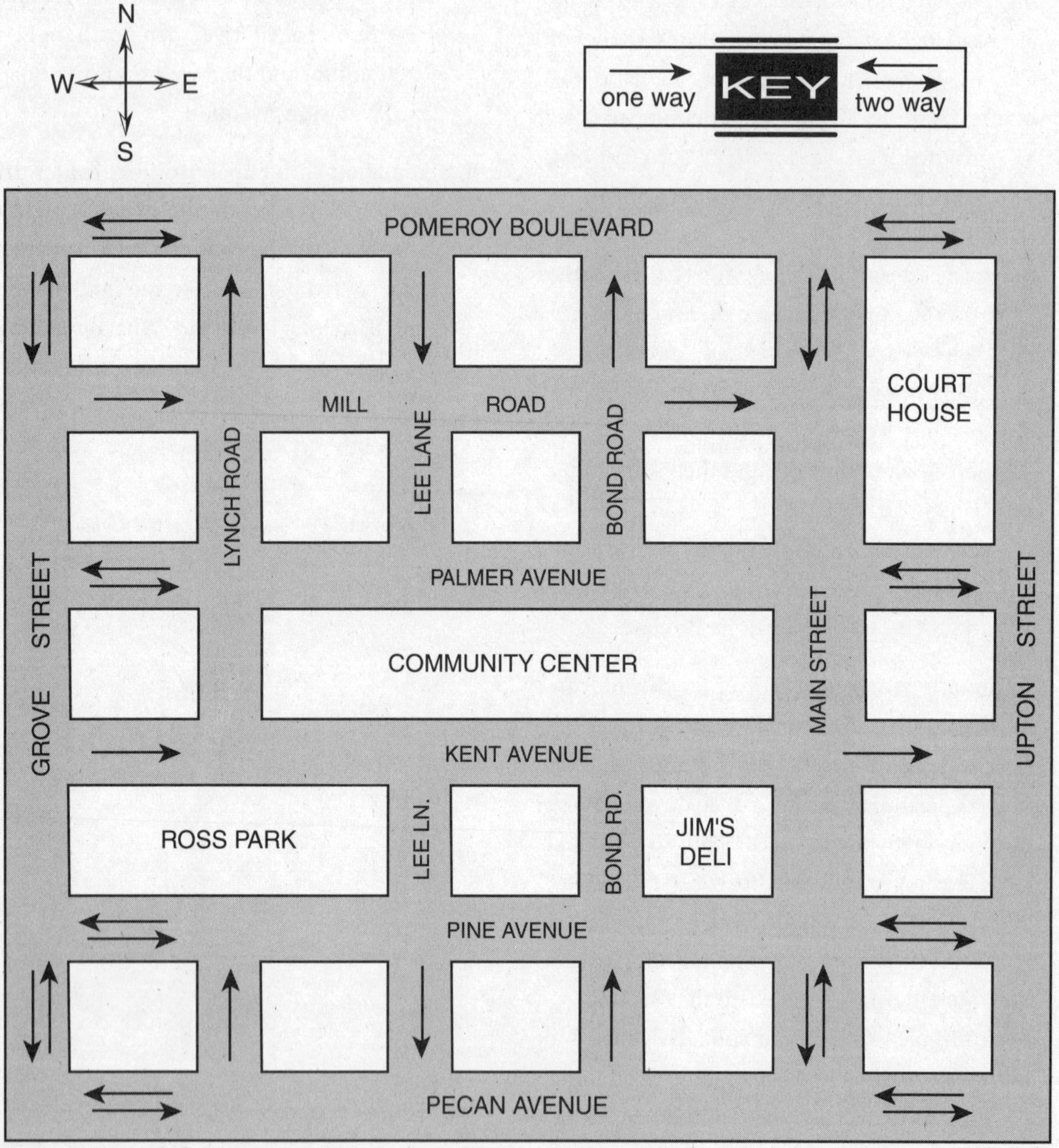

5. Sanitation Worker Tennyson is eastbound on Kent Avenue at Lee Lane. He receives a call about assistance needed for a pick-up at a residence located at the northeast corner of Lynch Road and Mill Road. What is the quickest route for Sanitation Worker Tennyson to take?
    a. continue east on Kent Avenue, then north on Main Street to Mill Road, and then west on Mill Road to the northeast corner of Lynch Road and Mill Road
    b. continue east on Kent Avenue, then north on Main Street, then west on Pomeroy Boulevard, and then south on Lynch Road
    c. continue east on Kent Avenue, then south on Main Street, then west on Pine Avenue, then north on Grove Street, and then east on Mill Road to Lynch Road
    d. continue east on Kent Avenue, then north on Main Street, then west on Palmer Avenue, and then north on Lynch Road to Mill Road

6. There has been heavy flooding in the city. As a result and on an emergency basis, some collection routes are being canceled or reassigned. Sanitation Workers McKay and Callihan are driving by the court house, northbound on Upton Street. They receive a call that their regular route is being canceled, and instead they are to begin pick-up at Ross Park on the Grove Street side of the park. What is the most direct legal route for Sanitation Workers McKay and Callihan to take?
    a. continue north on Upton Street, then drive west on Pomeroy Boulevard, then south on Main Street, and then west on Kent Avenue to Grove Street
    b. continue north on Upton Street, and then drive west on Pomeroy Boulevard, and then south on Grove Street to Ross Park
    c. continue north on Upton Street, then drive west on Pomeroy Boulevard, then south on Main Street, then west on Pecan Avenue, and then north on Grove Street to Ross Park
    d. make a U-turn on Upton Street, then go west on Palmer Avenue, and then south on Grove Street to Ross Park

7. Sanitation Worker Kenney has just finished lunch at Jim's Deli and is heading west on Pine Avenue to continue her route. She turns left on Lee Lane and then left again onto Pecan Avenue. She turns left on Main Street and finally turns right on Palmer Avenue. What direction is she facing?
    a. west
    b. south
    c. north
    d. east

SPATIAL CONCEPTS

Answer questions 8 and 9 based on the map below.

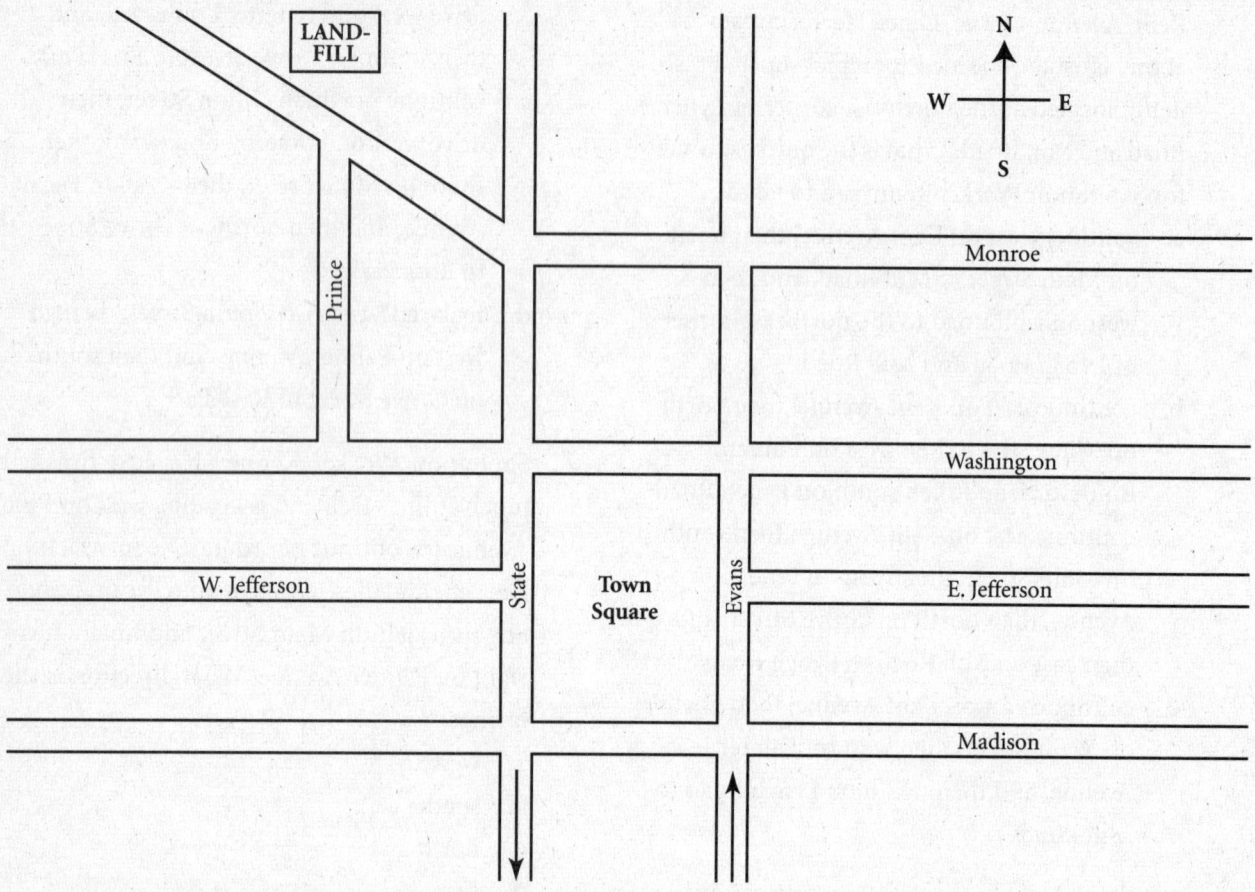

As indicated, State Street is one-way going south, and Evans Street is one-way going north. All other streets have two-way traffic.

8. A special collection truck is headed east on West Jefferson to make a pickup at the corner of Evans and East Jefferson. In order to travel the shortest distance without breaking traffic laws, the truck should turn
   a. right onto State, right onto Washington, right onto Evans.
   b. left onto State, left onto Madison, left onto Evans.
   c. right onto State, left onto Madison, left onto Evans.
   d. left onto State, left onto Evans, right onto East Jefferson.

9. A collection truck is headed in the direction of the landfill, which is located just off Monroe Street. The truck is already on Monroe, stopped at a red light at the intersection of Monroe and State. To reach the landfill, in which direction will the truck travel?
   a. northeast
   b. northwest
   c. southeast
   d. southwest

Answer question 10 based on the map below.

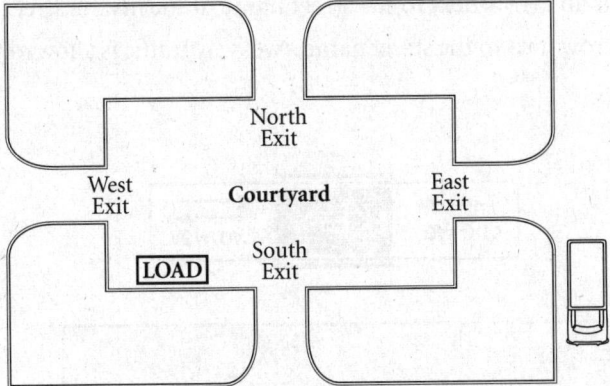

10. Which exit should a worker use to carry the load the shortest distance to the back of the truck?
    a. north
    b. south
    c. west
    d. east

SPATIAL CONCEPTS

The following map shows a section of the city where some public buildings are located. Each of the squares represents one city block. Street names are as shown. If there is an arrow next to the street name, it means the street is one way only in the direction of the arrow. If there is no arrow next to the street name, two-way traffic is allowed.

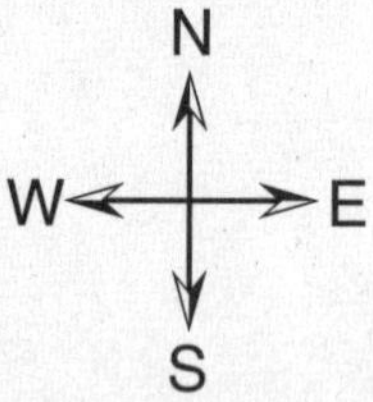

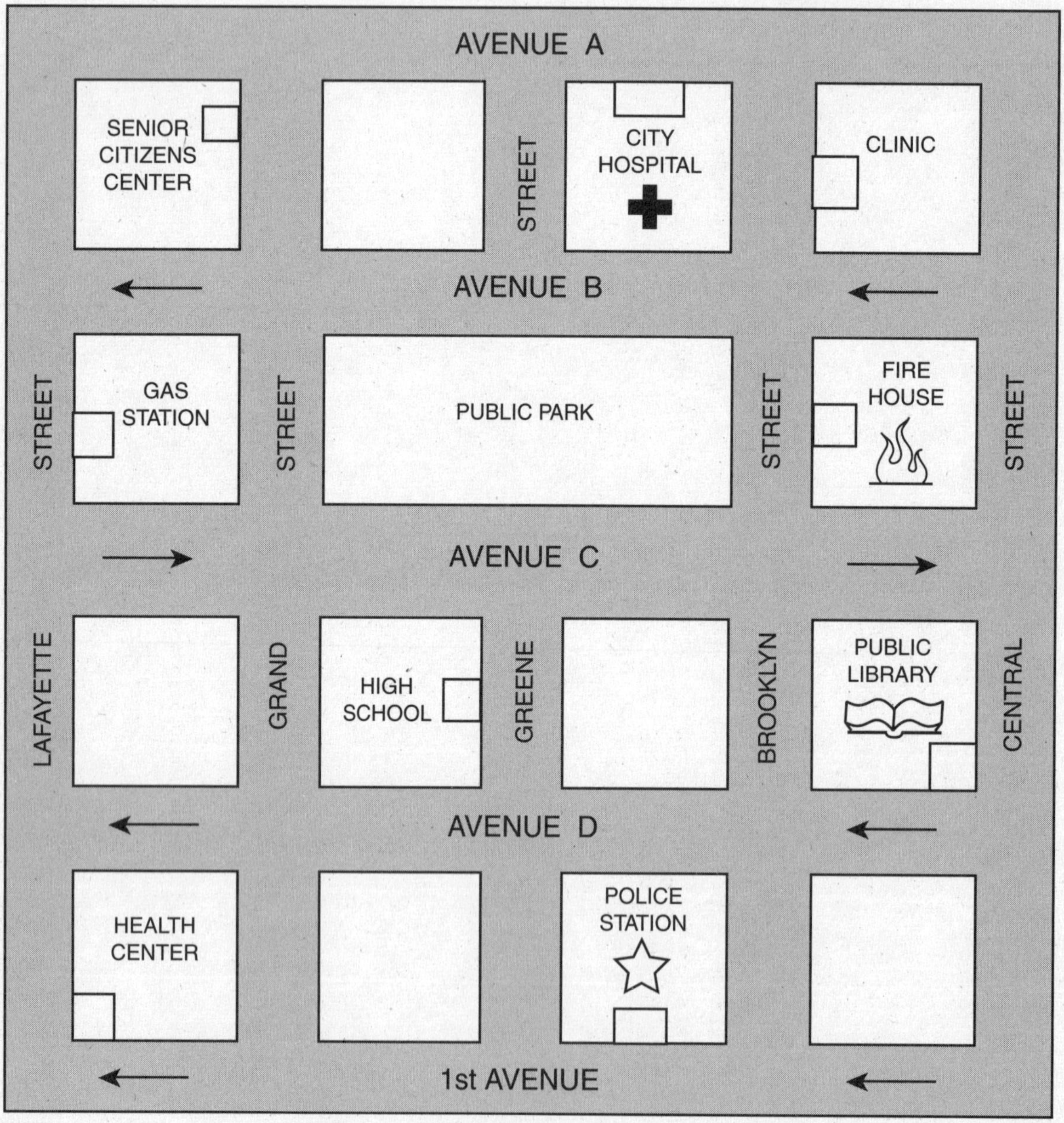

CHAPTER 4 • *LearningExpress Mechanical & Spatial Aptitude*

SPATIAL CONCEPTS

11. While you are on foot patrol, an elderly man stops you in front of the fire house and asks you to help him find the Senior Citizens Center. You should tell him to
    a. walk across the street to the Senior Citizens Center.
    b. walk south to Avenue C, make a right and walk west on Avenue C, make a right on Grand Street and walk up to the Senior Citizens Center.
    c. walk north to Avenue B and then west on Avenue B to the end of the park, make a right and go one block.
    d. walk north to Avenue B, then west on Avenue B to Lafayette Street, make a right and go one block.

12. The head librarian needs gasoline for his automobile. He is leaving the Avenue D garage exit from the library. His quickest legal route is to proceed
    a. north on Central Street to Avenue C and west on Avenue C to the gas station.
    b. west on Brooklyn Street to Avenue B and north on Avenue B to the gas station.
    c. west on Avenue D to Grand Street and north on Grand Street to the gas station.
    d. west on Avenue D to Lafayette Street and north on Lafayette Street to the gas station.

13. You are dispatched from the police station to an altercation taking place at the northwest corner of the public park. Which is the most direct legal route?
    a. east to Central Street, north on Central Street to Avenue B, and west on Avenue B to Grand Street
    b. west to Grand Street and north on Grand Street to Avenue B
    c. east to Brooklyn Street, north on Brooklyn Street to Avenue B, and west on Avenue B to Grand Street
    d. west to Greene Street, north on Greene Street to Avenue C, and east on Avenue C to Brooklyn Street

14. Your spouse is a nurse at the city hospital and goes to the public library every Monday as a volunteer. What would be the shortest legal route from the hospital to the library?
    a. west on Avenue A, south on Lafayette Street, east on Avenue C, and south on Central Street to the library entrance
    b. east on Avenue B and south on Central Street to the library entrance
    c. west on Avenue A, south on Lafayette Street, and east on Avenue D to the library entrance
    d. east on Avenue A and south on Central Street to the library entrance

15. After responding to a call at the fire house, you are ready to drive back to the police station for the end of your shift. What is the quickest legal route?
    a. south on Brooklyn Street and west on 1st Avenue to the police station
    b. north on Brooklyn Street, west on Avenue A, south on Lafayette Street, and east on 1st Avenue to the police station
    c. north on Brooklyn Street and east on 1st Avenue to the police station
    d. south on Brooklyn Street, west on Avenue C, south on Grand Street, and east on 1st Avenue to the police station

Answer questions 16–18 solely on the basis of the following map. The arrows indicate traffic flow; one arrow indicates a one-way street going in the direction of the arrow; two arrows represent a two-way street. You are not allowed to go the wrong way on a one-way street.

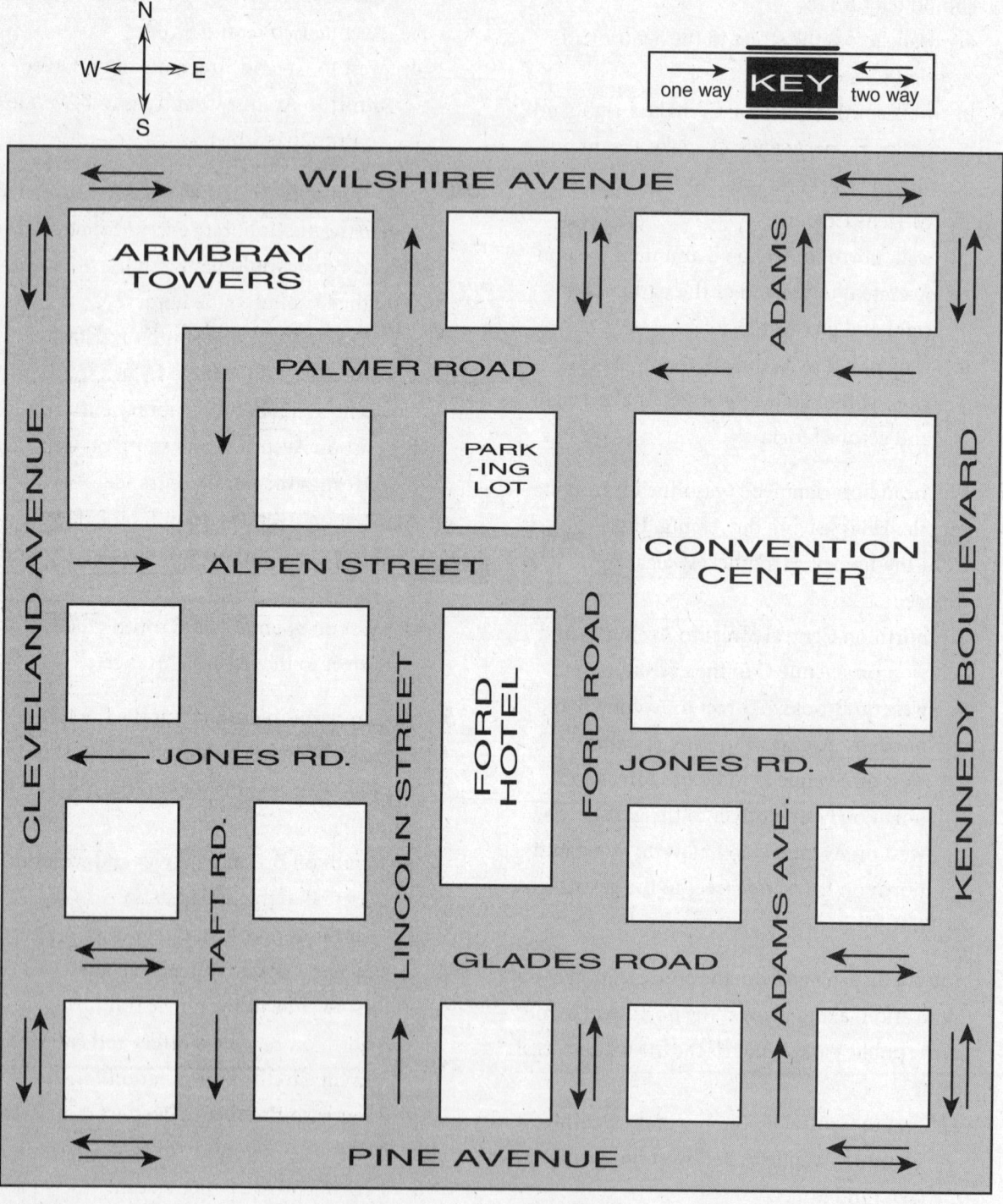

SPATIAL CONCEPTS

16. Officers Muldoon and Chavez are eating at Al's Cafe, which faces Jones Road. They get a call of a suspicious person at the Cleveland Avenue entrance to the Armbray Towers. What is their most direct route to the Armbray Towers?
   a. Go east on Jones Road, then south on Kennedy Boulevard, then west on Glade Road, then north on Cleveland Avenue to the Armbray Towers.
   b. Go west on Jones Road to Cleveland Avenue, then north on Cleveland to the Armbray Towers.
   c. Go west on Jones Road, then south on Ford Road, then west on Glade Road, then north on Cleveland Avenue to the Armbray Towers.
   d. Go west on Jones Road, then north on Glade Road, then west on Palmer Road, then south on Taft Road, then west on Jones Road, then north on Cleveland Avenue to the Armbray Towers.

17. Officers Chang and Parker are northbound on Lincoln Street and have just crossed Alpen Street. They receive a call about a two-car injury collision on Adams Avenue at Pine Avenue. What is their most direct route to the accident scene?
   a. Continue north on Lincoln Street, then east on Wilshire Avenue, then south on Ford Road, then east on Glade Road, then south on Adams Avenue to the accident scene.
   b. Continue north on Lincoln Street, then west on Palmer Road, then south on Taft Road, then east on Pine Avenue to the accident scene.
   c. Make a U-turn on Lincoln Street, and then go south on Lincoln Street, then east on Pine Avenue to the accident scene.
   d. Continue north on Lincoln Street, then east on Wilshire Avenue, then south on Kennedy Boulevard, then west on Pine Avenue to the accident scene.

18. Officer Tananga is southbound on Kennedy Boulevard. He makes a right turn onto Glade Road, then a left onto Taft Road, a right onto Pine Avenue, another right onto Cleveland Avenue, and then a right onto Wilshire Avenue. Which direction is he facing?
   a. west
   b. south
   c. east
   d. north

SPATIAL CONCEPTS

Answer questions 19 and 20 solely on the basis of the following map. The arrows indicate traffic flow; one arrow indicates a one-way street going in the direction of the arrow; two arrows represent a two-way street. You are not allowed to go the wrong way on a one-way street.

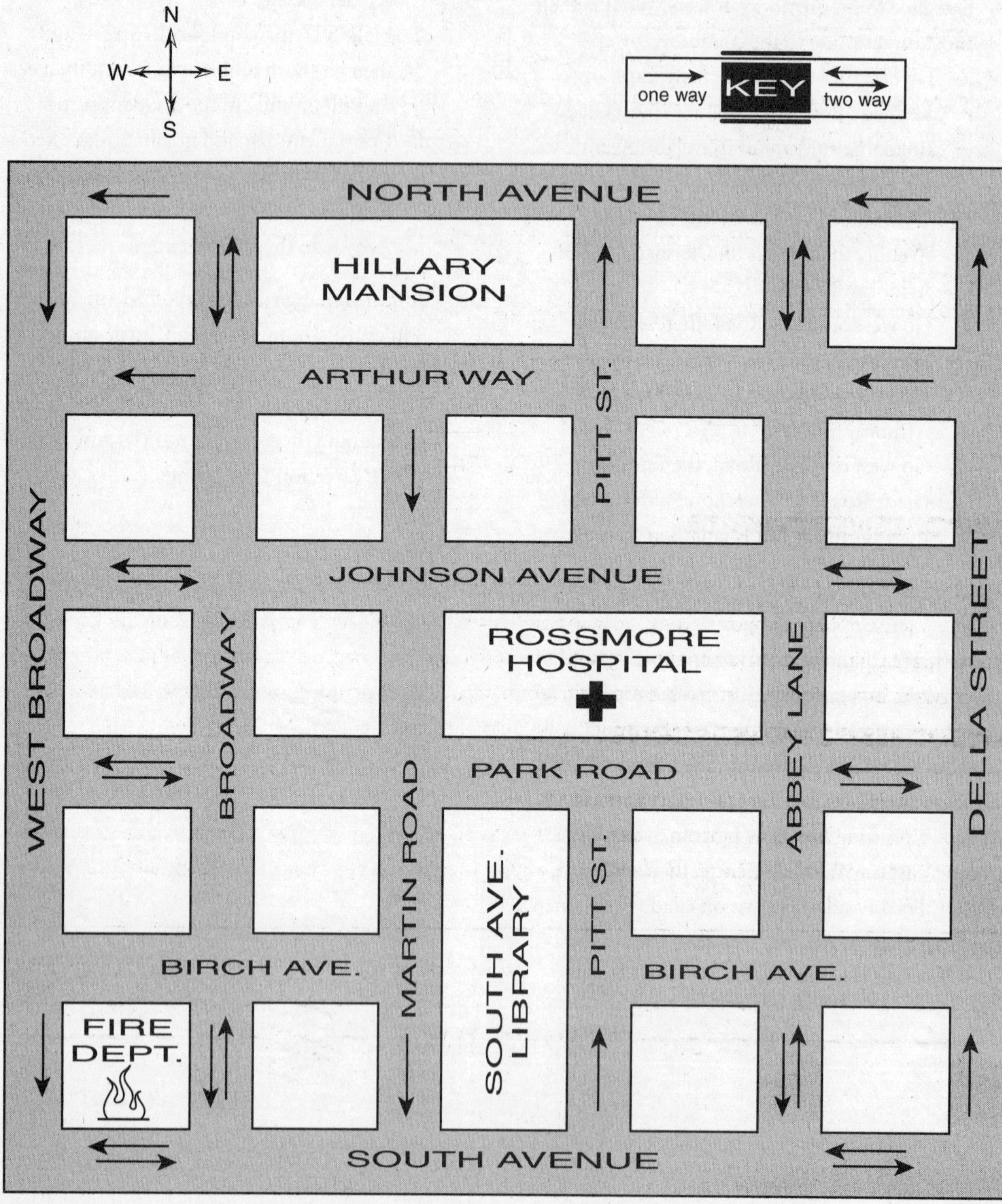

SPATIAL CONCEPTS

19. Officer Lazere is spending his lunch break at the South Avenue Library, which faces South Avenue. He gets a call to the Hillary Mansion, the entrance to which faces North Avenue. What is Officer Lazere's most direct route to the Hillary Mansion?
    a. Go east on South Avenue, then north on Abbey Lane to North Avenue, then west on North Avenue to the Hillary Mansion.
    b. Go east on South Avenue, then north on Pitt Street, then west on North Avenue to the Hillary Mansion.
    c. Go west on South Avenue, then north on West Broadway, then east on North Avenue to the Hillary Mansion.
    d. Go west on South Avenue, then north on Broadway to North Avenue, then east on North Avenue to the Hillary Mansion.

20. Officer Lew is southbound on Martin Road and has just crossed Park Road. Dispatch sends him to a residence at the corner of Arthur Way and Della Street. What is Officer Lew's most direct route to the residence?
    a. Make a U-turn on Martin Road and go north on Martin Road to Arthur Way, then east on Johnson Avenue to Della Street, then north on Della Street to the residence.
    b. Continue south on Martin Road, then east on South Avenue, then north on Pitt Street, then east on Park Road, then north on Abbey Lane, and then east on Arthur Way.
    c. Continue south on Martin Road, then east on South Avenue, then north on Della Street to the residence.
    d. Continue south on Martin Road, then north on Abbey Lane, then east on Arthur Way to the residence.

READING MAPS ANSWER EXPLANATIONS

1. **d.** The messenger travels two blocks farther to the south than she does to the north and two blocks farther to the east than she does to the west. Therefore, she finishes southeast of where she began, in Quadrant #4.

2. **c.** This is the simplest way around the one-way streets and Town Hall. Because Linda Lane is one-way the wrong way, some backtracking is inevitable. However, the residence is only one block from Barcelona Boulevard, and so turning east on Barcelona requires the least amount of backtracking. Choice **a** directs the sanitation workers to turn the wrong way down a one-way street. Choice **b** requires too much backtracking. Choice **d** leaves the workers on Barcelona Boulevard, not on Linda Lane.

3. **b.** This route is the most direct because it requires the fewest turns. Choice **a** leads the sanitation workers the wrong way on McMahon Street. Choice **c** is not correct because Canyon Drive is a one-way street south. Choice **d** takes the workers too far east.

4. **a.** If Shift Supervisor Richfield turns right onto James Avenue, she will be facing north. A left turn onto Linda Lane turns her west again, and a right turn onto Livingston Avenue turns her north. The final

LearningExpress Mechanical & Spatial Aptitude • CHAPTER 4

right turn onto Barcelona Boulevard turns her east.

5. d. This is the most direct route because it does not require any backtracking. Choice a is not correct because it would require Sanitation Worker Tennyson to go the wrong way on Mill Road. Choice b requires some backtracking and takes the worker the wrong way on Lynch Road. Choice c is not as direct because it requires the worker to move in the opposite direction from the call.

6. b. This is the fastest route, requiring the fewest turns. Choice a is not correct because Kent is a one-way street going east. Choice c requires too many turns and is not the most direct route. Choice d is not correct because Upton Street is one-way going north.

7. d. A left turn onto Lee Lane turns Sanitation Worker Kenney south. Another left turn onto Pecan Avenue turns her east. A left turn onto Main Street turns her north, and the final right turn onto Palmer turns her back east.

8. c. In choice a, a right onto State does not lead to Washington. Choices b and d would mean traveling the wrong way on a one-way street.

9. b. Using the directional guide for the map, it is easy to see that northwest is the only possible answer.

10. d. Carrying the load from west to east across the courtyard is the shortest distance to the back of the truck.

11. c. Choice a takes the man to the park, not to the Senior Citizens Center. Choice b takes the man too far south. Choice d takes him to Lafayette Street, while the entrance to the Senior Citizens Center is on Grand.

12. d. Choice a takes the librarian the wrong way on Avenue C. Choice b shows the wrong directions for the streets—Brooklyn Street runs north-south, and Avenue B runs east-west. Choice c leaves the librarian one block east of the gas station.

13. b. Choices a and c take you the wrong way on 1st Avenue. Choice d will get you to the southeast, not the northwest, corner of the park.

14. d. Choice a is less direct. Choice b does not start from the hospital and at any rate involves going the wrong way on Avenue B. Choice c is indirect and involves going the wrong way on Avenue D.

15. a. Choice b is less direct and involves going the wrong way on 1st Avenue. Choice c will lead away from 1st Avenue, not toward it. Choice d takes you the wrong way on Avenue C and 1st Avenue.

16. b. This is correct because it is the quickest and most direct route. Answer a has too many turns to be the most direct. Answer c is a one-way street going north and wouldn't be the right choice. Answer d takes the officers several blocks out of their way and is not the most direct.

17. b. This choice is correct because it is the quickest and most direct route. Choice a has too many turns and takes the officers the wrong way on Adams Avenue. Lincoln Street is a one-way street going north, so choice c is wrong. Choice d takes the officers several blocks out of their way and so is not the most direct.

SPATIAL CONCEPTS

18. c. A right turn onto Glade Road turns Officer Tananga west. The left onto Taft Road turns him south; the right onto Pine Avenue turns him west, the right onto Cleveland Avenue turns him back north, and the right onto Wilshire Avenue turns him east.

19. a. This is the most direct route to the Hillary Mansion, requiring the fewest changes in direction. Answer **b** requires the officer to drive through the Rossmore Hospital. Route **c** takes the officer the wrong way up West Broadway. Answer **d** takes the officer the wrong way on North Avenue.

20. c. This route requires the fewest number of turns. Answer **a** is wrong because Martin Road is a one-way street. Answer **b** requires a number of turns and goes the wrong way on Arthur Way. Answer **d** would mean traveling the wrong way on a one-way street.

C·H·A·P·T·E·R 5
INTERPRETING SYMBOLS

CHAPTER SUMMARY
There are several types of tests involving symbols and series. By design, symbol questions look intimidating, so we'll show you what to look for in order to crack the code on all sorts of questions. This chapter also addresses the sorting and classifying of figures and series tests involving reasoning.

LEARNINGEXPRESS MECHANICAL/SPATIAL EXAM ANSWER SHEET

SYMBOL SERIES

1. ⓐ ⓑ ⓒ ⓓ ⓔ	11. ⓐ ⓑ ⓒ ⓓ ⓔ	21. ⓐ ⓑ ⓒ ⓓ ⓔ
2. ⓐ ⓑ ⓒ ⓓ ⓔ	12. ⓐ ⓑ ⓒ ⓓ ⓔ	22. ⓐ ⓑ ⓒ ⓓ ⓔ
3. ⓐ ⓑ ⓒ ⓓ ⓔ	13. ⓐ ⓑ ⓒ ⓓ ⓔ	23. ⓐ ⓑ ⓒ ⓓ ⓔ
4. ⓐ ⓑ ⓒ ⓓ ⓔ	14. ⓐ ⓑ ⓒ ⓓ ⓔ	24. ⓐ ⓑ ⓒ ⓓ ⓔ
5. ⓐ ⓑ ⓒ ⓓ ⓔ	15. ⓐ ⓑ ⓒ ⓓ ⓔ	25. ⓐ ⓑ ⓒ ⓓ ⓔ
6. ⓐ ⓑ ⓒ ⓓ ⓔ	16. ⓐ ⓑ ⓒ ⓓ ⓔ	26. ⓐ ⓑ ⓒ ⓓ ⓔ
7. ⓐ ⓑ ⓒ ⓓ ⓔ	17. ⓐ ⓑ ⓒ ⓓ ⓔ	27. ⓐ ⓑ ⓒ ⓓ ⓔ
8. ⓐ ⓑ ⓒ ⓓ ⓔ	18. ⓐ ⓑ ⓒ ⓓ ⓔ	28. ⓐ ⓑ ⓒ ⓓ ⓔ
9. ⓐ ⓑ ⓒ ⓓ ⓔ	19. ⓐ ⓑ ⓒ ⓓ ⓔ	29. ⓐ ⓑ ⓒ ⓓ ⓔ
10. ⓐ ⓑ ⓒ ⓓ ⓔ	20. ⓐ ⓑ ⓒ ⓓ ⓔ	30. ⓐ ⓑ ⓒ ⓓ ⓔ

SYMBOL ANALOGIES

1. ⓐ ⓑ ⓒ ⓓ ⓔ	11. ⓐ ⓑ ⓒ ⓓ ⓔ	21. ⓐ ⓑ ⓒ ⓓ ⓔ
2. ⓐ ⓑ ⓒ ⓓ ⓔ	12. ⓐ ⓑ ⓒ ⓓ ⓔ	22. ⓐ ⓑ ⓒ ⓓ ⓔ
3. ⓐ ⓑ ⓒ ⓓ ⓔ	13. ⓐ ⓑ ⓒ ⓓ ⓔ	23. ⓐ ⓑ ⓒ ⓓ ⓔ
4. ⓐ ⓑ ⓒ ⓓ ⓔ	14. ⓐ ⓑ ⓒ ⓓ ⓔ	24. ⓐ ⓑ ⓒ ⓓ ⓔ
5. ⓐ ⓑ ⓒ ⓓ ⓔ	15. ⓐ ⓑ ⓒ ⓓ ⓔ	25. ⓐ ⓑ ⓒ ⓓ ⓔ
6. ⓐ ⓑ ⓒ ⓓ ⓔ	16. ⓐ ⓑ ⓒ ⓓ ⓔ	26. ⓐ ⓑ ⓒ ⓓ ⓔ
7. ⓐ ⓑ ⓒ ⓓ ⓔ	17. ⓐ ⓑ ⓒ ⓓ ⓔ	27. ⓐ ⓑ ⓒ ⓓ ⓔ
8. ⓐ ⓑ ⓒ ⓓ ⓔ	18. ⓐ ⓑ ⓒ ⓓ ⓔ	28. ⓐ ⓑ ⓒ ⓓ ⓔ
9. ⓐ ⓑ ⓒ ⓓ ⓔ	19. ⓐ ⓑ ⓒ ⓓ ⓔ	29. ⓐ ⓑ ⓒ ⓓ ⓔ
10. ⓐ ⓑ ⓒ ⓓ ⓔ	20. ⓐ ⓑ ⓒ ⓓ ⓔ	30. ⓐ ⓑ ⓒ ⓓ ⓔ

SORTING AND CLASSIFYING FIGURES

1. ⓐ ⓑ ⓒ ⓓ ⓔ	11. ⓐ ⓑ ⓒ ⓓ ⓔ	21. ⓐ ⓑ ⓒ ⓓ ⓔ
2. ⓐ ⓑ ⓒ ⓓ ⓔ	12. ⓐ ⓑ ⓒ ⓓ ⓔ	22. ⓐ ⓑ ⓒ ⓓ ⓔ
3. ⓐ ⓑ ⓒ ⓓ ⓔ	13. ⓐ ⓑ ⓒ ⓓ ⓔ	23. ⓐ ⓑ ⓒ ⓓ ⓔ
4. ⓐ ⓑ ⓒ ⓓ ⓔ	14. ⓐ ⓑ ⓒ ⓓ ⓔ	24. ⓐ ⓑ ⓒ ⓓ ⓔ
5. ⓐ ⓑ ⓒ ⓓ ⓔ	15. ⓐ ⓑ ⓒ ⓓ ⓔ	25. ⓐ ⓑ ⓒ ⓓ ⓔ
6. ⓐ ⓑ ⓒ ⓓ ⓔ	16. ⓐ ⓑ ⓒ ⓓ ⓔ	26. ⓐ ⓑ ⓒ ⓓ ⓔ
7. ⓐ ⓑ ⓒ ⓓ ⓔ	17. ⓐ ⓑ ⓒ ⓓ ⓔ	27. ⓐ ⓑ ⓒ ⓓ ⓔ
8. ⓐ ⓑ ⓒ ⓓ ⓔ	18. ⓐ ⓑ ⓒ ⓓ ⓔ	28. ⓐ ⓑ ⓒ ⓓ ⓔ
9. ⓐ ⓑ ⓒ ⓓ ⓔ	19. ⓐ ⓑ ⓒ ⓓ ⓔ	29. ⓐ ⓑ ⓒ ⓓ ⓔ
10. ⓐ ⓑ ⓒ ⓓ ⓔ	20. ⓐ ⓑ ⓒ ⓓ ⓔ	30. ⓐ ⓑ ⓒ ⓓ ⓔ

SERIES REASONING TEST

1. ⓐ ⓑ ⓒ ⓓ ⓔ	11. ⓐ ⓑ ⓒ ⓓ ⓔ	21. ⓐ ⓑ ⓒ ⓓ ⓔ
2. ⓐ ⓑ ⓒ ⓓ ⓔ	12. ⓐ ⓑ ⓒ ⓓ ⓔ	22. ⓐ ⓑ ⓒ ⓓ ⓔ
3. ⓐ ⓑ ⓒ ⓓ ⓔ	13. ⓐ ⓑ ⓒ ⓓ ⓔ	23. ⓐ ⓑ ⓒ ⓓ ⓔ
4. ⓐ ⓑ ⓒ ⓓ ⓔ	14. ⓐ ⓑ ⓒ ⓓ ⓔ	24. ⓐ ⓑ ⓒ ⓓ ⓔ
5. ⓐ ⓑ ⓒ ⓓ ⓔ	15. ⓐ ⓑ ⓒ ⓓ ⓔ	25. ⓐ ⓑ ⓒ ⓓ ⓔ
6. ⓐ ⓑ ⓒ ⓓ ⓔ	16. ⓐ ⓑ ⓒ ⓓ ⓔ	26. ⓐ ⓑ ⓒ ⓓ ⓔ
7. ⓐ ⓑ ⓒ ⓓ ⓔ	17. ⓐ ⓑ ⓒ ⓓ ⓔ	27. ⓐ ⓑ ⓒ ⓓ ⓔ
8. ⓐ ⓑ ⓒ ⓓ ⓔ	18. ⓐ ⓑ ⓒ ⓓ ⓔ	28. ⓐ ⓑ ⓒ ⓓ ⓔ
9. ⓐ ⓑ ⓒ ⓓ ⓔ	19. ⓐ ⓑ ⓒ ⓓ ⓔ	29. ⓐ ⓑ ⓒ ⓓ ⓔ
10. ⓐ ⓑ ⓒ ⓓ ⓔ	20. ⓐ ⓑ ⓒ ⓓ ⓔ	30. ⓐ ⓑ ⓒ ⓓ ⓔ

INTERPRETING SYMBOLS

SYMBOL SERIES

Yet another difficult question type when dealing with symbols and figures are symbol series questions. Very similar to symbol analogy questions, symbol series questions are solved in a similar manner. The main focus is to discover a relationship, recurring pattern, or continuing pattern.

SYMBOL SERIES INSTRUCTIONS

Each question below consists of two groups. The group on the left is made up of five symbols that have a relationship that progresses from left to right. The group on the right side of the page consists of five more symbols each with a letter above the choice. Your job is to study the group in the left column, determine the relationship between those symbols, and pick the symbol from the right column that you feel best continues the series.

SYMBOL SERIES SAMPLES

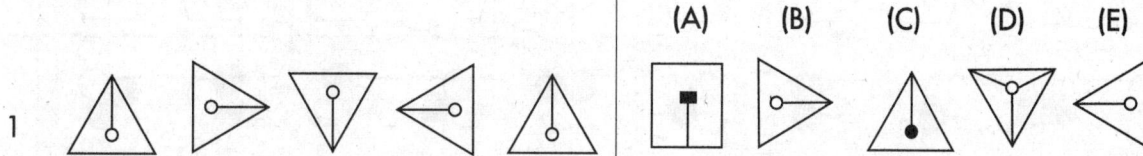

As you can see, each symbol on the left consists of a triangle, a line segment, and a circle. These symbols are extremely similar but are not exactly the same. As you study the group on the left you will notice that the change from each symbol to the next (moving left to right) is simply a rotation clockwise of 90 degrees again and again until the original symbol is repeated.

As this particular series moves on, notice that there are no other changes besides the rotation between the five symbols on the left. This is very important. Also notice that the first symbol and the fifth symbol are the same. This is all the evidence you need to assume that the second symbol and the answer are the same, making the answer **b**.

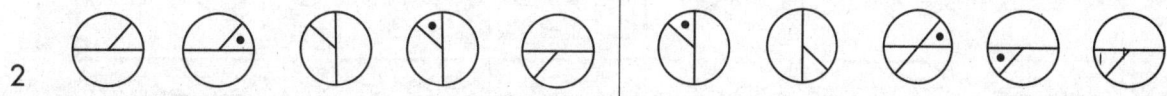

This question is just a little different. Each symbol on the left is made up of a circle with a bisecting line and another line that produces a wedge. These symbols also rotate as they progress left to right, but this time they rotate counter-clockwise with every other turn.

Notice the second symbol in the group is the same as the first, except for the addition of the black dot in the center of the wedge. Also notice that the third symbol is a rotated version of the first symbol, but without the dot added in the second symbol. The dot only appears in every other symbol. According to the pattern, each symbol rotated counterclockwise is followed by the same symbol only with a dot in the wedge section. It is safe to say, at this point, that the answer would be similar to the fifth symbol with a dot added. Choice **d** is the correct answer.

LearningExpress Mechanical & Spatial Aptitude • CHAPTER 5

INTERPRETING SYMBOLS

30 PRACTICE QUESTIONS

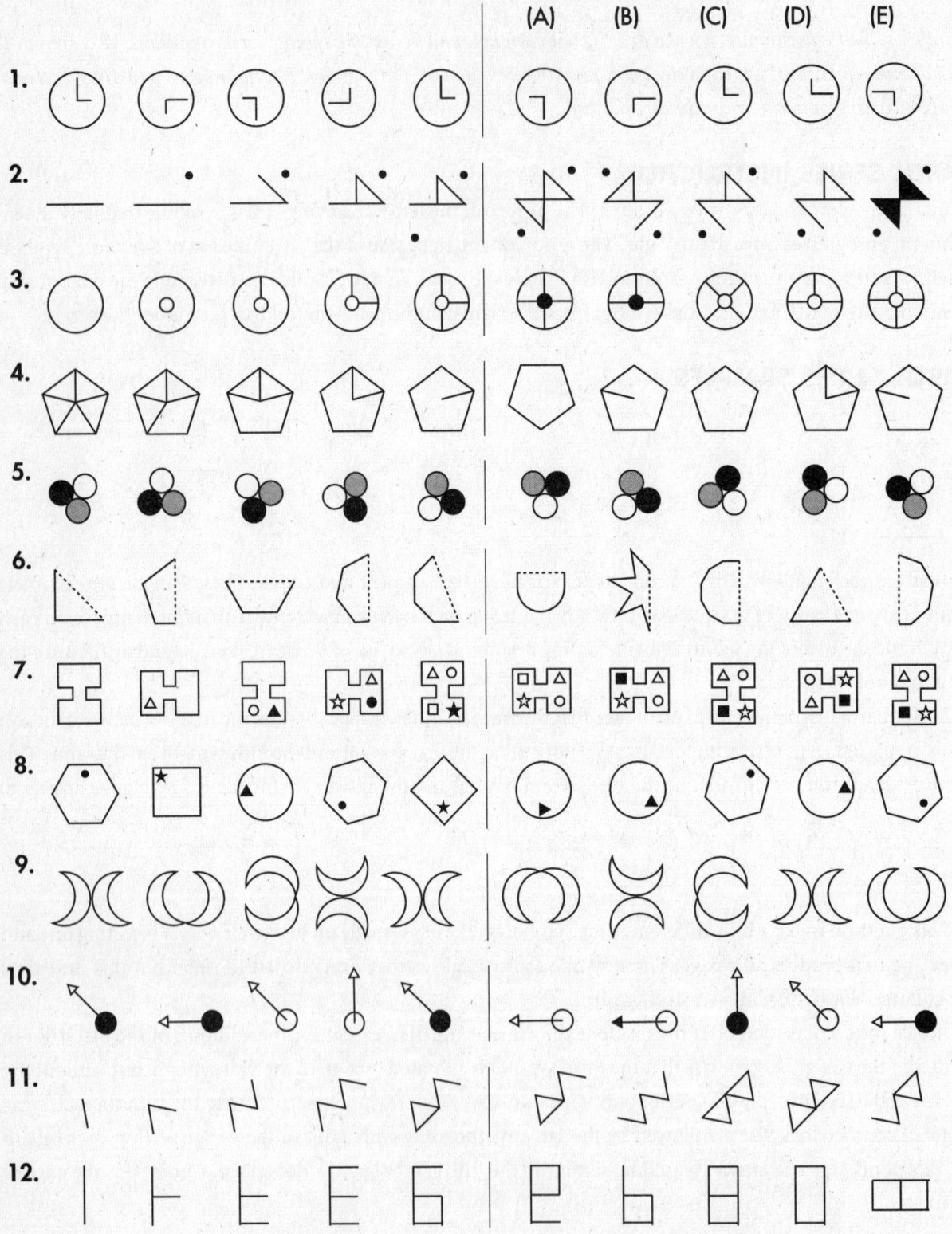

CHAPTER 5 • LearningExpress Mechanical & Spatial Aptitude

INTERPRETING SYMBOLS

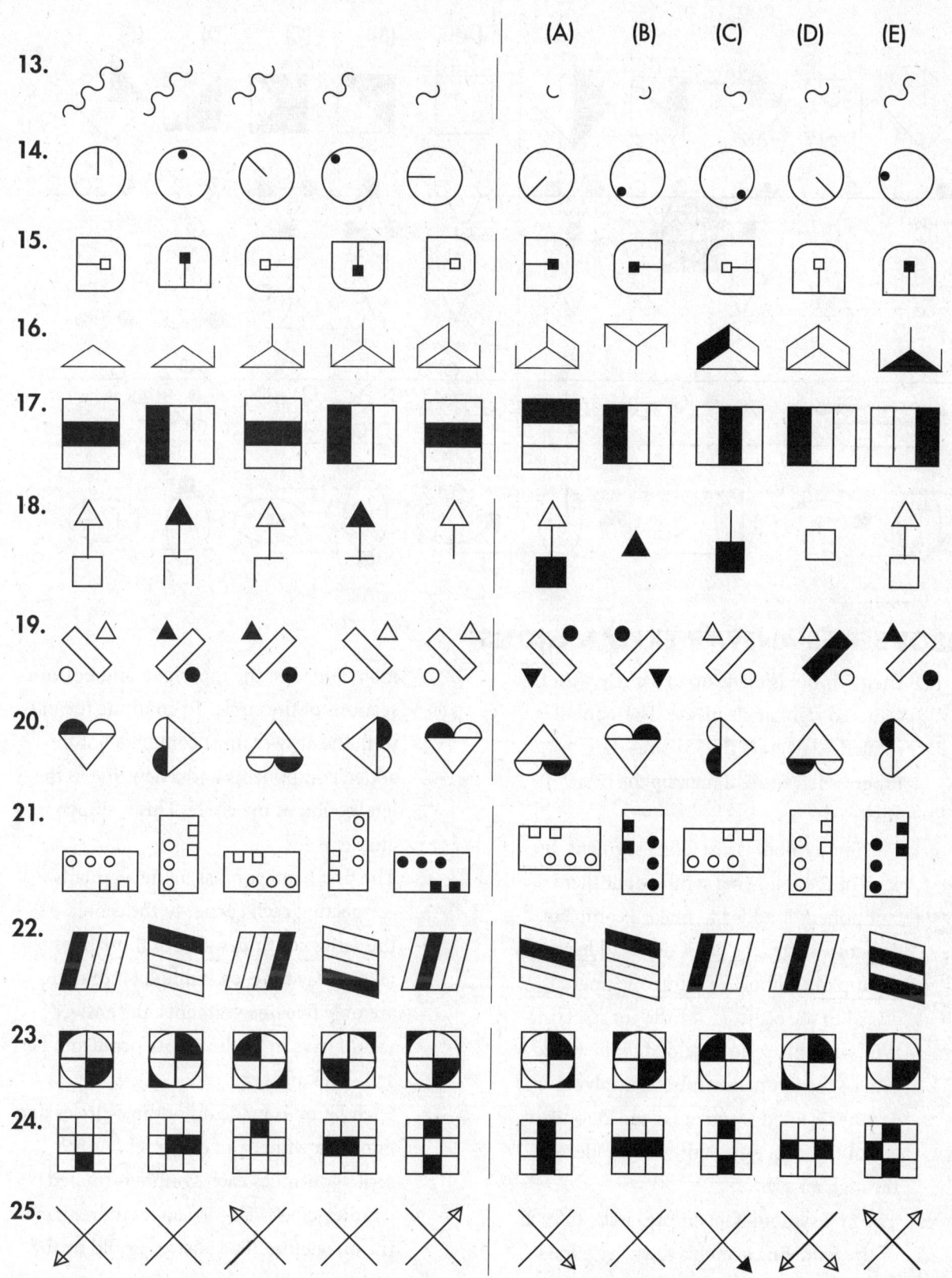

INTERPRETING SYMBOLS

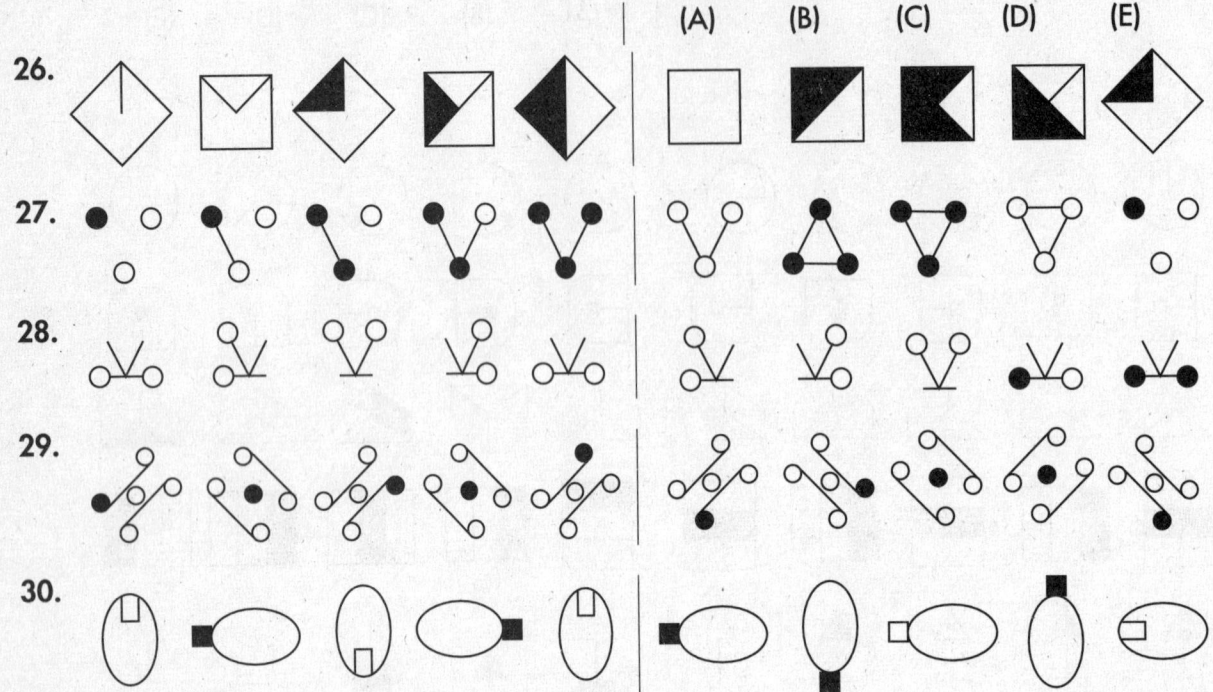

SYMBOL SERIES ANSWER EXPLANATIONS

1. **b.** Each symbol is made up of a circle with a centered right angle inside. The symbol is rotated 90 degrees clockwise as they progress left to right making the best answer **b**.

2. **c.** The first symbol is just a line segment. In each of the following symbols another component is added to make a complete structure. After the black dot is added to the top of symbol 2, a slanted segment is added to the right side of the constructing symbol. A black dot is added to the bottom of the figure in symbol 5 implying another slanted segment be added to the left of the structure. This is best reflected through answer **c**.

3. **e.** The first symbol is an empty circle. In each of the following symbols there are added pieces being put inside the circle. In each of the last 3 symbols there is a line segment added to the top, right, and bottom sections of the circle. To continue the pattern, the answer must contain all of the added components and a new line in the left section of the circle. This is shown in answer **e**.

4. **c.** The first pentagon has 5 line segments connecting each corner to the center. As the series continues, one of those lines is taken away for each symbol. Since there are only five line segments, the answer would have to be the empty pentagon, best shown in answer **c**.

5. **a.** Each figure is made up of three circles one gray, one white, and one black. As the series continues each symbol is rotated counter-clockwise 45 degrees more than the one before. The answer would be the fifth symbol but rotated 45 degrees, answer **a**.

CHAPTER 5 • LearningExpress Mechanical & Spatial Aptitude

INTERPRETING SYMBOLS

6. e. Each symbol is half a polygon cut at the dotted line. Symbol 1 is half a square, symbol 2 is a pentagon, symbol 3 is a hexagon, and so on. Each of the shapes in the series has one more original (before being split in half) side than the last. Since symbol 5 has 4 sides (8 original) then the answer would have to have 4 and a half sides (9 original). Answer **e**.

7. d. The symbols in this series are being rotated counter-clockwise, a component is being added for each symbol, and each component is shaded black after it appears in its second symbol. The square is added in symbol 5. The answer should have a shaded square in the appropriate spot according to the pattern of rotation. This is shown in answer **d**.

8. b. This series is made up of three different shapes each with another shaded shape rotating around the perimeter. As the series progresses the whole shape is rotated 45 degrees counter-clockwise (shown in the polygons). The circle is next in the series making the answer **b**.

9. a. Each symbol in the series rotates counter-clockwise as do the two half moons. The symbol rotates on one turn and switches the way each moon faces each other at every turn. Since symbol 5 had just been rotated, the next symbol should have the moons switch appropriately, best shown in answer **a**.

10. e. Each figure is made up of an arrow connected to a circle that faces one of three ways, horizontal, diagonal, or vertical. The arrow changes position for each symbol in the series in this pattern; horizontal, diagonal, vertical, diagonal, horizontal, etc. The circle is shaded in groups of two as the symbols progress. The first two we shaded black, the second two are blank, the fifth is again shaded. The answer must be shaded, and according to the position of the arrow shown in symbol 5 should be in a horizontal position. Answer **e**.

11. d. A line segment is added to each figure as the series progresses. In symbol 5, a line is added to close a triangle. The answer should include the next line that would close the second triangle, best shown in answer **d**.

12. c. A line segment is added to each figure as the series progresses. In symbol 5, a line is added to close the square. The answer should include the next line that closes the second square, best shown in answer **c**.

13. b. Figure 1 is made up of several half-circle segments. In each progressing symbol, one of these segments is taken away in an alternating fashion, one from the top, then one from the bottom. In figure 5 there are only two segments left implying the answer can only have one segment. Following the pattern of removal, the answer is **b**.

14. e. Each symbol is a circle with either a line or a shaded dot inside. The figure rotates 45 degrees counter-clockwise in every other symbol. For each symbol not rotated, the line is replaced with a dot. The line in symbol 5 is set at the "9 o'clock" position. The answer should have a dot replacing the line in symbol 5, making the answer **e**.

INTERPRETING SYMBOLS

15. e. The series is simply a symbol rotated 90 degrees counter-clockwise. Every other symbol has a shaded square instead of a blank one. Since symbol 5 is not shaded, the answer must be rotated 90 degrees more than symbol 5 and have a shaded square inside, best shown in answer **e**.

16. d. The first symbol in this series is a triangle. As the series progresses, vertical lines are added in the next three symbols. In symbol 5, a diagonal line is added that connects the left most vertical line and the one added to the center. Following the pattern shown, the answer should have another added diagonal line that would connect the right most vertical line and the line in the center. This is best reflected in choice **d**.

17. b. The figures in this series are a simple rectangle separated into three sections, one of which is shaded. The rectangles alternate between the position of symbol 1 to that of symbol 2. The shaded region also only alternates between two positions. Since symbol 5 is in the original position, the answer would be choice **b**.

18. b. The symbols in this series consist of a triangle and 4 lines that make up a square and another line connecting the two shapes. A line is taken away from each figure as the series progresses. Also, the triangle alternates between shaded and unshaded for each symbol. Since the fifth symbol was not shaded and only has one line left to be taken away, the answer must consist of just a triangle that is shaded. Choice **b**.

19. e. This series consists of two similar figures, one unshaded figure with a triangle, a circle, and a rectangle between. The other figure is the same as the first. But, it is reflected over a vertical plane, and the circle and triangle are shaded. The pattern shows one of the unshaded figures then two shaded and two unshaded. According to the pattern, two more shaded figures should appear, so the best answer choice is **e**.

20. c. The figures are simply rotated 90 degrees counter-clockwise. Since the pattern is not broken and the fifth symbol is the same as the first, the answer must be the same as the second symbol. Choice **c**.

21. e. The figures in this series are similar rectangles with shapes inside, rotated counter-clockwise. The fifth symbol is back at the original position but it has shaded shapes inside. The answer which best fits the pattern is **e**.

22. a. The symbols in this series consist of quadrilaterals that are separated into 4 sections, one of which is shaded. The symbols are rotated clockwise throughout the series. Symbol 5 is back to the position of symbol 1 but has a different section shaded. Following the pattern shown in the first 4 symbols, the answer is **a**.

23. d. The figures in this series are rotated 90 degrees counter-clockwise without the two shaded regions changing positions. Following the simple pattern the answer is **d**.

24. b. Figure 1 consists of a square divided into 9 sections, one of which is shaded. Figure 2 consists of the same shaded square just

INTERPRETING SYMBOLS

rotated 90 degrees with the center square shaded also. In figure 3, the symbol is again rotated 90 degrees, but the center square is no longer shaded. In figure 4, the pattern continues. Figure 5 adds another shaded square. The answer should be rotated 90 degrees more than figure 5 and also have the center square shaded, best shown in answer **b**.

25. b. Figure 1 consists of two line segments and an arrowhead at the end of one line. Figure 2 is just two line segments. Figure 3 is similar to figure 1, but the arrowhead has moved clockwise to the end of the adjacent line. Figure 4 again is two lines without the arrowhead. Following the pattern through the series, the answer would be **b**.

26. d. As each square is rotated 45 degrees counter-clockwise, a line segment is added to every other symbol in the series. As the lines close, a shape inside the figures (shown in symbol 2 and 3) is shaded in the next symbol of the series (shown in symbol 3 and 4). Following the pattern, the answer should be a 45–degree counter-clockwise rotation of the fifth symbol with an added segment, which is choice **d**.

27. c. The first symbol in this series consists of 3 circles, one of which is shaded. The second symbol adds a line that connects the shaded circle with one of the two blank circles. The third symbol shades the circle that has just been connected to the previously shaded circle. The fourth symbol adds another line that connects the last blank circle to the circle shaded previously. Following the pattern the answer should have all three circles shaded and connected by another added line. This is best shown through choice **c**.

28. a. Each figure consists of two circles that move clockwise to each adjacent line end as the series matures. Since the fifth figure is the same as the first, and the pattern is not interrupted, the answer is best shown in choice **a**.

29. c. Each symbol consists of a line segment with circles on each end that are reflected diagonally over a circle. One of the circles in each figure is shaded, moving first from left to right, then back to the middle in figure 4, then up. The proposed pattern change would imply up to down, the next symbol needed in the series would be similar to each of the other symbols that have the shaded circle in the center (2 and 4). The answer is **c**.

30. a. This series consists of two different symbols, one that is horizontal and has a shaded region outside of the ellipse and the other which is vertical and has a blank section inside the ellipse. These symbols alternate starting with the vertical ellipse. Each time they appear is reflected over a vertical axis. Since symbol 5 was a vertical ellipse and symbol 4 horizontal with a shaded region on the right side, the answer would be **a**.

Symbol Analogies

Analogies are comparisons of two separate scenarios that have a likeness or a defined pattern similar to each other. To the test-taker, analogies involving symbols seem to take on an undeserved, more fearful appearance. Mistakes in questions like these are common but can be avoided as long as the test taker's focus is to define a relationship between the first scenario and the second. On the other hand, improving your prowess with questions like these might improve such things as graphical instruction interpretation, pattern recognition, and logical decisions.

SYMBOL ANALOGY INSTRUCTIONS

In this exercise there are three groups. In Group 1 there are symbols which share a common characteristic. In Group 2 symbols may look the same, but they do not share the characteristic as those in Group 1. From the information provided to you in symbol form in the first two groups, choose an answer from the lettered column on the right that shares the trait which is characteristic of Group 1.

Symbol Analogy Samples

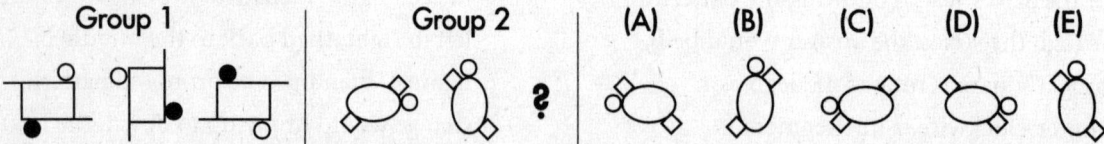

The symbols in Group 1 show a particular pattern that should apply to symbols in Group 2. By following this pattern you should be able to pick the third symbol in Group 2 from the answer column.

The symbols in Group 1 are rotating 90 degrees counter-clockwise. This is reflected in the first two steps in Group 2. This would leave choice **c** as your answer.

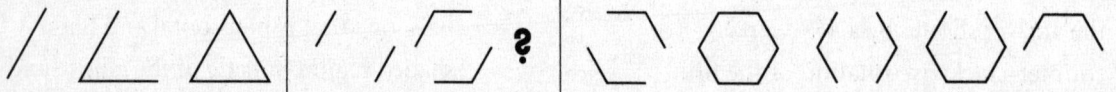

In Group 1, each symbol adds a line segment to complete a whole shape by the third figure in the group. In Group 2, parallel lines are being added to the shape according to the first two symbols. According to the pattern set in Group 1, the answer should complete a shape that relates to the symbols in Group 2. This leaves answer **b** as the only correct choice.

INTERPRETING SYMBOLS

30 PRACTICE QUESTIONS

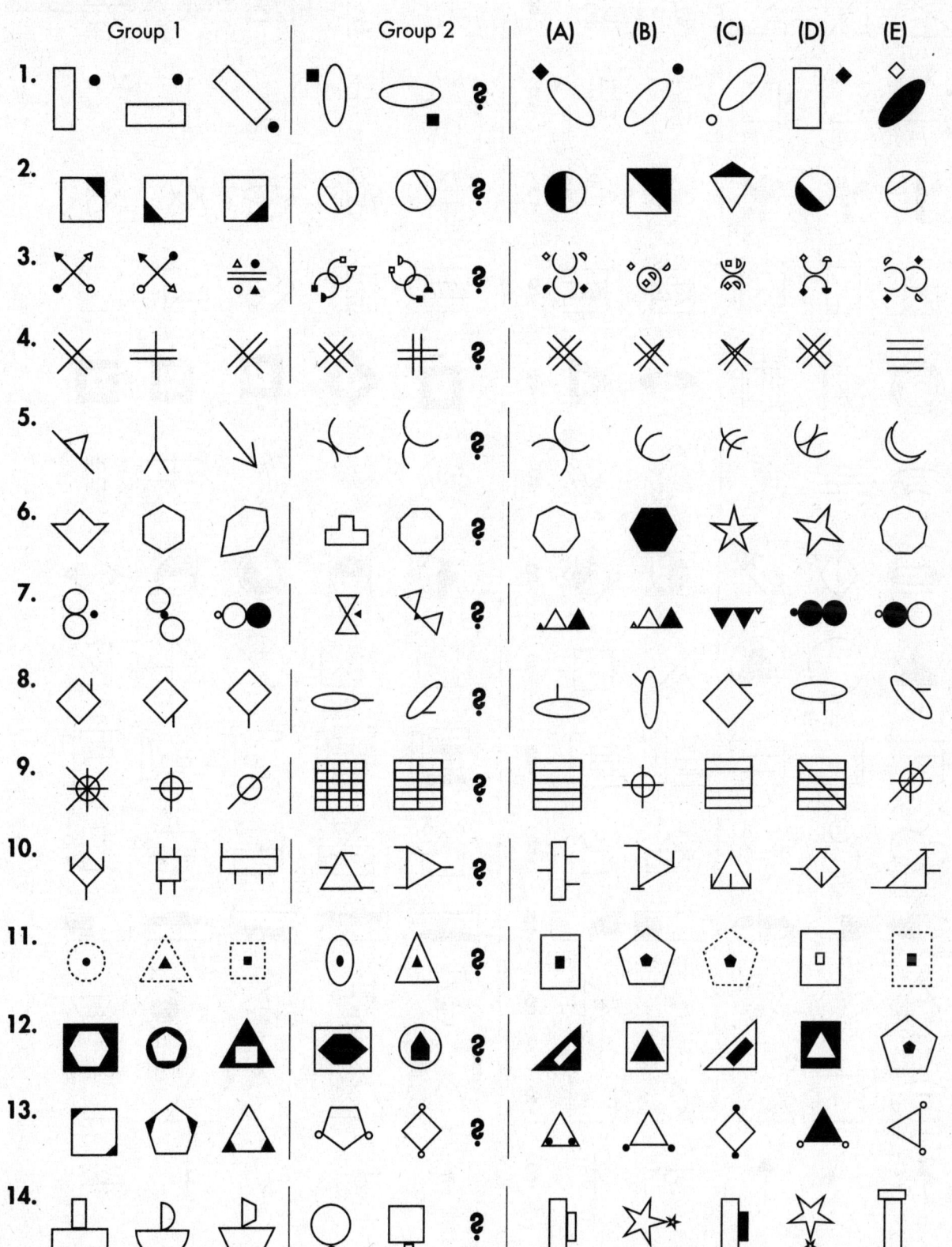

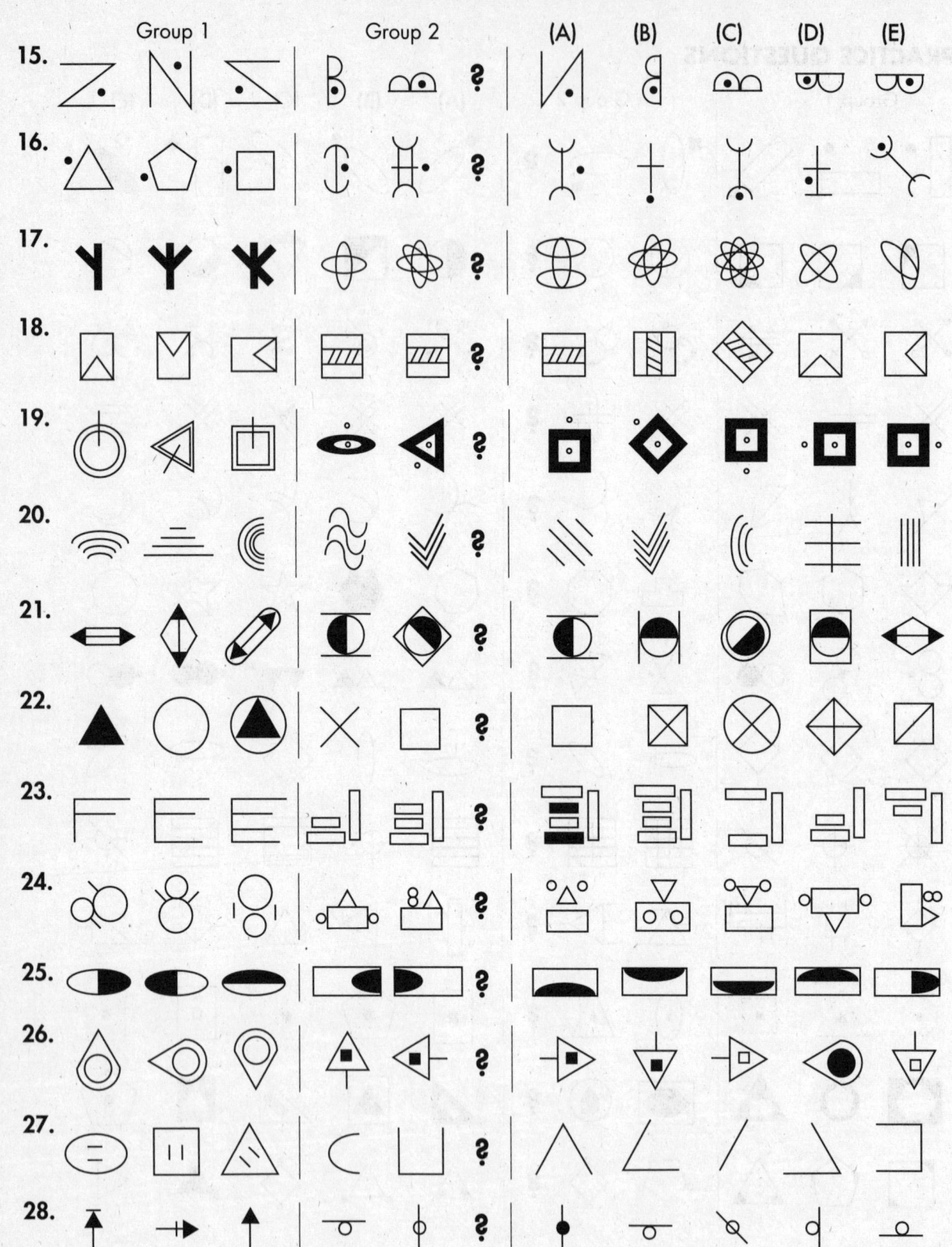

INTERPRETING SYMBOLS

	Group 1	Group 2	(A)	(B)	(C)	(D)	(E)
29.	△ □ ⬠ (with X)	⬡ ⯃ (with S) ?	☆ S	⬡ S	⬣ S	⬠ S	⯃ S
30.	⊘ ⊙ (in circles)	◇ ◇ (with squares) ?	◇	◇	◇	◇	◇

SYMBOL ANALOGIES ANSWER EXPLANATIONS

1. **a.** In Group 1, each symbol consists of an empty rectangle and a small shaded dot. In Group 2 each symbol consists of an empty ellipse and a small shaded square. Choice **a** is the only choice that fits.

2. **e.** Each symbol in Group 1 is a square with a shaded region. Each figure in Group 2 is a circle with a non-shaded region. Choice **e** can be the only correct choice.

3. **a.** The first two symbols in Group 1 consist of two lines, one shaded circle, one non-shaded circle, a shaded triangle, and a non-shaded triangle. The third symbol has all of these parts but none are touching the other. In Group 2, the first symbols consist of two $\frac{3}{4}$ circles and one shaded half-circle, one non-shaded half-circle, one shaded square, and one non-shaded square. The answer must be all the parts in the symbols of group 2, but none can be touching one another. The answer is **a**.

4. **a.** Each symbol in Group 1 consists of just three lines (two running parallel to each other and the other intersecting). The symbols in Group 2 consist of only 4 lines (two sets of parallel lines which intersect). The only logical answer is choice **a**.

5. **b.** Group 1 consists of symbols that contain one straight line and two smaller straight lines that make an acute angle. Group 2 consists of one quarter-circle and one-half of a circle. The only choice that has these components would be choice **b**.

6. **d.** Each symbol in Group 1 is made up of six sides. Each symbol in Group 2 is made up of eight sides. Choice **d** is the only answer that fits Group 2.

7. **b.** Group 1 consists of three circles, two big and one small, one of which is shaded. Group 2 consists of three triangles, two big and one small, one of which is shaded. Choice **b** is the best choice.

8. **e.** Each symbol in Group 1 is a rotated square with a vertical line extending from it. In Group 2 each symbol is an ellipse with a horizontal line extending from it. Choice **e** is the answer.

9. **a.** Group 1 consists of circles that are being intersected by lines. The first symbol has 4 lines, the second has 2 lines, and the third has 1 line. In Group 2 the first rectangle is separated into 20 sections, the second into 10, so the answer must be separated into 5 sections, choice **a**.

LearningExpress Mechanical & Spatial Aptitude • CHAPTER 5

INTERPRETING SYMBOLS

10. e. In Group 1, each symbol is a square with 4 vertical lines extending from it. Group 2 has symbols with 3 horizontal lines extending from it. The best answer is choice **e**.

11. a. Each figure in Group 1 is a dotted symbol with a shaded shape inside and follows the pattern of ellipse, triangle, and quadrilateral. In Group 2, each symbol has solid lines with a shaded shape inside and contains an ellipse, and a triangle. Since a quadrilateral follows the pattern and the lines need to be solid, the only possible answer is choice **a**.

12. c. Each symbol in Group 1 consists of a shaded figure with a blank shape inside, following the pattern of quadrilateral, circle, and triangle. Each symbol in Group 2 is a blank figure with a shaded shape inside following the same pattern. This makes choice **c** the only right answer.

13. e. Each figure in Group 1 has two shaded regions inside. Each figure in Group 2 has two blank circles outside the shape. This would make choice **e** the right answer.

14. d. Each symbol in Group 1 consists of a shape and its miniature, rotated counter clockwise and placed on top. In Group 2, the same pattern is followed but the smaller shape is placed underneath the bigger one. Choice **d** is only one that fits.

15. b. In Group 1, the second symbol is a 90-degree counter-clockwise rotation of the first symbol. The third symbol is a vertical reflection of the first symbol. In Group 2 the symbols follow the same pattern. This would make choice **b** the answer.

16. a. In Group 1, the shaded dot is always on the left side of the figure. In Group 2, the shaded dot is on the right side of the figure making choice **a** the only possible answer.

17. c. In Group 1, each symbol adds a segment of the shape. Group 2 follows that pattern and makes choice **c** the best answer.

18. b. In Group 1, the second symbol is a 180-degree rotation of the first symbol. The third symbol is a 90-degree rotation of the first symbol. Group 2 follows the same pattern making **b** the only appropriate answer.

19. a. In Group 1, the first symbol consists of two ellipses, one inside the other, with a line intersecting the top half of the ellipse. The second symbol consists of two triangles, one inside the other, with a diagonal line intersecting the shape at the bottom. The third symbol is a square drawn the same way, but with a line again intersecting through the top. In Group 2, the symbols are similar and follow a similar pattern but replace the line that intersected the symbols in Group 1 with two circles. Following the analogy, the answer must be **a**.

20. c. Each symbol in Group 1 consists of 4 line segments. Each symbol in Group 2 only has 3, making choice **c** the best answer.

21. c. Group 1 shows a double-sided arrow connected by three lines, then encased in a quadrilateral, then encircled by an ellipse. Group 2 follows the same pattern, which makes choice **c** the only answer.

INTERPRETING SYMBOLS

22. b. The first two symbols in Group 1 are separate and the last symbol includes both. The first two symbols in Group 2 follow the same pattern, making **b** the answer.

23. b. In Group 1, each figure is made up of line segments. The first symbol has 3 lines, the second has 4 lines, and the third has 5 lines. In Group 2, the symbols are made up of blank rectangles but follow a similar pattern. The best answer is **b**.

24. a. Group 1 consists of two circles and two diagonal lines, but the third symbol has all the components separated. Group two consists of two circles, a triangle, and a rectangle, but follows the same pattern making the answer **a**.

25. b. The symbols in Group 1 consist of an ellipse with a shaded half. The symbols in Group 2 are rectangles that contain the missing shaded half from Group 1. Judging from the missing half in the third symbol of Group 1, the answer must be answer **b**.

26. b. Each figure in Group 1 consists of a pointed shape with a blank circle inside. In Group 2, each symbol consists of a pointed object with a shaded figure inside. The figures in Group 1 are rotated 90 degrees counter-clockwise. The figures in Group 2 follow a similar pattern implying that choice **b** is the answer.

27. d. In Group 1 each symbol has a set of parallel lines inside. In Group 2, each shape has a missing line according to which side of the shape the open end of the parallel lines inside the symbols of Group 1 are pointing to. This pattern would make choice **d** correct.

28. e. The first symbol in Group 1 consists of an arrow and a horizontal line, the second has an intersecting vertical line, and the third has a horizontal line at the bottom of the arrow. In Group 2, the symbols consist of one circle but the lines follow a similar pattern making **e** the proper selection.

29. a. In Group 1, the first symbol is a triangle with an "X" in the bottom left-hand corner, the second is a square with an "X" in the bottom right, the third is a pentagon with an "X' in the top corner. In Group 2 the first symbol has 6 sides with an "S" in the bottom left corner, the second has 8 sides with an "S" in the bottom right corner, so the answer has to be a 10 sided figure with an "S" in the top corner, answer **a**.

30. a. In Group 1, each symbol is a circle bisected with one black dot in one half; the second has two dots in the same half; the third has three. In Group 2, each symbol is a square bisected with one blank square inside a half; the second has three blank squares in the same half. Since they follow similar patterns, the answer must have five squares in the same half, leaving only choice **a** as your answer.

INTERPRETING SYMBOLS

SORTING AND CLASSIFYING FIGURES

*Many people find symbol-based questions to be somewhat intimidating or confusing or **both**. If you are among these people, don't feel alone. The concept of interpreting written or drawn symbols is intentionally created in a manner that would make the answer obvious to some while distracting and confusing to others. A comforting thought is the fact that there is always a logical answer and with practice the answer gets easier to find.*

Figure classification questions, such as the ones in this chapter, are another exercise meant to develop your ability to find relationships in groups of symbols and shapes. These questions focus on characteristics shared by two groups *and* characteristics unique to one group but not the other. Although these may be among the toughest questions, they prove to be one of the better measuring devices for aptitude in interpreting symbols and shapes.

SORTING AND CLASSIFYING FIGURES INSTRUCTIONS

In this exercise, each question consists of three sets of symbols, Group 1, Group 2, and the answer choices. The symbols in Group 1 all share a similar trait which make them characteristic to one another. The symbols in Group 2 may look somewhat like those in the previous group but DO NOT share the trait found in Group 1. After studying the symbols in both Groups, choose the answer choice that best fits Group 1.

Sorting and Classifying Figures Samples

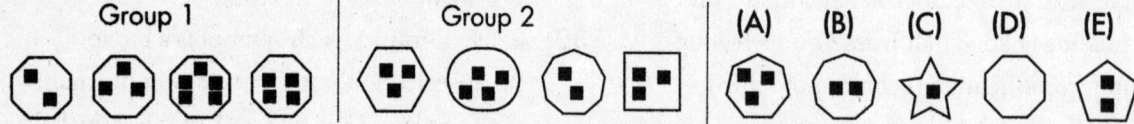

Both Groups 1 and 2 contain four symbols with block boxes inside. Because both groups have four symbols with black boxes, that is a common trait of both groups. That eliminates black boxes in symbols as a possible answer.

However, all four symbols in Group 1 are in the shape of octagons while Group 2 contains no symbols shaped as octagons. The trait of the four octagon-shaped symbols that exists in Group 1 does NOT exist in Group 2.

The answer is **d**, the octagon shape.

Each symbol in Group 1 has only one similar characteristic. They all have two triangles inside a blank shape. Just to double-check this as our answer, none of the symbols in Group 2 have two triangles inside a blank shape. The only choice with more than one triangle inside is choice e.

INTERPRETING SYMBOLS

30 PRACTICE QUESTIONS

1. Group 1 | Group 2 | (A) (B) (C) (D) (E)

LearningExpress Mechanical & Spatial Aptitude • CHAPTER 5

INTERPRETING SYMBOLS

	Group 1	Group 2	(A) (B) (C) (D) (E)

16–30. [Visual symbol-matching exercises]

INTERPRETING SYMBOLS

SORTING AND CLASSIFYING FIGURES ANSWER EXPLANATIONS

1. **d.** In Group 1 all of the symbols contain an ellipse, a triangle, and quadrilateral. Answer **d** is the only possible answer.
2. **e.** Each figure in Group 1 is made of three separate shapes, one of which is shaded. Answer **e** is the only choice fitting that description.
3. **a.** Each symbol in Group 1 has one side represented by a dotted line. Choice **a** is the only answer that fits.
4. **e.** Each symbol in Group 1 consists of one whole arrow and one split arrow in random order. Choice **e** is the only choice with the appropriate components.
5. **e.** Each symbol in Group 1 is a star. Choice **e** is the only star.
6. **a.** Each figure in Group 1 only consists of two components (a large blank shape with another inside). Choice **a** is the only symbol that fits.
7. **c.** Each symbol in Group 1 has a shape at the end of each line. Choice **c** is the answer.
8. **b.** Each symbol in Group 1 has a shaded shape with a blank shape touching on two sides. Choice **b** fits that description.
9. **d.** Each figure in Group 1 has more shaded space than white space. Only choice **d** has that trait.
10. **b.** In each symbol in Group 1, the shaded figure is on top. Choice **b** is the only answer that fits.
11. **d.** Each symbol in Group 1 is a single line intersecting itself. This is only shown in choice **d**.
12. **c.** Each symbol in Group 1 has two separate arrows on separate lines connected in between. Choice **c** is the only fit.
13. **a.** All the symbols in Group 1 can be reflected over a vertical line of symmetry. Only choice **a** fits.
14. **b.** Each symbol in Group 1 is separated into three parts. This is shown in choice **b**.
15. **a.** Each symbol consists of two circles with two horizontal lines and one vertical line, which is only shown in choice **a**.
16. **c.** Each symbol in Group 1 has an even number of circles, which is only reflected in choice **c**.
17. **d.** Each symbol in Group 1 has two black dots exactly opposite each other through the shape. Choice **d** is the only choice that reflects this.
18. **c.** Each figure in Group 1 has the same number of lines inside as outside. This is shown in choice **c**.
19. **b.** Each symbol in Group 1 consists of one vertical line. Choice **b** is the only answer.
20. **c.** Each symbol in Group 1 consists of a star and a shaded shape. This is shown in choice **c**.
21. **a.** Each shape consists of two diagonal lines which is shown in choice **a**.
22. **c.** Each symbol in Group 1 consists of an "H" figure that is only shown in answer **c**.
23. **d.** Each figure in Group 1 has four sections. This is shown in choice **d**.
24. **b.** Each figure consists of a $\frac{3}{4}$ open circle, a black dot, and a line segment which is shown only in choice **b**.
25. **a.** Each symbol in Group 1 has shapes that reflect over a line. Shaded shapes turn white when reflected and white figures

turn shaded when reflected. This is shown only in choice **a**.

26. **e.** Each symbol in Group 1 consists of an "X" figure that is shown in choice **e**.

27. **e.** Each symbol in Group 1 can be reflected over a vertical axis. Choice **e** is the only answer.

28. **b.** Each symbol in Group 1 consists of a right angle (90 degrees). This is only reflected in choice **b**.

29. **a.** Each individual symbol in Group 1 consists of only one shape. Figure 1 has only quadrilaterals; figure 2 is only triangles, etc. Choice **a** is the answer.

30. **d.** Each figure in Group 1 has two round sides. This is only reflected in choice **d**.

SERIES REASONING TEST

Tests that determine your ability to reason in a series or sequence come up often in mechanical/spatial exams. One type of Series questions involves a series of numbers, which may entail addition, subtraction, multiplication, division, and/or identification of a random number inserted in the sequence; for example: 12 24 48 9 3 6 12 9... Here the first numbers are multiplied by 2, then the random number 9 is inserted, then you multiply by 2 again, and then 9 is inserted. Every fourth number is 9. Here is an example of a typical number series question.

NUMBER SERIES

1. 3 6 7 21 18 10 30 ___
   a. 5
   b. 20
   c. 23
   d. 27

Answer: d. This is an alternating sequence, requiring multiplication and subtraction. In each set, the second number is 3 times the first number. The third number is 3 less than the second number.

Another kind of Series question uses a series of letters in a pattern. Usually these questions use the letters' alphabetical order as a base. To make matters more complicated, sometimes a number will be thrown into the letter series. For example: rather than A B F, the series might read A3B2F4. Try this sample letter series question.

LETTER SERIES

1. FHJ JLN NPR ___ VXZ
   a. RSU
   b. SUW
   c. RTV
   d. TUV

Answer: c. The letters in each set of three are in alphabetical order, but one letter is skipped. For example, the first set is F (skip G), H (skip I), J. The second set begins with J, which is the last letter of the previous set. This pattern repeats. Note that this item asks you to fill in the blank and not to add to the end of the sequence. Because the last letter repeats, the set that is missing must begin with an "R." Immediately, this rules out choices **b** and **d**.

30 PRACTICE QUESTIONS

1. Look at this series: 10, 34, 12, 31, ___, 28, 16,... What number should fill the blank?
   a. 14
   b. 18
   c. 30
   d. 34

INTERPRETING SYMBOLS

2. Look at this series: 17, ___, 28, 28, 39, 39, . . . What number should fill the blank?
   a. 50
   b. 39
   c. 25
   d. 17

3. Look at this series: 0.15, 0.3, ___, 1.2, 2.4, . . . What number should fill the blank?
   a. 4.8
   b. 0.006
   c. 0.6
   d. 0.9

4. Look at this series: J14, L16, ___, P20, R22, . . . What letter and numbers should fill the blank?
   a. S24
   b. N18
   c. M18
   d. T24

5. Look at this series: QPO, NML, KJI, ___, EDC, . . . What letters should fill the blank?
   a. HGF
   b. CAB
   c. JKL
   d. GHI

6. Look at this series: 3 11 19 | 36 44 52 | 68 ___ 84, . . . What number should fill the blank?
   a. 60
   b. 72
   c. 76
   d. 92

7. Look at this series: 72 67 61 | 50 55 49 | 38 33 ___, . . . What number should fill the blank?
   a. 22
   b. 27
   c. 28
   d. 31

8. Look at this series: 44 44 50 | 62 62 68 | 81 ___ 87, . . . What number should fill the blank?
   a. 74
   b. 81
   c. 84
   d. 93

9. Look at this series: 0.2 0.04 0.0016 | 0.3 0.09 0.0081 | 0.1 0.01 ___, . . . What number should fill the blank?
   a. 0.0001
   b. 000.1
   c. 0.02
   d. 0.2

10. Look at this series: 2 3 4 | 12 13 4 | 22 ___ 4, . . . What number should fill the blank?
    a. 3
    b. 5
    c. 21
    d. 23

11. Look at this series: 90 30 27 | 12 4 1 | 27 9 ___, . . . What number should fill the blank?
    a. 1
    b. 3
    c. 6
    d. 16

LearningExpress Mechanical & Spatial Aptitude • CHAPTER 5

INTERPRETING SYMBOLS

12. Look at this series: 5 7 21 | 10 12 36 | 8 10 ___, ... What number should fill the blank?
    a. 12
    b. 24
    c. 28
    d. 30

13. Look at this series: QAR RAS SAT TAU ___, ... What letters should fill the blank?
    a. UAV
    b. UAT
    c. TAS
    d. TAT

14. Look at this series: DEF DEF_2 DE_2F_2 ___ $D_2E_2F_3$, ... What letters should fill the blank?
    a. DEF_3
    b. D_3EF_3
    c. D_2E_3F
    d. $D_2E_2F_2$

15. Look at this series: VAB WCD XEF ___ ZIJ, ... What letters should fill the blank?
    a. AKL
    b. UHG
    c. YGH
    d. GHW

16. Look at this series: BOC COB DOE EOD ___, ... What letters should fill the blank?
    a. FOG
    b. DOG
    c. DOF
    d. FOE

17. Look at this series: LML NON PQP RSR ___, ... What letters should fill the blank?
    a. TUT
    b. RTR
    c. STS
    d. TRT

18. Look at this series: ZA_5 Y_vB XC_6 W_3D___, ... What letters should fill the blank?
    a. E_7V
    b. V_2E
    c. VE_5
    d. VE_7

19. Look at this series: 44, 44, 50, 50, 56, ... What number should come next?
    a. 44
    b. 48
    c. 56
    d. 62

20. Look at this series: 50, 5, 40, 10, 30, ... What number should come next?
    a. 15
    b. 18
    c. 25
    d. 35

21. Look at this series: 66, 59, 52, 45, 38, ... What number should come next?
    a. 29
    b. 31
    c. 32
    d. 35

INTERPRETING SYMBOLS

22. Look at this series: 102, 112, 123, 135, … What number should come next?
  a. 146
  b. 148
  c. 150
  d. 149

23. Look at this series: $\frac{1}{6}, \frac{1}{3}, \frac{1}{2}, \frac{2}{3}$ … What number should come next?
  a. 1
  b. $\frac{4}{6}$
  c. $\frac{5}{6}$
  d. $\frac{8}{9}$

24. Look at this series: V, VIII, XI, XIV, … What Roman numeral should come next?
  a. IX
  b. XX
  c. XV
  d. XVII

25. Look at this series: 33, 31, 27, 25, 21, … What number should come next?
  a. 17
  b. 19
  c. 20
  d. 24

26. Look at this series: 21, 9, 21, 11, ___, 13, … What number should fill the blank?
  a. 12
  b. 15
  c. 21
  d. 23

27. Look at this series: 2, 5, 28, 8, 11, 20, 14, … What number should come next?
  a. 12
  b. 17
  c. 23
  d. 28

28. Look at this series: 7, 10, 8, 11, 9, ___, 10, … What number should fill the blank?
  a. 7
  b. 11
  c. 12
  d. 13

29. Look at this series: 2, 6, 18, 54, … What number should come next?
  a. 108
  b. 148
  c. 162
  d. 216

30. Look at this series: 1000, 200, 40, … What number should come next?
  a. 8
  b. 10
  c. 15
  d. 20

LearningExpress Mechanical & Spatial Aptitude • CHAPTER 5

SERIES REASONING ANSWER EXPLANATIONS

1. **a.** This is a simple alternating addition and subtraction series. The first series begins with 10 and adds 2; the second begins with 34 and subtracts 3.
2. **d.** In this simple addition with repetition series, each number in the series repeats itself, and then increases by 11 to arrive at the next number.
3. **c.** This is a simple multiplication series. Each number is 2 times greater than the previous number.
4. **b.** In this series, the letters progress by 2, and the numbers increase by 2.
5. **a.** This series consists of letters in a reverse alphabetical order.
6. **c.** In this simple addition series, each number is 8 more than the previous number.
7. **b.** In this subtraction series, subtract 5 from the first number and 6 from the second number in each segment.
8. **b.** This is an alternation-with-repetition series, in which each number repeats itself and then increases by 6.
9. **a.** This is a simple multiplication series. In each segment, the numbers are multiplied by themselves. The last segment is $0.1 \times 0.1 = 0.01$; $0.01 \times 0.01 = 0.0001$.
10. **d.** This is an addition series, with a random number, 4, interpolated as every third number. In each segment, the second number is 1 more than the first number, and 4 is always the third number.
11. **c.** This is an alternating division and subtraction series, in which the first number is divided by 3 and the third number is 3 less than the second number.
12. **d.** Here is an addition and multiplication series. Two are added to the first number. The second number is then multiplied by 3.
13. **a.** In this series, the third letter is repeated as the first letter of the next segment. The middle letter, A, remains static. The third letters are in alphabetical order, beginning with R.
14. **d.** In this series, the letters remain the same: DEF. The subscript numbers follow this series: 1,1,1; 1,1,2; 1,2,2; 2,2,2; 2,2,3.
15. **c.** There are two alphabetical series here. The first series is with the first letters only: VWXYZ. The second series involves the remaining letters: AB, CD, EF, GH, IJ.
16. **a.** The middle letters are static, so concentrate on the first and third letters. The series involves an alphabetical order with a reversal of the letters. The first letters are in alphabetical order: A, B, C, D, E, F. The second and forth segments are reversals of the first and third segments. The missing segment begins with a new letter.
17. **a.** This series consists of a simple alphabetical order with the first two letters of all segments: L, M, N, O, P, Q, R, S, T, U. The third letter of each segment is a repetition of the first letter.
18. **d.** There are three series to look for here. The first letters are alphabetical in reverse: Z, Y, X, W, V. The second letters are in alphabetical order, beginning with A. The number series is as follows: 5, 4, 6, 3, 7.
19. **c.** This is an alternation with repetition series, in which each number repeats itself, then increases by 6.

INTERPRETING SYMBOLS

20. a. This is an alternating addition and subtraction series. In the first pattern, 10 is subtracted from each number to arrive at the next. In the second, 5 is added to each number to arrive at the next.

21. b. This is a simple subtraction series; each number is 7 less than the previous number.

22. b. In this addition series, 10 is added to the first number, 11 is added to the second number; 12 is added to the third number; and so forth.

23. c. This is a simple addition series. Each number increases by $\frac{1}{6}$.

24. d. This is a simple addition series; each Roman numeral is 3 more than the previous number.

25. b. This is an alternating subtraction series. First 2 is subtracted, then 4, then 2, and so on.

26. c. In this alternating repetition series, the random number 21 is interpolated every other number into an otherwise simple addition series that increases by 2, beginning with the number 9.

27. b. Two series alternate here, with every third number following a different pattern. In the main series, 3 is added to each number to arrive at the next. In the alternating series, 8 is subtracted from each number to arrive at the next.

28. c. This is a simple alternating addition and subtraction series. In the first pattern, 3 is added; in the second, 2 is subtracted.

29. c. This is a simple multiplication series. Each number is three times more than the previous number.

30. a. This is a simple division series. Each number is divided by 5.

C·H·A·P·T·E·R 6
DIAGNOSTIC TEST—PRACTICE WHAT YOU HAVE LEARNED

CHAPTER SUMMARY

If you've worked diligently through this book, here's where it all pays off. No, we are not going to actually give you money, we're going to give you something better than money: an all-encompassing practice test. This test combines all the skills you have practiced in this book. You can see how much you learned and analyze what topics you need to go back and brush up on. Good luck!

LEARNINGEXPRESS MECHANICAL/SPATIAL EXAM ANSWER SHEET

DIAGNOSTIC TEST

#						#						#					
1.	ⓐ	ⓑ	ⓒ	ⓓ	ⓔ	28.	ⓐ	ⓑ	ⓒ	ⓓ	ⓔ	55.	ⓐ	ⓑ	ⓒ	ⓓ	ⓔ
2.	ⓐ	ⓑ	ⓒ	ⓓ	ⓔ	29.	ⓐ	ⓑ	ⓒ	ⓓ	ⓔ	56.	ⓐ	ⓑ	ⓒ	ⓓ	ⓔ
3.	ⓐ	ⓑ	ⓒ	ⓓ	ⓔ	30.	ⓐ	ⓑ	ⓒ	ⓓ	ⓔ	57.	ⓐ	ⓑ	ⓒ	ⓓ	ⓔ
4.	ⓐ	ⓑ	ⓒ	ⓓ	ⓔ	31.	ⓐ	ⓑ	ⓒ	ⓓ	ⓔ	58.	ⓐ	ⓑ	ⓒ	ⓓ	ⓔ
5.	ⓐ	ⓑ	ⓒ	ⓓ	ⓔ	32.	ⓐ	ⓑ	ⓒ	ⓓ	ⓔ	59.	ⓐ	ⓑ	ⓒ	ⓓ	ⓔ
6.	ⓐ	ⓑ	ⓒ	ⓓ	ⓔ	33.	ⓐ	ⓑ	ⓒ	ⓓ	ⓔ	60.	ⓐ	ⓑ	ⓒ	ⓓ	ⓔ
7.	ⓐ	ⓑ	ⓒ	ⓓ	ⓔ	34.	ⓐ	ⓑ	ⓒ	ⓓ	ⓔ	61.	ⓐ	ⓑ	ⓒ	ⓓ	ⓔ
8.	ⓐ	ⓑ	ⓒ	ⓓ	ⓔ	35.	ⓐ	ⓑ	ⓒ	ⓓ	ⓔ	62.	ⓐ	ⓑ	ⓒ	ⓓ	ⓔ
9.	ⓐ	ⓑ	ⓒ	ⓓ	ⓔ	36.	ⓐ	ⓑ	ⓒ	ⓓ	ⓔ	63.	ⓐ	ⓑ	ⓒ	ⓓ	ⓔ
10.	ⓐ	ⓑ	ⓒ	ⓓ	ⓔ	37.	ⓐ	ⓑ	ⓒ	ⓓ	ⓔ	64.	ⓐ	ⓑ	ⓒ	ⓓ	ⓔ
11.	ⓐ	ⓑ	ⓒ	ⓓ	ⓔ	38.	ⓐ	ⓑ	ⓒ	ⓓ	ⓔ	65.	ⓐ	ⓑ	ⓒ	ⓓ	ⓔ
12.	ⓐ	ⓑ	ⓒ	ⓓ	ⓔ	39.	ⓐ	ⓑ	ⓒ	ⓓ	ⓔ	66.	ⓐ	ⓑ	ⓒ	ⓓ	ⓔ
13.	ⓐ	ⓑ	ⓒ	ⓓ	ⓔ	40.	ⓐ	ⓑ	ⓒ	ⓓ	ⓔ	67.	ⓐ	ⓑ	ⓒ	ⓓ	ⓔ
14.	ⓐ	ⓑ	ⓒ	ⓓ	ⓔ	41.	ⓐ	ⓑ	ⓒ	ⓓ	ⓔ	68.	ⓐ	ⓑ	ⓒ	ⓓ	ⓔ
15.	ⓐ	ⓑ	ⓒ	ⓓ	ⓔ	42.	ⓐ	ⓑ	ⓒ	ⓓ	ⓔ	69.	ⓐ	ⓑ	ⓒ	ⓓ	ⓔ
16.	ⓐ	ⓑ	ⓒ	ⓓ	ⓔ	43.	ⓐ	ⓑ	ⓒ	ⓓ	ⓔ	70.	ⓐ	ⓑ	ⓒ	ⓓ	ⓔ
17.	ⓐ	ⓑ	ⓒ	ⓓ	ⓔ	44.	ⓐ	ⓑ	ⓒ	ⓓ	ⓔ	71.	ⓐ	ⓑ	ⓒ	ⓓ	ⓔ
18.	ⓐ	ⓑ	ⓒ	ⓓ	ⓔ	45.	ⓐ	ⓑ	ⓒ	ⓓ	ⓔ	72.	ⓐ	ⓑ	ⓒ	ⓓ	ⓔ
19.	ⓐ	ⓑ	ⓒ	ⓓ	ⓔ	46.	ⓐ	ⓑ	ⓒ	ⓓ	ⓔ	73.	ⓐ	ⓑ	ⓒ	ⓓ	ⓔ
20.	ⓐ	ⓑ	ⓒ	ⓓ	ⓔ	47.	ⓐ	ⓑ	ⓒ	ⓓ	ⓔ	74.	ⓐ	ⓑ	ⓒ	ⓓ	ⓔ
21.	ⓐ	ⓑ	ⓒ	ⓓ	ⓔ	48.	ⓐ	ⓑ	ⓒ	ⓓ	ⓔ	75.	ⓐ	ⓑ	ⓒ	ⓓ	ⓔ
22.	ⓐ	ⓑ	ⓒ	ⓓ	ⓔ	49.	ⓐ	ⓑ	ⓒ	ⓓ	ⓔ	76.	ⓐ	ⓑ	ⓒ	ⓓ	ⓔ
23.	ⓐ	ⓑ	ⓒ	ⓓ	ⓔ	50.	ⓐ	ⓑ	ⓒ	ⓓ	ⓔ	77.	ⓐ	ⓑ	ⓒ	ⓓ	ⓔ
24.	ⓐ	ⓑ	ⓒ	ⓓ	ⓔ	51.	ⓐ	ⓑ	ⓒ	ⓓ	ⓔ	78.	ⓐ	ⓑ	ⓒ	ⓓ	ⓔ
25.	ⓐ	ⓑ	ⓒ	ⓓ	ⓔ	52.	ⓐ	ⓑ	ⓒ	ⓓ	ⓔ	79.	ⓐ	ⓑ	ⓒ	ⓓ	ⓔ
26.	ⓐ	ⓑ	ⓒ	ⓓ	ⓔ	53.	ⓐ	ⓑ	ⓒ	ⓓ	ⓔ						
27.	ⓐ	ⓑ	ⓒ	ⓓ	ⓔ	54.	ⓐ	ⓑ	ⓒ	ⓓ	ⓔ						

DIAGNOSTIC TEST

79 PRACTICE QUESTIONS
Shop Arithmetic

1. A length of rope 3 feet 4 inches long was divided in 5 equal parts. How long was each part?
   a. 1 foot 2 inches
   b. 10 inches
   c. 8 inches
   d. 6 inches

2. Plattville is 80 miles west and 60 miles north of Quincy. How long is a direct route from Plattville to Quincy?
   a. 100 miles
   b. 120 miles
   c. 140 miles
   d. 160 miles

3. A builder has 27 cubic feet of concrete to pave a sidewalk whose length is 6 times its width. The concrete must be poured 6 inches deep. How long is the sidewalk?
   a. 9 feet
   b. 12 feet
   c. 15 feet
   d. 18 feet

4. A floor plan is drawn to scale so that $\frac{1}{4}$ inch represents 2 feet. If a hall on the plan is 4 inches long, how long will the actual hall be when it is built?
   a. 2 feet
   b. 8 feet
   c. 16 feet
   d. 32 feet

5. All of the rooms in a building are rectangular, with 8-foot ceilings. One room is 9 feet wide by 11 feet long. What is the combined area of the four walls, including doors and windows?
   a. 99 square feet
   b. 160 square feet
   c. 320 square feet
   d. 72 square feet

Tool Knowledge
Put the correct letter next to the description of the tools.

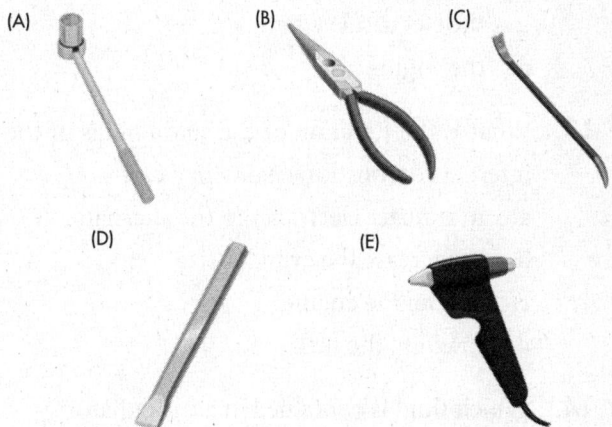

6. used with hammer to notch or chip away stone ___

7. used to crimp wire ends to fit into screw terminals ___

8. used with glue stick to apply adhesive ___

9. used to remove nails or open crates ___

10. used with sockets to loosen or tighten nuts and/or bolts ___

Mechanical Knowledge

11. Which of the following automotive systems uses lubrication fluid?
    a. the transmission system
    b. the exhaust system
    c. the suspension system
    d. the electrical system

12. Which automotive system uses fuses and an alternator?
    a. the steering system
    b. the cooling system
    c. the electrical system
    d. the engine

13. What is the function of the spark plugs in the internal combustion engine in a car?
    a. to transfer electricity to the alternator
    b. to increase the cylinder size
    c. to cool the engine
    d. to ignite the fuel

14. Which fluid is contained in a car radiator?
    a. transmission fluid
    b. cooling fluid
    c. brake fluid
    d. steering fluid

15. What is the primary function of the water pump in a car?
    a. to circulate coolant
    b. to evacuate waste water
    c. to remove exhaust
    d. to filter water

Mechanical Insight

16. What is the most accurate statement regarding the relationship between weight and density?
    a. Weight equals density divided by volume.
    b. A bathroom scale cannot measure density.
    c. Density can be measured in pounds.
    d. All of the above.

17. Expansion is to contraction as
    a. pressure is to density.
    b. acceleration is to deceleration.
    c. weight is to center of gravity.
    d. direction is to velocity.

18. The center of gravity of a baseball bat would be best described as
    a. near the grip.
    b. near the fat end.
    c. near the skinny end.
    d. at the top.

19. Which is heavier, five pounds of feathers or five pounds of lead?
    a. The feathers are heavier.
    b. The lead is heavier.
    c. They weigh the same.
    d. It is not possible to compare the two.

20. Which material is best suited for use as a boat anchor?
    a. metal
    b. foam
    c. wood
    d. glass

DIAGNOSTIC TEST

Hidden Figures

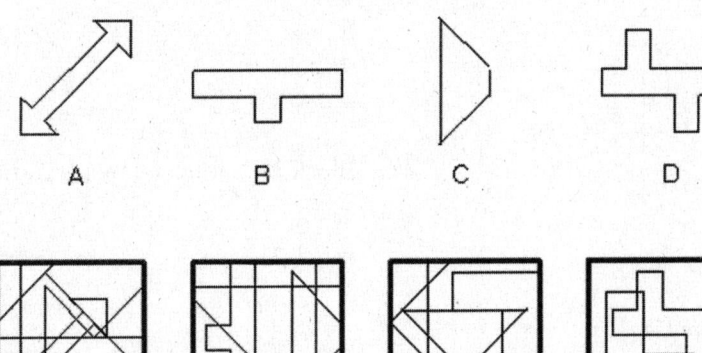

Figure J-3

Use Figure J-3 for questions 21–25:

21. The hidden figure in block 21 is ___.
    a. A
    b. B
    c. C
    d. D
    e. E

22. The hidden figure in block 22 is ___.
    a. A
    b. B
    c. C
    d. D
    e. E

23. The hidden figure in block 23 is ___.
    a. A
    b. B
    c. C
    d. D
    e. E

24. The hidden figure in block 24 is ___.
    a. A
    b. B
    c. C
    d. D
    e. E

25. The hidden figure in block 25 is ___.
    a. A
    b. B
    c. C
    d. D
    e. E

DIAGNOSTIC TEST

Block Counting

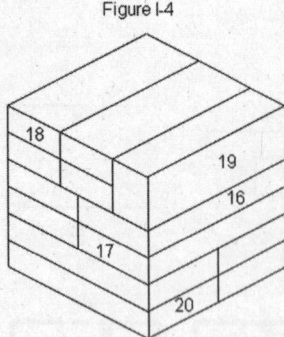

Figure I-4

For questions 26–30, refer to Figure I-4

26. Block 26 is touched by ___ other blocks.
    a. 2
    b. 3
    c. 4
    d. 5
    e. 6

27. Block 27 is touched by ___ other blocks.
    a. 2
    b. 3
    c. 4
    d. 5
    e. 6

28. Block 28 is touched by ___ other blocks.
    a. 2
    b. 3
    c. 4
    d. 5
    e. 6

29. Block 29 is touched by ___ other blocks.
    a. 2
    b. 3
    c. 4
    d. 5
    e. 6

30. Block 30 is touched by ___ other blocks.
    a. 2
    b. 3
    c. 4
    d. 5
    e. 6

Rotated Blocks

31.

a.

b.

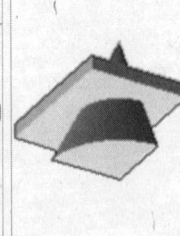
c.

d.

e.

32.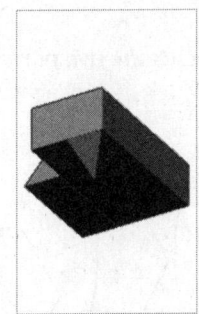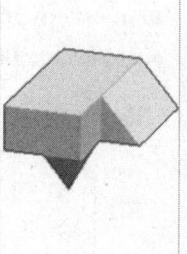

a. b. c. d. e.

33.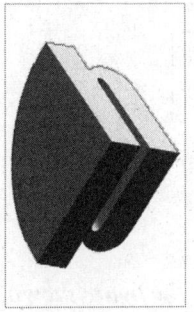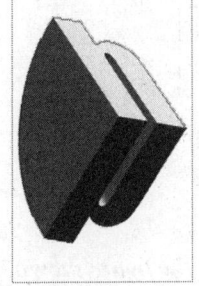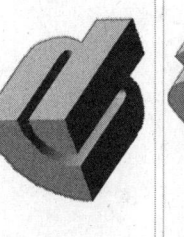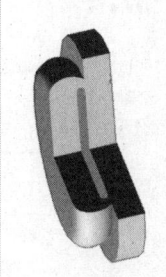

a. b. c. d. e.

34.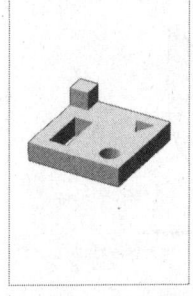

a. b. c. d. e.

35.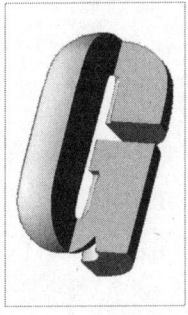

a. b. c. d. e.

Matching Pieces and Parts

In questions 36–37 below, select the single answer choice that represents the two parts that join together to make the given whole. Pieces may be reflected and/or rotated.

36.

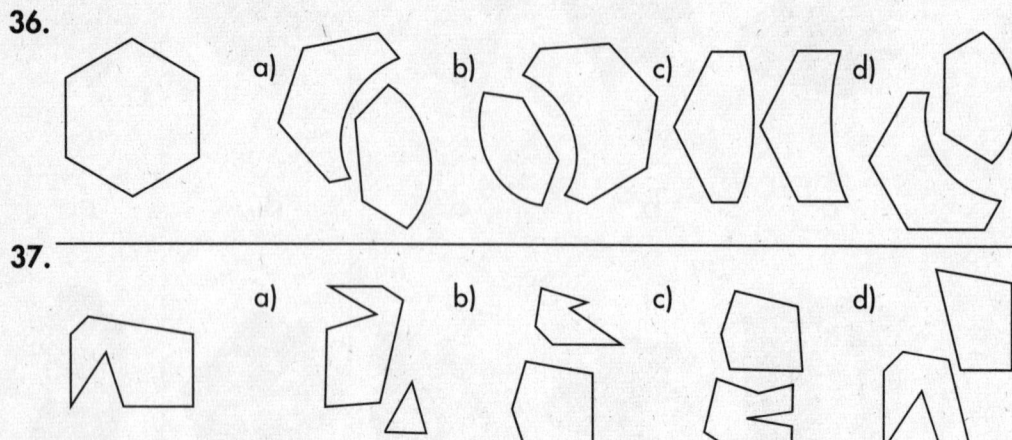

37.

In questions 38–39 below, pick the two answer choices that will come together to make the figure shown. Pieces may be reflected and/or rotated.

38.

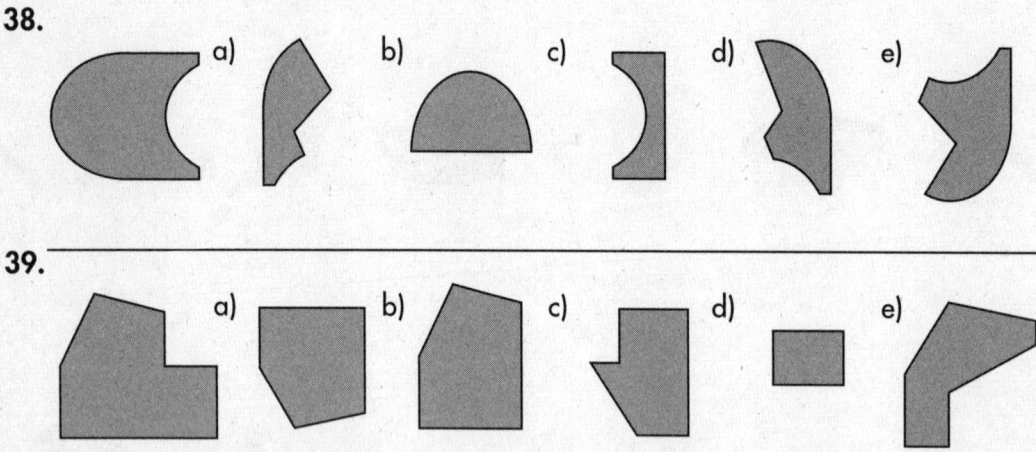

39.

DIAGNOSTIC TEST

In question 40 below, four pieces are given. Choose the answer choice that represents a figure comprised of all four pieces. Pieces may be rotated and/or reflected.

40.

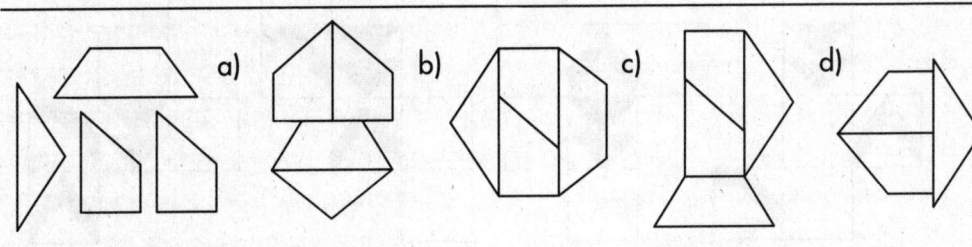

Spatial Analysis

41. 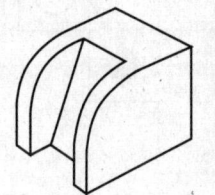 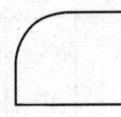 a. 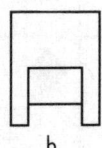 b. 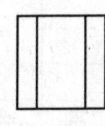 c. 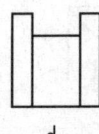 d.

42. 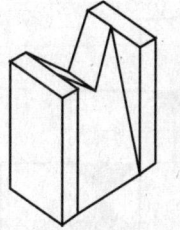 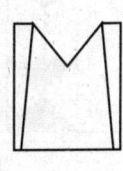 a. 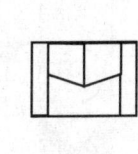 b. 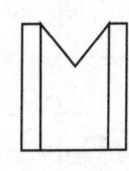 c. 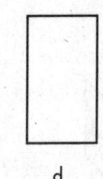 d.

43. 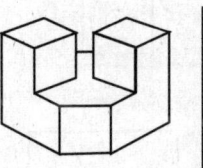 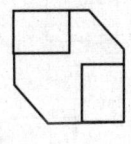 a. 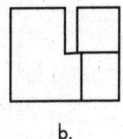 b. 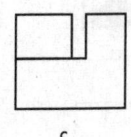 c. 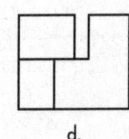 d.

44. 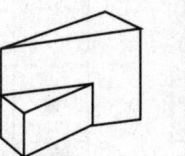 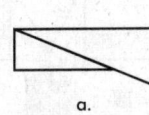 a. 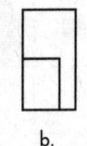 b. 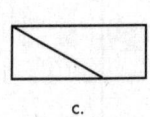 c. 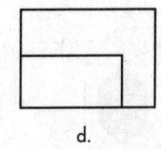 d.

45. 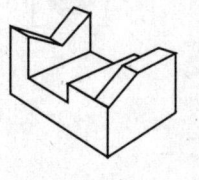 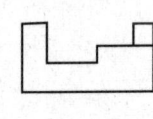 a.  b. 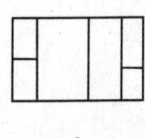 c. 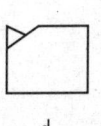 d.

Understanding Patterns

46.

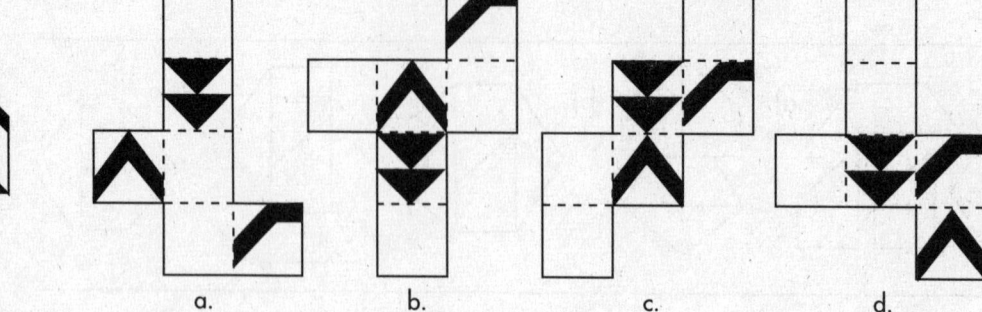

47.

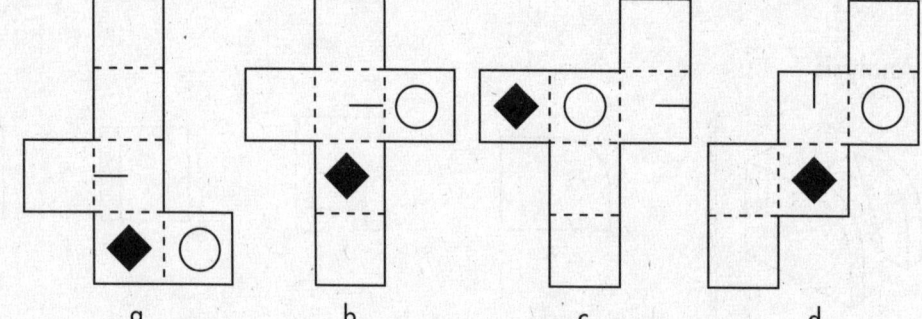

48.

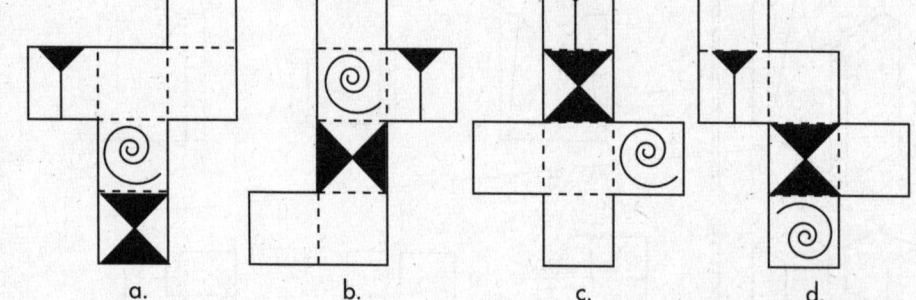

49.

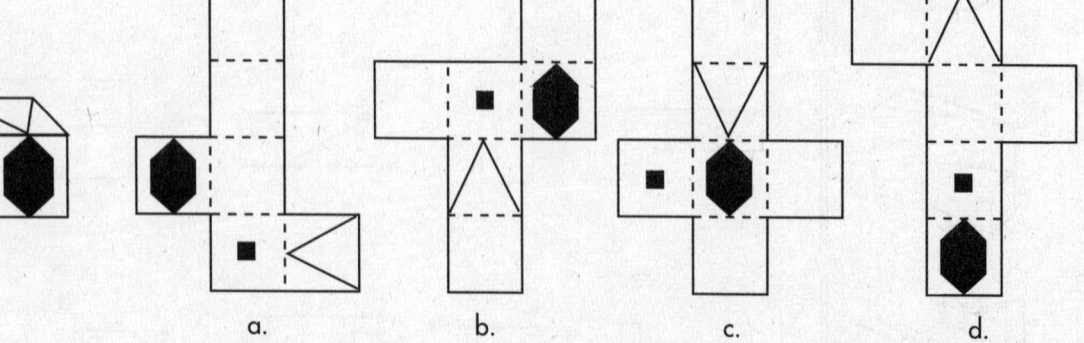

50.

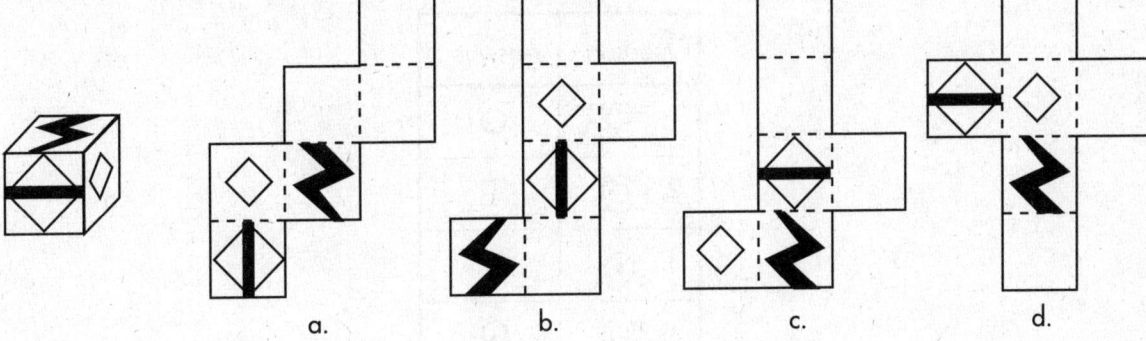

Eye-Hand Coordination
4 LETTER-SYMBOL QUESTIONS

Reference Code

Letter	A	B	C	D	E	F	G	H	I	J
Code	⬠•	◉	▽	▽	⊡	⬡	⬠	▲•	◇	△
Letter	K	L	M	N	O	P	Q	R	S	T
Code	⬡	⊙	△	⬠•	◁	☆	⬡	⬡	▽	⊚

Questions

Question	Answer
1. ◁	
2. ⬡	
3. ⬡•	
4. ⬡	

DIAGNOSTIC TEST

Answers

Question	Answer
1. ◁	O
2. ⬡	T
3. ⬢	L
4. ⬠	Q

Letter	A	B	C	D	E	F	G	H	I	J
Code	⬠	▣	▽	▽	▣	⬡	⬠	△	◇	△
Letter	K	L	M	N	O	P	Q	R	S	T
Code	⬡	⬢	△	⬠	◁	☆	⬡	⬡	▽	⬡

↑ 3   ↑ 1   ↑ 4   ↑ 2

3 EXAMINING OBJECTS QUESTIONS

The Sorting Code above is a graphical summary for the following Sorting Code. Read the code carefully.

CHAPTER 6 • LearningExpress Mechanical & Spatial Aptitude

Sorting Code for Boxes 1 through 4:

Box 1: Ship
All packages placed in this box must satisfy each of the following requirements
- The two pieces are the same weight.
- The two pieces are the same shape.
- The two pieces are free from defects.

Box 2: Fail
All packages placed in this box contain two defective pieces. Regardless of weight or shape, if both pieces inside a package are defective, put them in Box 2.
Note: A "defect" is displayed as a black circle on the piece. See the graphic code above.

Box 3: Recycle
All packages placed in this box contain one defective piece. Regardless of shape or weight, if one piece of the pair is defective, put the package in Box 3.

Box 4: Discount
All packages placed in this box contain non-defective pieces that do not match in weight or shape.

In the questions below, you are presented with a package containing two pieces. Use the above sorting code to determine which box each package needs to be placed in.

51.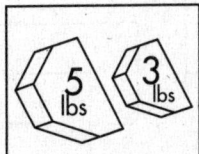
    a. Box 1
    b. Box 2
    c. Box 3
    d. Box 4

52.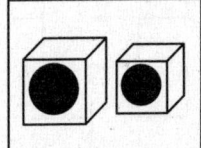
    a. Box 1
    b. Box 2
    c. Box 3
    d. Box 4

53.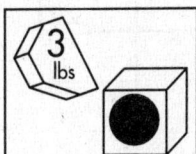
    a. Box 1
    b. Box 2
    c. Box 3
    d. Box 4

MAZES

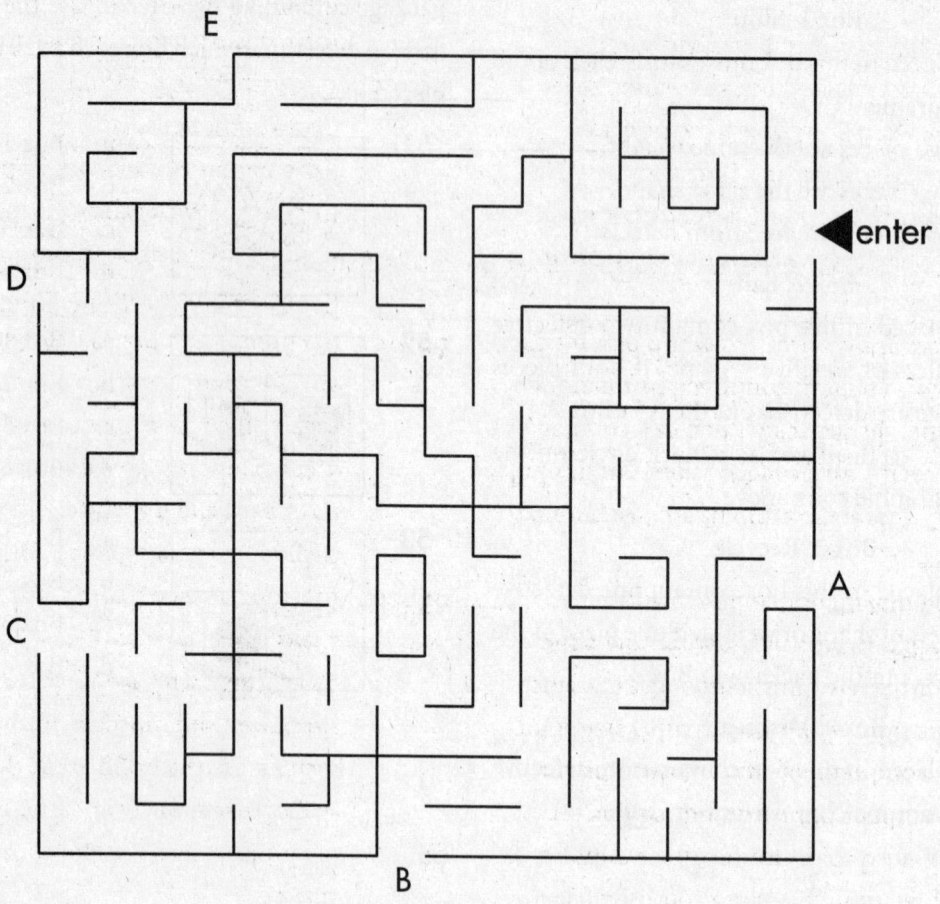

54. Follow the maze above and mark the letter that correctly represents the way out of the maze. ___

DIAGNOSTIC TEST

Reading Maps

Answer questions 55–59 based on the map and the information below.

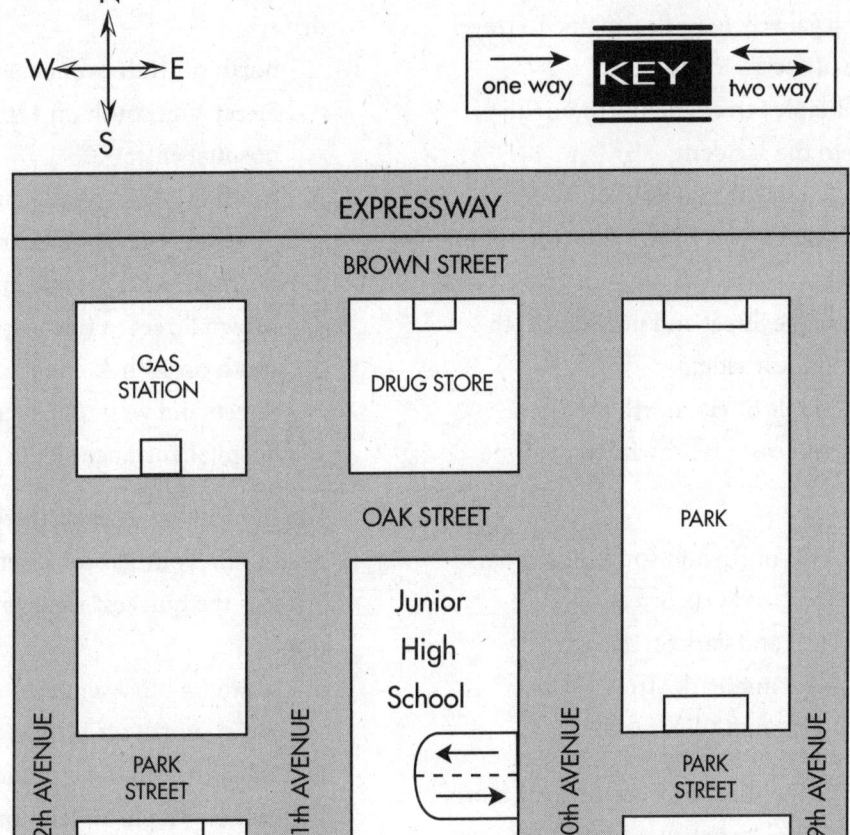

This is a map of a section of the city where some public buildings are located. Each of the squares represent one city block. Street names are as shown. If there is an arrow next to the street name, it means the street is one way only, in the direction of the arrow. If there is no arrow next to the street name, two-way traffic is allowed.

LearningExpress Mechanical & Spatial Aptitude • CHAPTER 6

55. There has been a vehicular accident at the corner of Brown Street and 9th Avenue and gasoline is leaking from one of the cars. What is the most direct legal way for a fire engine to travel to the scene of the accident?
    a. east on Maple Street and north on 9th Avenue to the accident
    b. west on Maple Street, north on 12th Avenue, and east on Brown Street to the accident
    c. east on Maple Street and north on 11th Avenue to the accident
    d. west on Maple Street, north on 11th Avenue, and east on Brown Street to the accident

56. What streets run north and south of the park?
    a. Brown Street and Oak Street
    b. Maple Street and Park Street
    c. Brown Street and Park Street
    d. Green Street and Oak Street

57. If you were giving directions to the drug store from the hospital, what would be the most direct, legal route?
    a. east on Maple Street, north on 9th Avenue, and west on Brown Street to the store entrance
    b. west on Maple Street, north on 10th Avenue, and west on Brown Street to the store entrance
    c. west on Green Street, north on 12th Avenue, and east on Brown Street to the store entrance
    d. east on Oak Street, north on 11th Avenue, and east on Brown Street to the store entrance

58. Someone at the junior high school has been injured and needs to go to the hospital. What directions would you give to the ambulance driver?
    a. north on 10th Avenue, west on Brown Street, and south on 12th Avenue to the hospital entrance
    b. south on 10th Avenue and west on Green Street to the hospital entrance
    c. north on 10th Avenue and south on Brown Street to the hospital entrance
    d. south on 10th Avenue, west on Maple Street, and west on Green Street to the hospital entrance

59. You are leaving work at the police station and need to fill your gas tank before you go home. What is the quickest legal route to the gas station?
    a. south on 9th Avenue, west on Maple Street, north on 11th Avenue, and west on Oak Street to the entrance
    b. east on Maple Street, north on 10th Avenue, and west on Oak Street to the entrance
    c. north on 9th Avenue and west on Brown Street to the entrance
    d. north on 9th Avenue, west on Park Street, north on 10th Avenue, and west on Oak Street to the entrance

DIAGNOSTIC TEST

Symbol Series

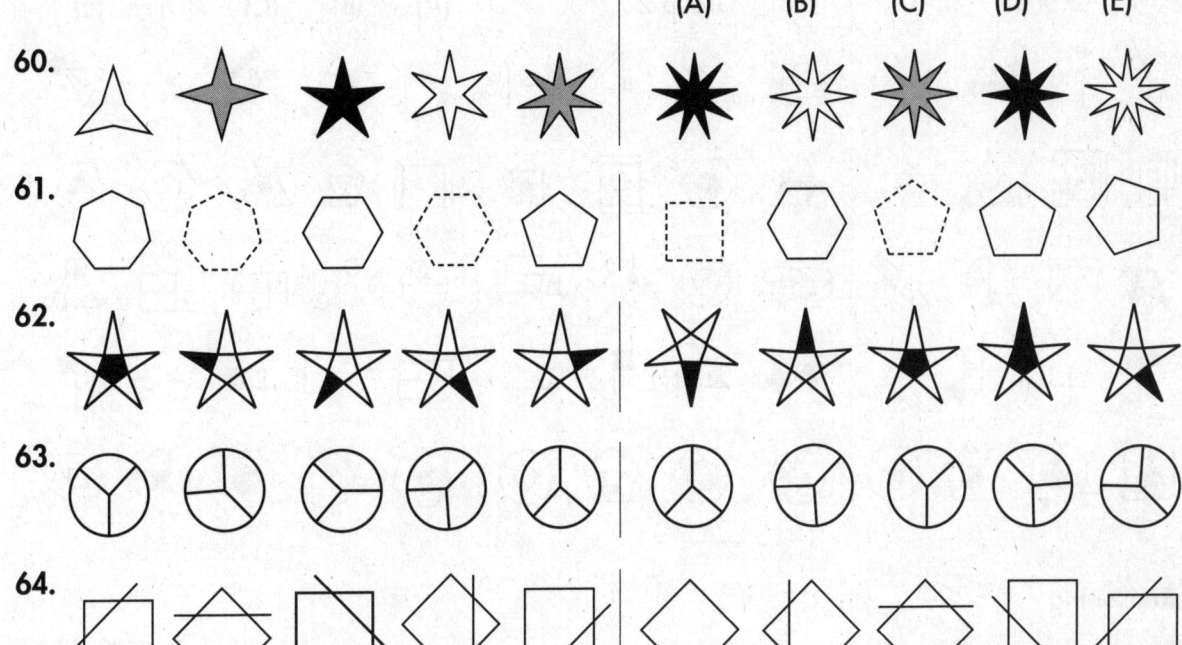

Symbol Analogies

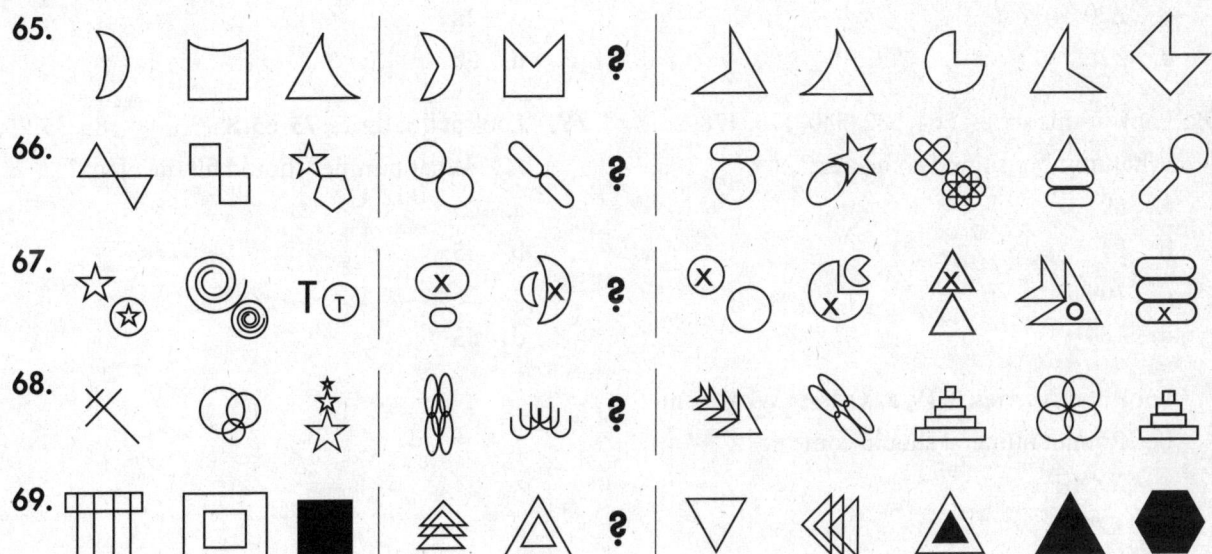

Sorting and Classifying Figures

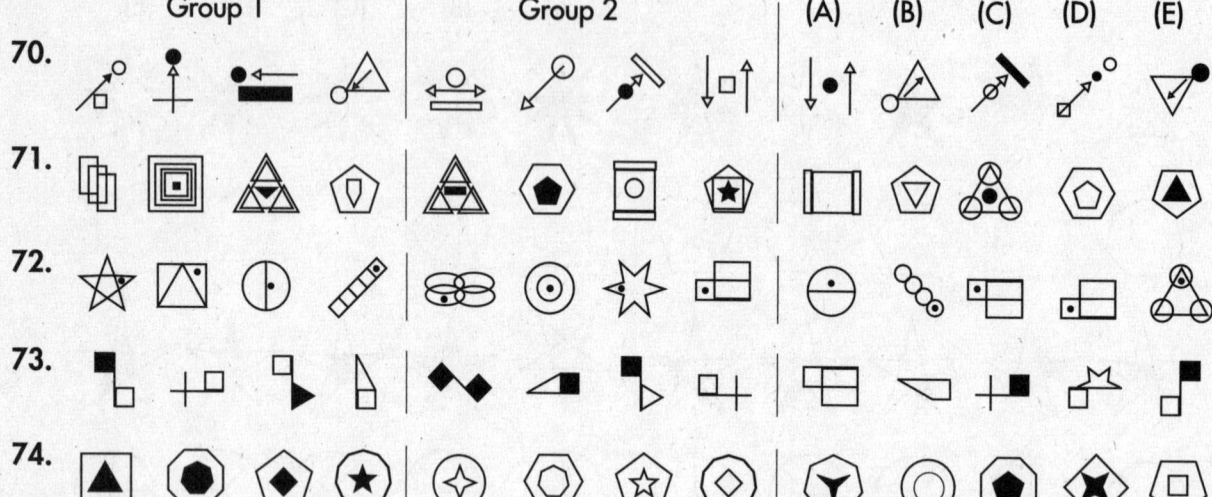

Series Reasoning

75. Look at this series: U32, V29, W26, X23, ... What number should come next?
  a. Y20
  b. Y17
  c. Z20
  d. Z26

76. Look at this series: 664, 332, 340, 170, 178, ... What number should come next?
  a. 89
  b. 94
  c. 109
  d. 184

77. Look at this series: 2, IV, 8, XVI, ... What number/Roman numeral should come next?
  a. XXXII
  b. XIX
  c. 16
  d. 32

78. Look at this series: 17, ___, 28, 28, 39, 39, ... What number should fill the blank?
  a. 6
  b. 17
  c. 28
  d. 50

79. Look at this series: 75, 65, 85, 55, ___, 85, 35, 25, ... What number should fill the blank?
  a. 25
  b. 45
  c. 65
  d. 85

DIAGNOSTIC TEST ANSWER EXPLANATIONS

Shop Arithmetic

1. **c.** Three feet 4 inches equals 40 inches; 40 divided by 5 is 8.
2. **a.** The distance between Plattville and Quincy is the hypotenuse of a right triangle with sides of length 80 and 60. The length of the hypotenuse equals the square root of ($80^2 + 60^2$), which equals the square root of (6,400 + 3,600), which equals the square root of 10,000, which equals 100 miles.
3. **d.** The volume of concrete is 27 cubic feet. Volume is length times width times depth, or (L)(W)(D), so (L)(W)(D) = 27. We're told that the length L is 6 times the width W, so L equals 6W. We're also told that the depth is 6 inches, or 0.5 feet. Substituting what we know about the length and depth into the original equation and solving for W, we get (L)(W)(D) = (6W)(W)(0.5) 27. $3W^2 = 27$. $W^2 = 9$, so W = 3. To get the length, we remember that L equals 6W, so L equals (6)(3), or 18 feet.
4. **d.** Four inches is equal to 16 quarter inches. Each quarter inch is 2 feet, so 16 quarter inches is 32 feet.
5. **c.** Each 9-foot wall has an area of 9(8) or 72 square feet. There are two such walls, so those two walls combined have an area of 144 square feet. Each 11-foot wall has an area of 11(8) or 88 square feet, and again there are two such walls: 88 (2) = 176. Finally, add 144 and 176 to get 320 square feet.

Tool Knowledge

6. **d.** Choice **d** is a stone chisel used with a hammer to notch or chip stone.
7. **b.** A pair of needle nose pliers is shown in choice **b**. These pliers have a multitude of uses including handling electrical wiring.
8. **e.** A common glue gun is represented in choice **e**. By melting a stick of glue, the glue gun is used to apply a hot adhesive.
9. **c.** Choice **c** is a pry bar which has many uses from removing nails to separating wood planks.
10. **a.** The tool represented in choice **a** is a socket wrench. This tool can be used to tighten and loosen any size nut or bolt easily by changing the size of the socket.

Mechanical Knowledge

11. **a.** The transmission has many moving parts (gears and shafts), which must be lubricated by transmission fluid in order to prevent excessive wear and allow the parts to move smoothly.
12. **c.** The fuses are used as links in the electrical system to prevent damage to other key components. The alternator is used to recharge the battery when the car is running.
13. **d.** The spark plug sends a spark into the cylinder, igniting the fuel.
14. **b.** The radiator is part of the cooling system. The cooling fluid is stored in the radiator and is then pumped through the cooling system by the water pump. As air passes over the radiator, the fluid is cooled, which prevents engine overheating.
15. **a.** The water pump pumps the engine coolant (a combination of water and

antifreeze) out of the radiator and around the engine block in order to cool the engine.

Mechanical Insight

16. **b.** Choice **a** is not correct, as weight is equal to density multiplied by volume. Choice **c** is not correct, as density is measured in weight (pounds) per unit volume.
17. **b.** Expansion and contraction are opposites, as are acceleration and deceleration. The other choices are not opposites.
18. **b.** The center of gravity is the place on an object where there is equal weight on either side.
19. **c.** Weight is measured in pounds, and the question states that both the feathers and the lead weigh five pounds.
20. **a.** Foam and wood float and would therefore make poor boat anchors. Glass is not strong enough to be used as a boat anchor.

Hidden Figures

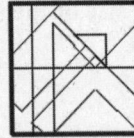 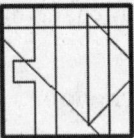 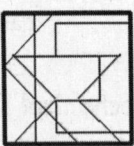 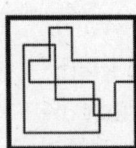 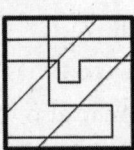

21. a   22. c   23. e   24. d   25. b

Block Counting

26. **c.** Block 26 touches two blocks above, one block to the left, and one block below.
27. **c.** Block 27 touches one block above, one block to the left, and two blocks below.
28. **a.** Block 28 touches one block to the right and one block below.
29. **b.** Block 29 touches two blocks to the left and one block below.
30. **a.** Block 30 touches one block above and one block to the right.

Rotated Blocks

31. b
32. a
33. b
34. a
35. c

Matching Pieces and Parts

36. c.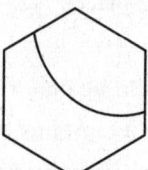

37. b.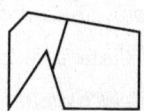

38. a + e.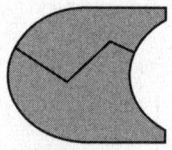

39. b + d.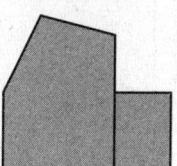

40. b.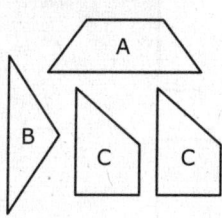

Spatial Analysis

41.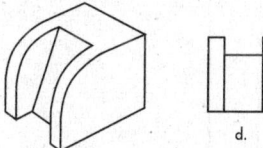

42.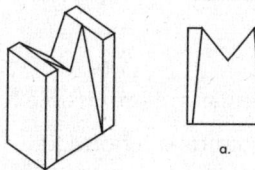

43.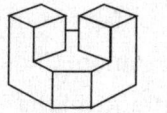

44.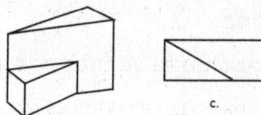

45.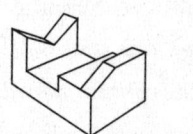

Understanding Patterns

46.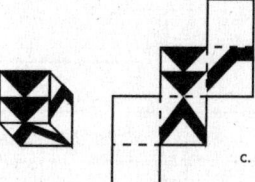

47.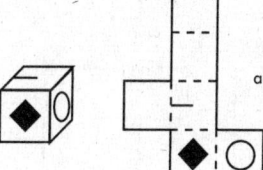

48.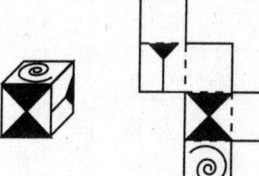

49.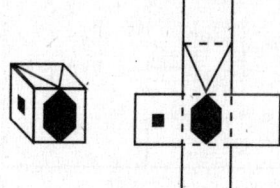

50.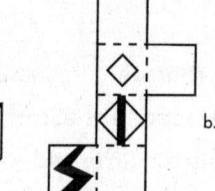

DIAGNOSTIC TEST

Eye-Hand Coordination

51. **d.** This package should go into Box 4 (Discount) because the two pieces are non-defective and do not have the same weight. The Sorting Code states: *All packages placed in this box contain non-defective pieces that do not match in weight or shape.*

52. **b.** Because both pieces are damaged, this package should be placed into Box 2 (Fail).

53. **c.** This package should be placed into Box 3 (Recycle) because it contains *one* damaged piece. The Sorting Code states: *All packages placed in this box contain one defective piece. Regardless of shape or weight, if one piece of the pair is defective, put the package in Box 3.*

54.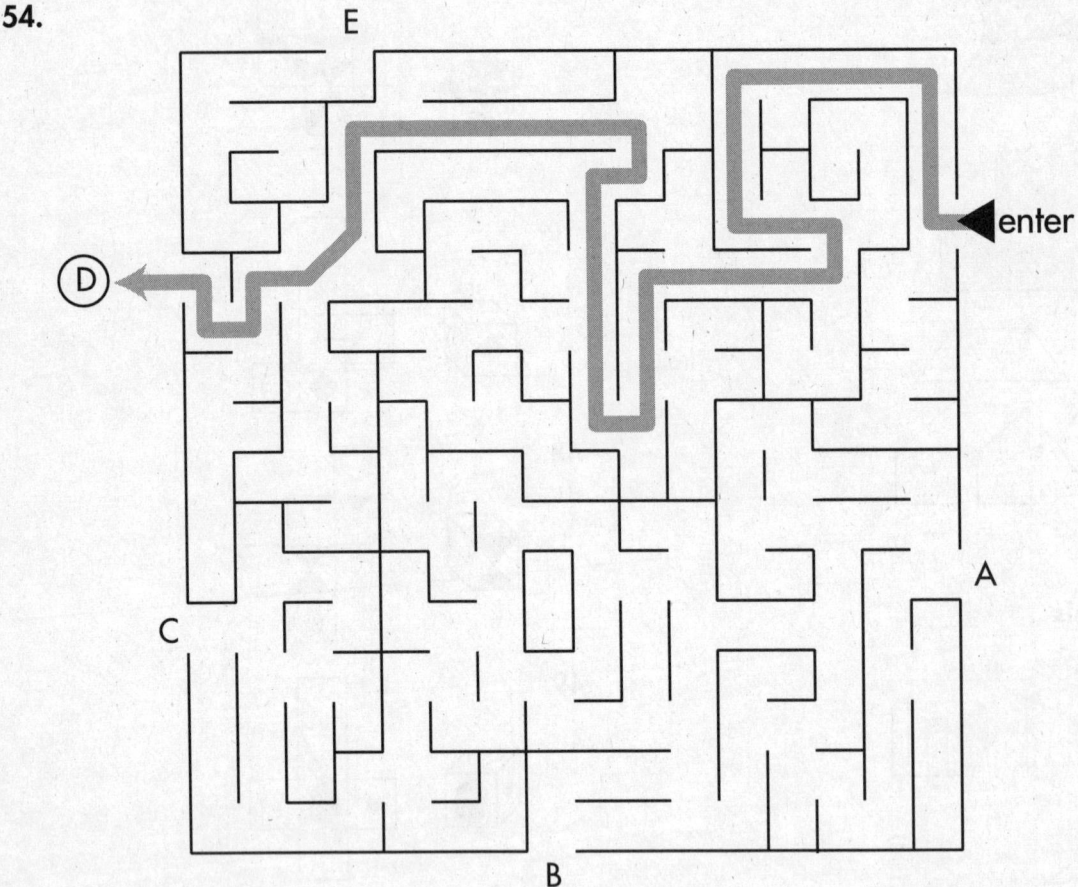

Reading Maps

55. **a.** The other routes are impossible or illegal.
56. **c.** Brown Street and Park Street are the two streets that run north and south of the park.
57. **a.** The other routes are impossible or illegal.
58. **b.** The other routes are impossible (choices **c** and **d**) or circuitous (choice **a**).
59. **d.** Choice **a** takes you the wrong way on Maple Street. Choice **b** starts from the fire house, not the police station. Choice **c** will not get you to the entrance of the gas station.

DIAGNOSTIC TEST

Symbol Series

60. d. Each symbol is a star. As the series matures the symbols follow a shading pattern (white, gray, black) and also add a point to the star in each step. Since the fifth symbol is gray and has seven points, the answer must be black and have eight points, which is choice **d**.

61. c. The pattern in this series consists of a seven-sided shape for the first symbol, a similar shape but with a dotted line for the second symbol, and six-sided figure for the third with a dotted line version for the fourth. The fifth symbol has five sides implying that the next figure will be the same but with dotted lines instead. Answer **c**.

62. b. In this series, the symbols are five pointed stars each with a shaded region. In symbol two, the shaded region begins a counter-clockwise pattern continued throughout the rest of the series. Answer **b** best fits the pattern.

63. d. Each symbol consists of a circle divided into thirds. As the series matures each symbol is rotated 45 degrees counter-clockwise. The answer must be a 45-degree counter-clockwise rotation of symbol five, which is best shown in choice **d**.

64. a. Each symbol consists of the same figure simply rotated 45 degrees clockwise. The answer is a 45-degree clockwise rotation of symbol five, which is best represented as choice **a**.

Symbol Analogies

65. d. In each of the symbols of Group 1, an elliptical shape has been cut from each figure and follows a pattern of circle, square, and triangle. In Group 2, each of the symbols shows a triangular shape has been cut out, but follows the same pattern of shapes, which makes choice **d** the answer.

66. c. In Group 1, each symbol consists of two shapes that connect at corners to make up each figure. In Group 2, the symbols consist of shapes connected at round ends of each shapes. This would leave **c** as the best answer.

67. b. In Group 1, each figure consists of a big shape and a small shape with each symbol having the small shape circled. In Group 2, the symbols follow a similar pattern but each of the bigger shapes are marked with an "X" making choice **b** the answer.

68. c. In Group 1, the first symbol is made up of three lines; the second symbol is made up of three circles; and the third three stars. In Group 2, each symbol is made up of five similar shapes, making choice **c** the only answer that fits.

69. d. The first figure in Group 1 is made up of three quadrilaterals, the second is made up of two, and the third is made up of one shaded quadrilateral. In Group 2, the symbols are made up of triangles that follow the same pattern. This would leave choice **d** as the only logical response.

Sorting and Classifying Figures

70. d. Each symbol in Group 1 has an arrow pointed at a circle. The only choice with this trait is choice **d**.

71. a. Each individual symbol in Group 1 consists of only its kind. Figure 1 has only quadrilaterals; figure 3 has only triangles, etc. Choice **a** is the answer.

72. b. Each symbol in Group 1 has a black dot in the right most section of the shape which is only reflected in choice **b**.

73. d. Each symbol in Group 1 consists mainly of a blank square with a line along its left side rotated about with added embellishments. Choice **d** has these same components.

74. a. Each figure in Group 1 has a blank shape, and a shaded shape inside with one less side than its surrounding shape. This is reflected through choice **a**.

Series Reasoning

75. a. In this series, the letters progress by one; the numbers increase by three.

76. a. This is an alternating multiplication and addition series: First, divide by two, and then add eight.

77. d. This is an alternating multiplication series. Each number is two times more than the previous number. Roman numerals alternate with Arabic numbers.

78. b. In this simple addition with repetition series, each number in the series repeats itself, and then increases by 11 to arrive at the next number.

79. b. This is a simple subtraction series in which a random number, 85, is interpolated as every third number. In the subtraction series, ten is subtracted from each number to arrive at the next.

Achieve Test Success With LearningExpress

Our acclaimed series of academic and other job related exam guides are the most sought after resources of their kind. Get the edge with the only exam guides to offer the features that test-takers have come to expect from LearningExpress—The Exclusive LearningExpress Advantage:

- **THREE** Complete practice tests based on official exams
- Vital review of skills tested and hundreds of sample questions with full answers and explanations
- The exclusive LearningExpress Test Preparation System—must know exam information, test-taking strategies, customized study planners, tips on physical and mental preparation and more.

Easy to Use & Understand

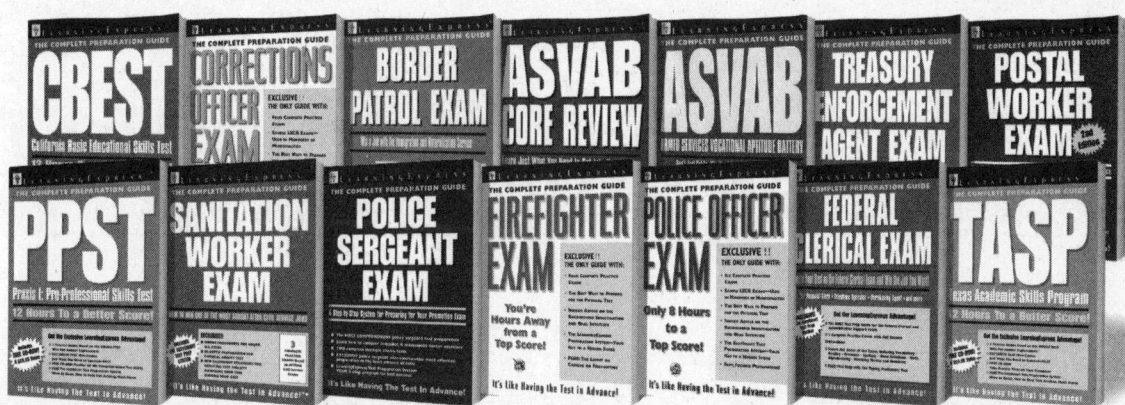

ASVAB, 2/e
336 pages • 8 1/2 x 11 • paper
$19.95/ISBN: 1-57685-332-2
(Available October 2000) (Includes FREE CD-Rom)

ASVAB Core Review
208 pages • 8 1/2 x 11 • paper
$12.95 • ISBN: 1-57685-155-9

Border Patrol Exam
256 pages • 8 1/2 x 11 • paper
$19.95 • ISBN: 1-57685-140-0

CBEST
272 pages • 8 1/2 x 11 • paper
$18.95 • ISBN: 1-57685-115-X
(Includes FREE CD-Rom)

Corrections Officer Exam
304 pages • 8 _ x 11 • paper
$14.95 • ISBN: 1-57685-295-4

Federal Clerical Exam
288 pages • 8 1/2 x 11 • paper
$14.95 • ISBN: 1-57685-101-X

Firefighter Exam
304 pages • 8 1/2 x 11 • paper
$14.95 • ISBN: 1-57685-294-6

Police Officer Exam
384 pages • 8 1/2 x 11 • paper
$14.95 • ISBN: 1-57685-207-5

Police Sergeant Exam
288 pages • 8 1/2 x 11 • paper
$18.95 • ISBN: 1-57685-335-7
(Available November 2000)

Postal Worker Exam, 2/e
288 pages • 8 1/2 x 11 • paper
$14.95 • ISBN: 1-57685-331-4
(Available September 2000)

PPST-Praxis I
272 pages • 8 1/2 x 11 • paper
$18.95 • ISBN: 1-57685-136-2
(Includes FREE CD-Rom)

Sanitation Worker Exam
224 pages • 8 1/2 x 11 • paper
$12.95 • ISBN: 1-57685-047-1

TASP
272 pages • 8 1/2 x 11 • paper
$18.95 • ISBN: 1-57685-114-1
(Includes FREE CD-Rom)

Treasury Enforcement Agent Exam
272 pages • 8 1/2 x 11 • paper
$18.95 • ISBN: 1-57685-139-7

To Order: Call 1-888-551-JOBS
LearningExpress C/O PROTOCOL
5005 Kingsley Drive
Cincinnati, OH 45227

Also available at your local bookstore. Prices Subject to Change Without Notice.

LEARNINGEXPRESS®
LearnATest.com™